VICTORY DEFERRED

The War on Global Poverty (1945-2003)

Robert F. Clark

University Press of America,® Inc.
Lanham · Boulder · New York · Toronto · Oxford

Copyright © 2005 by
University Press of America,® Inc.
4501 Forbes Boulevard
Suite 200
Lanham, Maryland 20706
UPA Acquisitions Department (301) 459-3366

PO Box 317
Oxford
OX2 9RU, UK

Library of Congress Control Number: 2004114180
ISBN 0-7618-3072-3 (paperback : alk. ppr.)

♾™ The paper used in this publication meets the minimum
requirements of American National Standard for Information
Sciences—Permanence of Paper for Printed Library Materials,
ANSI Z39.48—1984

To Marie

and also,

to the one billion people of the planet who survive on less than one dollar a day.
You deserve better.

CONTENTS

Preface

Encouragingly, as exemplified by the United Nations' Millennium Development Goals, poverty reduction has risen to near the top of the world's agenda. Because, distressingly, extreme poverty on a global scale will persist for the foreseeable future.

Despite impressive global economic growth in recent decades, close to half of the world's current population of six billion people lives on the equivalent of $2 a day or less and around one billion of them eke out their existence on $1 a day or less. If global economic integration is meant to benefit all, rather than leaving so many marginalized, then there is work to be done.

And, in fact, much is being done.

A comprehensive bibliography on poverty and what the world is doing about it would result in a book by itself. The flood of publications shows no sign of abating. Why one more?

Publications about global poverty for the most part are rooted in disciplines like development economics and sociology; after cursory attention to historical factors, they quickly become problem-focused and solution-oriented.

Understandably, the histories of international bodies like the United Nations and World Bank examine global poverty through their own institutional lenses.

Hence, it is not easy from the extant literature to sift out a cross-cutting historical perspective on the emergence of poverty as a global concern and the evolution of approaches to overcoming it.

In this book, I synthesize the more specialized literature into a narrative covering the past six decades. While tapping into other disciplines, this is mainly an administrative history, with emphasis on the antipoverty roles of bilateral, multilateral and global organizations. From this "database", I sift out trends in theory, research, policy, programs and resource allocation.

The book has three intended audiences. First, the new generation of paid workers and volunteers in the world's war on poverty. They may be found in the ministries of developing countries, aid agencies in developed countries, multilateral and global organizations like the United Nations and World Bank, and national and international non-governmental organizations. This history is meant to provide them with useful background and context for their endeavors.

Second, social welfare policy analysts, economists, legislators and journalists who focus on global issues. To complement their expertise in particular issues and areas, they may find value in this broader history. While mainly descriptive, in places the book challenges the conventional wisdom about global poverty in an attempt to spur new lines of inquiry among researchers and policy analysts.

Third, it could serve as a textbook (possibly primary but most likely supplementary) for graduate courses on international issues in fields like public administration, public policy, political science, and social work.

Acknowledgments

My previous histories of the U.S. War on Poverty raised my awareness of global poverty and provided the impetus for this work.[1] There is little new here. Instead the book synthesizes the information and insights produced by others. I am deeply indebted to all the authors listed in the bibliography—and *their* sources.

The Martha Washington Branch of the Fairfax County Public Library in Virginia obtained many of the materials I used for research. I must also tip my hat to that marvelous Internet search engine, Google, and the astonishing openness of the many public and private entities it led me to. These resources proved indispensable to a deskbound writer. An unnamed outside reviewer provided a valuable critique.

As with my previous books, my wife Marie provided indispensable feedback and loving support. This book remains my sole responsibility, including its errors of fact, omission or interpretation.

Robert F. Clark
Alexandria, Virginia
September 1, 2004

ENDNOTE

1. *Maximum Feasible Success: A History of the Community Action Program* (Washington, DC: National Association of Community Action Agencies, 2000) and *The War on Poverty: History, Selected Programs and Ongoing Impact* (Lanham, MD: University Press of America, 2002).

Introduction

On December 10, 1948, the General Assembly of the United Nations proclaimed the Universal Declaration of Human Rights.[1] Article 25 launches the world's war on poverty.

> "(1) Everyone has the right to a standard of living adequate for the health and well-being of himself and of his family, including food, clothing, housing and medical care and necessary social services, and the right to security in the event of unemployment, sickness, disability, widowhood, old age or other lack of livelihood in circumstances beyond his control. (2) Motherhood and childhood are entitled to special care and assistance. All children, whether born in or out of wedlock, shall enjoy the same social protection."

By today's standards the language is a bit quaint, even sexist. But the basic concept is not. Freedom from economic poverty is a universally recognized human right.

Recognized, yes. Achieved, by no means. With approximately a billion people around the globe living on the equivalent of $1 a day or less, it is clear that extreme poverty on a large scale will persist into the foreseeable future. The world has the economic resources and technological capacity to end poverty. There is even a considerable international consensus around the goal. Global security is one incentive.

Threats to national and global security come from disparities between rich and poor countries, international economic and financial fluctuations, environmental degradation, and extreme poverty. Addressing these threats requires engagement by all members of the international community. Eliminating extreme poverty in particular would go a long way towards making the world a more secure place for all.

So how, and how well, is the world waging war on global poverty?

The Mixed Blessings of Globalization

The early years of the twenty-first century serve as a symbolically useful vantage point from which to assess the world's war on poverty. In many respects the previous six decades have produced encouraging progress in real income, life expectancy, infant survival, education, housing, health care, and nutrition.

Globalization has helped integrate the production and distribution of goods, services, capital, and new ideas. Some observers blame globalization for exacerbating unemployment and poverty, others see it as an opportunity to overcome these problems. The evidence supports both views.

Technology has fueled global advances in transportation, communications and information. Systems of production have become linked internationally as richer countries outsource labor-intensive activities. The combination of technology and cheaper labor has improved productivity. The forces of global trade, private capital flows, and technological innovation continue to benefit nations with the ability to adapt.

While benefiting many individuals, population groups and countries, globalization has marginalized others. More than one billion persons, nearly one-fourth of the total population in developing countries, live in extreme poverty, defined as living on less than $1 a day. They are stranded across a digital divide, lacking access to the information and communications technologies that drive modern economies.[2]

Increasingly, developing countries are shifting from production based on low-wage labor toward higher-end manufacturing. In this process, poor persons with the requisite skill sets can benefit. The rest fall by the economic wayside.

Hypocritically, advanced industrialized countries of the West "have pushed poor countries to eliminate trade barriers, while keeping up their own barriers."[3] As a consequence, poor countries lose export income from the sale of those basic commodities on which their economies depend. Unregulated speculative flows of capital into and out of poor countries have "left behind collapsed currencies and weakened banking systems."[4]

Thanks to increased mobility and information-sharing, people who once could compare themselves only to their close neighbors are more than ever aware of the living standards of others in their own country and elsewhere in the world. They are also more sensitive to asymmetrical economic relationships between developing and developed countries in areas like trade.

Globalization does not routinely generate jobs where large concentrations of people live. Every year millions of people cross their national borders in search of greater freedom and economic security elsewhere. However, the expansion of transnational corporations and the freer flow of trade, capital and technology have not been matched by freer labor flows.

Worldwide, there are an estimated eighty-six million economically active migrants. About two in five go from one developing country to another.[5] Migration policies and patterns are weighted against the flow of unskilled labor from developing to developed countries. This fosters migration outside regular channels, through means like illegal entry, unauthorized overstays and smuggling.

International migration can be a positive experience for developing countries, which typically cannot provide enough jobs internally for their growing labor forces. Remittances from abroad benefit families and the economy as a whole. They appear to have a statistically significant effect on poverty reduction in the migrants' countries of origin.[6]

However, millions of poor migrants face living and working conditions far inferior to those of nationals in their destination countries. They perform physically demanding and hazardous duties for low pay during short and irregular periods of work. They are more easily victimized by violent crime, racial and ethnic discrimination, child neglect, sexual abuse and social exclusion. They are less likely to have access to education, health care and sanitary conditions. They lack wage protection, social security and the right to form trade unions.[7]

Globalization has fostered the spread of democratic values, civil and human rights and cultural diversity while threatening to overwhelm them in the long run. "[T]he nation-state, as a bedrock economic political institution, is steadily losing control over international flows of people, goods, funds and technology."[8] Underdeveloped countries are the least able to cope with these forces.

Crushing debt burdens leave some developing countries with little room for maneuver. Increased crime and corruption have characterized some aspects of globalization in some parts of the world. Few developing countries have adapted to onrushing technologies in computers, robotics, telecommunications and medicine.

Poverty, Terrorism and 9/11

Coping with terrorism has become the top national security issue for the United States of America. The country devotes enormous resources to countering terrorist threats, particularly from the al Qaeda network and its affiliates.

Arab and Muslim resentment is fueled by the perception that the United States is anti-Muslim. Among various other factors, America's policy choices in the Israeli-Palestinian conflict and its war in Iraq are cited to reinforce the message. While Islam itself does not teach terrorism, fundamentalists seize on such grievances to justify terrorist actions.

Social and economic conditions in the Middle East create a receptive audience for the antagonism toward the United States and its allies. "The combined gross domestic product of the 22 countries in the Arab League is less than the GDP of Spain...One-third of the broader Middle East lives on less than two dollars a day."[9]

The United States learned from its investigation into the terrorist attack of September 11, 2001 that "weak states, like Afghanistan, can pose as great a danger to our national interests as strong states. Poverty does not make poor people into terrorists and murderers. Yet poverty, weak institutions and corruption can make weak states vulnerable to terrorist networks and drug cartels within their borders."[10]

The government's 9/11 Commission echoed this view. "Terrorism is not caused by poverty. Indeed, many terrorists come from relatively well-off families. Yet when people lose hope, when societies break down, when countries fragment, the breeding grounds for terrorism are created."[11]

The current clash between Islamist terror networks and the economically advanced societies of the West is at risk of metastasizing into a broader conflict between the have and have-not peoples of the world.

As the world's sole superpower and a principal force in globalization, the United States has a special responsibility to work to "spread its benefits to all, including the poorest, while addressing its negative consequences."[12] Apart from the moral imperative that drives them, policies aimed at reducing global poverty are tied directly to U.S. national security interests.

Poverty, Population and Global Protest

The United States, however hegemonic in world affairs, cannot afford to act alone. Through the forces of globalization, "American national security is becoming increasingly blended with issues of global well-being."[13] Global well-being is dependent on global cooperation. This is due in no small part to population pressures.

"The addition of eighty million people each year to an already overcrowded globe is exacerbating the problems of pollution, desertification, underemployment, epidemics and famine."[14] While the proportion of the world's population living in extreme poverty has declined, the absolute number has not. Although the evidence is not conclusive, living standards within and among countries appear to have widened over the past decades.[15]

Out of the world's 200 countries, 124 are democracies and most of the world lives in market economies. The converse is that 76 countries are not democratic and many so-called democracies are fragile at best.

Disenchantment with democratic governance has taken hold in parts of the developing world. People are dissatisfied with political leaders seen as unaccountable, corrupt and indifferent to social and economic problems. Political polarization between the haves and the have-nots "has become a feature of our world."[16]

While market economies have fostered growth and expanded individual opportunities, they do not automatically open to everyone a "fair chance to participate . . . and exploit their potential to the full."[17]

The poor in particular are handicapped by deficits in education, training, access to health care, personal security, basic infrastructure services and employment.[18] Four-fifths of the world's population lives on one-fifth of the world's income.

The persistence of poverty and income inequality has triggered a backlash against the harsher forces of globalization. Protests are directed at various international organizations and rich countries like the United States that are seen as tolerating, if not actually abetting, unfettered free market capitalism, unfair trade relationships and crushing debt burdens on developing countries.

Without improvement in the economic conditions of poor people in poor countries, economic globalization will be accompanied by political polarization. Poor people do not instigate terrorism; but terrorists find it easier to hide in poor countries.

If moral suasion does not suffice, the self-interest of developed nations suggests that winning the war on global poverty is an international imperative. The national security interests of rich and poor countries alike is tied to the eradication of extreme global poverty.[19]

One Goal, Multiple Agendas

The task of eliminating poverty will extend into the foreseeable future. Progress against poverty will depend on the creation, sustainability and cross-fertilization of institutional structures that survive the fashions of global policy development. It will also depend on the emergence of a new paradigm.

The goal of global poverty reduction has achieved priority status on the world's radar screen. However, the means for accomplishing the goal have become enmeshed in other agendas—sustainable development, population planning, gender equity, good governance, market reform and promotion of democratic values, to name a few.

Progress in these areas, all meritorious, can have demonstrably positive effects on poverty reduction. Coalitions of interests allied around the goal of poverty reduction can yield a useful synergy. The world's extremely poor by themselves do not constitute a powerful political constituency and therefore benefit from their alliances with other interest groups.

However, international bodies like the United Nations and the World Bank risk being overwhelmed by the demands placed on them. In the aggregate they appear incapable of dealing politically with the emerging global economic architecture. In their poverty reduction strategies, they seek to satisfy all interests and offend none.

The proliferation of causes linked however plausibly to poverty reduction seems to be generating a kind of goal indigestion. It remains to be shown that all this shared global energy will result in the world's poorest people achieving greater economic self-sufficiency.

This Book's Scope and Limitations

In this book I synthesize the more specialized literature on global poverty into a narrative covering the past six decades. While tapping into other disciplines, this is mainly an administrative history, with emphasis on the antipoverty roles of government-sponsored multilateral and global organizations.

I devote disproportionate attention to the poverty-fighting efforts of global bodies like the United Nations and the World Bank and their regional counterparts. Essentially these are organizations whose members consist of national governments that have come together in voluntary association to pursue common goals.

The proclamations, research, policy perspectives, programs and projects of these bodies in some sense reflect the world's official "mindset" about poverty. The history and underpinnings of that mindset help illuminate past successes and failures as well as the world's prospects for winning its war on poverty.

Because of the book's global perspective, I do not cover adequately many of the individual antipoverty programs supported by governments of developing countries, communities within those countries, and organizations comprising "civil society" (churches, foundations, non-profit agencies, educational institutions, and others occupying the space between citizens and their governments).

International non-governmental organizations have functioned as test-beds for innovative projects and as passionate advocates for the poor in international settings. In some cases they started with humanitarian relief missions but over time adopted more long-term strategies and programs for global poverty reduction. Increasingly they operate through networks of like-minded organizations.

My treatment of these non-governmental organizations is also limited. Arguably, the world's war on poverty has two distinct story lines. One focuses on official entities with a public policy perspective like the United Nations and the World Bank. The other emphasizes the role of private, voluntary non-governmental organizations. This book highlights the former.

With respect to non-governmental organizations, the choices at the extremes are to cover them comprehensively or cover them not at all. The former would obscure the book's main theme. The latter would exclude entities whose impact on global poverty has been significant and whose interactions with official aid entities have increased in recent decades.[20]

For this book, in addition to surveying some larger trends, I have selected several large non-governmental organizations with relatively long histories and sketched the evolution and impact of their approach to global poverty. The ones

I highlight are Oxfam, Caritas Internationalis, Christian Aid, CARE, World Vision and ACCION.

Their particular histories indicate to some extent the scope, growth and influence of international non-governmental organizations. Apologies to others whose good works I have failed to include or have shortchanged.

Chapter Overviews

The treatment of the period of this history decade-by-decade is convenient in the absence of any generally accepted classification. In places, I do not hesitate to leapfrog years or even decades to sustain the narrative flow.

Of necessity, there is ongoing interplay among the themes of poverty, development, growth and globalization. The subject is large; hence, the book is *a* history, not *the* history of the world's war on poverty. If successful, it will stimulate additional work along similar lines.

Chapter 1 begins somewhat fancifully by inviting the reader to imagine herself as the President of Peñuria dealing with a succession of visitors from various bilateral and multilateral aid organizations. It goes on to provide an overview of global poverty and examines the many meanings of poverty, including its nonmonetary aspects. It describes the evolution of various theories of development and the role of foreign aid (or, by its more formal name, official development assistance).

Chapter 2 covers the creation of the United Nations and the Bretton Woods institutions. It references President Truman's Point Four address, which launched the era of development. It concludes with treatment of the world's newly independent nations and their efforts to overcome internal poverty while fostering economic growth as well as the emergence of international relief organizations like Oxfam, CARE and Caritas Internationalis.

Chapter 3 discusses the economic thinking of the 1950s with its emphasis on urban industrialization (and hence de-emphasis of agriculture and rural enterprise) as key to development. The World Bank slowly came to grips with its role as a development organization, while at the same time preserving an image of hard-nosed financial soundness.

By 1960, the world stage was augmented with new players like the Organization for Economic Cooperation and Development (OECD), Special United Nations Fund for Economic Development (SUNFED) which evolved into the United Nations Development Programme (UNDP), and the World Bank's soft loan window, the International Development Association.

In the 1960s, it was assumed that significant public sector involvement was required to accelerate growth in developing nations. Chapter 4 devotes attention to the First Development Decade of the United Nations, the emergence of the Non-Aligned Movement, and the World Bank's increasing emphasis not just on "development" but on direct poverty reduction

The role of Robert McNamara as the Bank's president in fostering this antipoverty orientation is highlighted. The chapter also covers trade and balance of payments issues and the contributions of global, regional and bilateral aid agencies. Attention is paid to, environmental concerns related to poverty reduction and the impact of the Green Revolution.

Chapter 5 shows how progress against poverty was slowed by the breakdown of the Bretton Woods agreements on international exchange rates, declining flows of official development assistance, the rising price of oil and a borrowing binge among developing nations. New international approaches to poverty first advocated by the International Labour Organization stressed the importance of meeting the basic needs of people for employment, income, education, health care, housing, and, interestingly, culture.

The mixed motives of donor nations like the United States are examined. The chapter focuses on the emergence of structural adjustment approaches to economic stability in developing countries and their adverse impact on the poor.

In Chapter 6, the effects of neoliberal prescriptions are highlighted. A recession in the early years of the 1980s compounded the difficulties of developing nations. The United Nations launched a Second Development Decade. Under pressure from the Reagan Administration, the World Bank and the International Monetary Fund emphasized structural adjustment. The chapter devotes attention to the Baker and Brady plans, designed to alleviate the woes of highly indebted nations.

Late in the decade, the World Bank's adjustment loans began to incorporate more provisions for health, education and social safety nets to protect the poor. The chapter notes the contributions of the United Nations in promoting worldwide awareness of poverty and making its eradication a global imperative.

Chapter 7 describes a shift of emphasis in the 1990s at the World Bank and related entities from structural adjustment to poverty reduction. Bilateral and multilateral aid for development projects began to be provided more systematically. The varied and often creative approaches to poverty reduction adopted by different United Nations agencies are described.

The expansion of microcredit schemes is highlighted with emphasis on organizations like the Grameen Bank and ACCION. The chapter covers international activities like the World Food Summit, the World Bank's Heavily Indebted Poor Countries Initiative (HIPC), the Copenhagen Declaration, creation of the World Trade Organization and the adoption in 2000 of the UN's Millennium Development Goals.

Chapter 8 provides evidence of constructive forward movement in pursuit of the Millennium Development Goals. The United Nations has focused attention on the needs of the world's fifty least developed countries. The President of Tunisia proposed the creation of a World Solidarity Fund to combat poverty and finance development.

At the same time, there are impediments to progress. Poverty reduction is enmeshed with other goals (e.g. overall development, environmental protection, gender equity), all worthy but all in competition for their share of resources. Aid projects remain uncoordinated. How long a global war on poverty will remain high on the international agenda is uncertain.

The concluding chapter summarizes and interprets the major themes and trends that can be drawn from the prior six decades. Despite international goodwill and some measurable progress, I contend that the war on global poverty is unwinnable on its present course. The Millennium Development Goals for poverty reduction are modest at best.

In what to praise and what to criticize about poverty reduction efforts, I have tried to be even-handed. If the book succeeds on these terms, the reader may wonder what solution the author would offer.

Let me tip my hand here. The shortest path to the reduction of extreme global poverty is to subsidize personal income. Accordingly, I favor what for my lifetime will remain a political chimera, namely some version of a negative income tax designed on a global scale and implemented through the United Nations. I elaborate on this approach in the final chapter.

There is some ground to cover between here and there.

ENDNOTES

1. Adopted and proclaimed by General Assembly resolution 217 A (III), December 10, 1948.
2. To reinforce the point, half of the world's population has never used a telephone and Montreal has more telephones than the entire country of Bangladesh. See Canadian International Development Agency (2001) 5.
3. Stiglitz, Joseph E. (2002) 6.
4. Ibid.: 7.
5. International Labour Organization (2004a) 7. The ILO emphasizes the provisional nature of these estimates.
6. Adams, Richard H. Jr. and John Page (2003). In their study of seventy-four developing countries, the authors find that, on average, a 10 percent increase in the share of international remittances in a country's Gross Domestic Product will lead to a 1.6 percent decline in the share of people living in extreme poverty ($1 a day).
7. International Labour Organization (2004a) 23, 45-47.
8. U.S. Central Intelligence Agency (2003).
9. National Commission on Terrorist Attacks Upon the United States (2004) 376.
10. United States Government (2002). Statements are contained in transmittal letter by President George W. Bush.
11. National Commission on Terrorist Attacks Upon the United States (2004) 378.
12. United States Conference of Catholic Bishops (2003) 15.
13. Brzezinski, Zbigniew (2004) 4.
14. U.S. Central Intelligence Agency (2003).
15. Townsend, Peter (2000) 3.
16. United Nations (2001) 13.
17. United Nations (2001) 37.
18. Ibid.
19. Alarmist sentiments? Not to the government of the United States. Under the National Security Strategy of U.S. President George W. Bush, September 2002, development

assistance has been elevated as the third pillar of U.S. national security, along with defense and diplomacy. Broad-based development assistance rather than targeted antipoverty initiatives is advocated as the surest path to poverty reduction. See U.S. Agency for International Development (2003).

20. For an insightful study of how non-governmental organizations are evolving to deal with extreme poverty and other issues in response to globalization, see Lindenberg, Marc and Coralie Bryant (2001).

1

Poverty Globally

You Are the President of Peñuria

We begin with a piece of fiction.

Imagine yourself as president of a small landlocked developing country, call it Peñuria. Forty percent of your population of twenty million people lives on incomes of less than a dollar a day.

Nearly three-quarters of the extreme poverty population of eight million souls comes from a single ethnic group, the Havents. They have become restive at the recent decline in public spending for education, health care, affordable housing and social security.

By contrast, your legislature is made up of citizens all of whom come from the top quintile of the income distribution, all of whom are men and nine-tenths of whom come from the country's dominant ethnic group, the Posh. They are generally unsympathetic to demands from the poor that involve more government spending and higher taxes.

These legislators and their political supporters are wary of proposed economic reforms aimed at benefiting small labor-intensive producers (the poor) and diverting resources from larger, technology-driven producers (themselves).

Your economy depends on the export of a single commodity, cotton. However, the world's largest developed country subsidizes its domestic cotton producers. They are able to sell their cotton at home and abroad at reduced prices.

Your country must therefore contend with declining global market share even as it lowers prices in an effort to remain competitive. Your balance of payments is unfavorable, since your expenditures for consumer goods, services, industrial equipment and technology far outstrip your revenues. Your country is deeply in debt having borrowed heavily to finance domestic development and import purchases while meeting the basic needs of your citizens.

On this particular day several people are waiting in your outer office. Six are officials from bilateral aid agencies from developed countries (United States, Canada, France, Japan, Sweden, United Kingdom), one is from a regional development bank, one is from the World Bank and two are from specialized United Nations Agencies, the United Nations Development Programme and the International Labour Organization.

First into your office is an official from the Agency for International Development in the United States of America.

I'll be brief, he promises, since others are waiting. Our agency is prepared to make a $200 million grant to Peñuria. That averages out to $10 per person. Your eyes light up.

He goes on. Your country must submit a proposal that identifies its poverty reduction needs while spelling out a strategy that is consistent with the terms of the U.S. Foreign Assistance Act. This Act spells out thirty different objectives.

We will of course need to measure, monitor and evaluate your progress in meeting these objectives. You can expect regular visits from our aid teams. You will need to design and implement a poverty reduction tracking and reporting system.

Noting your anxiety, he immediately becomes reassuring. Not to worry, he says, we will provide you with the necessary technical support. We urge you to spend a portion of the grant funds on a contract with one of our large multinational corporations that specializes in information and communications technologies.

You are left with mixed feelings as he departs.

This official is followed by his counterparts from Canada, France, Japan, Sweden, United Kingdom, each making a similar presentation. You begin adding up the number of different reports your ministries will have to prepare for these different donors. There will be a lot of overlap and duplication because each donor defines terms differently, uses different categories to record data and varies in its reporting schedules.

While you are mulling over these factors, your chief of staff announces that the representative from the World Bank group has arrived. She speaks on behalf of the International Development Association and the International Monetary Fund. This unusual circumstance is due to a sudden shortfall in the World Bank's travel budget.

Since Peñuria is characterized by the United Nations as a "least developed country," she explains, it qualifies for concessional lending rates from the International Development Association and from the International Monetary Fund's Poverty Reduction and Growth Facility.

As a condition of assistance, Peñuria must commit to a program of good governance, macroeconomic stability, and economic growth as the underpinning for its poverty reduction agenda. Poverty reduction must occur within a comprehensive development framework.

The bilateral aid agencies, the representative reports, have all subscribed to the World Bank's poverty reduction strategy agenda. Global antipoverty programs are being coordinated for the first time in history. There will of course be some variations from one donor country to another in its expectations and reporting requirements, but this is a huge step forward.

Just complete Peñuria's poverty reduction strategy paper, submit the draft to Bank staff for review, and, once it passes muster, you will be on your way. Be sure that the document reflects a consensus among all groups in society, above all the Posh and the Havents. Also, make sure that poverty reduction takes place within the overall comprehensive development framework we have previously discussed with you as well as, of course, any domestic priorities you may have set.

You ask, what is left of our national sovereignty? She replies that the Bank and other donors all want you and your people to feel a sense of pride and ownership in these documents. The Bank stands ready to provide training and technical assistance and to share its knowledge and expertise.

Later a representative from the regional development bank is ushered in. She stresses the importance of regional economic integration and offers low-interest, long-term loans to aid in the development of a regional common market.

Your schedule for the following morning includes a series of brief meetings with officials from specialized agencies of the United Nations. These include the United Nations Development Programme, United Nations Conference on Trade and Development, United Nations Children's Fund, United Nations Educational Scientific and Cultural Organization and the International Labour Organization.

Your afternoon will be devoted to a more heterogeneous group of development partners. A spokesperson for your country's Civil Society Coalition, representing trade unions, religious entities, and nonprofit service organizations will come in after lunch. Later you will meet with an official from a transnational corporation that may build a manufacturing facility in your country, providing, of course, that conditions are ripe and the incentives are sufficient.

Finally you will meet with a vice-president of an international financial institution that is weighing whether to make a large commercial loan to a group in your agricultural sector. You know that these private capital flows far outstrip the amount of official development assistance your country receives.

They also tend to dictate critical aspects of your country's domestic and foreign policy, such as environmental protection, workers' rights and international trade. You start thinking about the end of your one six-year term in office, which is not far off.

For the moment, the meetings with your various development partners have ended. You as president go back to the task at hand—preparing the annual budget for submission to the legislature. Once again, the legislative session is bound to be contentious.

As you take pen in hand, you let your mind drift back.

How did the world's war on poverty come to this?

Poverty as a "Time Bomb"

"Poverty in all its forms is the greatest single threat to peace, democracy, human rights and the environment. It is a time bomb against the heart of liberty; but it can be conquered, and we have the tools in our hands to do so, if only we have the courage and focus to make use of them."[1]

This is the view not of a militant protest group but of a pillar of the international establishment, the World Trade Organization. Developing countries with high rates of extreme poverty tend to be politically unstable. They do not make reliable trading partners and hence find themselves ever more marginalized by the forces of globalization.

Their economic problems exacerbate internal civil conflicts and trigger wars with neighboring countries. Witness Rwanda, Burundi, Sudan, Sri Lanka, Congo-Zaire and Haiti.

Poor countries are easily overwhelmed by the devastation from hurricanes, drought or volcanic eruptions. Their urgent efforts to build their economies can lead to deforestation, desertification, air and water pollution and other forms of environmental degradation.

In a rapidly integrating world, such conditions and their effects are not confined within national borders. International money launderers, slave traders, drug cartels and terrorist networks operate from poor countries with weak institutions. Finally, the time it takes to spread an emerging disease from a poor country to a rich one or vice versa is as short as a plane ride.[2]

In the global economy, "poverty in the midst of plenty is one of the central challenges....Fighting poverty is both a moral imperative and a necessity for a stable world."[3] The 2000 United Nations Millennium Summit, attended by representatives from 191 countries, adopted the goal of reducing the proportion of the world's population in poverty by one half by 2015.[4]

Even if the goal is met, an uncertain prospect at best, an unacceptable number of people will continue to live in desperate circumstances.

Demography, Gross Domestic Product and Poverty

From 1950 to 2000 inclusive, the world's population grew from an estimated 2.5 billion to 6.1 billion people. Over the same period, the world's gross domestic product (GDP) grew from an estimated $5.3 trillion to $36.5 trillion. In other words, despite a world population in 2000 that was 2.4 times larger than it was in 1950, the world's wealth increased much more—nearly sevenfold. World population experienced a 1.7 percent annual growth rate, world per capita GDP a 2.1 percent annual growth rate.[5] (See Table 1.)

While both population and per capita GDP grew everywhere, the rate of growth varied between these two dimensions and among the world's regions. In Western Europe, from 1950 to 2000, the population grew at an annual rate of only 0.5 percent while per capita GDP surged by 2.5 percent. In Africa, by contrast, population grew by 2.5 percent a year while per capita GDP went up at only a 1.0 percent annual rate.[6]

The contrast is made starker when one considers that in 1950, Western Europe's per capita GDP was five times larger than Africa's—$4,579 compared to $894. In 2000, Western Europe's per capita GDP had become *thirteen* times larger—$19,002 compared to $1,464. In Western Europe, the rich few got much richer while in Africa the many poor got only slightly less poor.[7]

If $1 a day signifies extreme (that is, subsistence-level) poverty, then $2 a day is at least "severe" poverty. "Half the world—nearly three billion people—live on less than two dollars a day."[8]

By that standard, more people are poor today than were alive in 1950. By 2025, the world's population will have increased by an estimated two billion people. Of these 97 percent will have been born in the developing countries.[9]

Table 1. Population (Millions) and Per Capita Gross Domestic Product (GDP/PC)[1]: Region, World for Selected Years.

Region[3]	1950	1960	1970	1980	1990	2000	AGR[2]
I							
-Pop.	305	326	352	367	378	391	0.5%
-GDP/PC	4,579	6,896	10,195	13,197	15,966	19,002	2.8%
II[3]							
-Pop.	176	212	242	270	298	337	1.3%
-GDP/PC	9,268	10,961	14,560	18,060	22,345	27,065	2.1%
III							
-Pop.	88	99	108	117	122	121	0.6%
-GDP/PC	2,111	3,070	4,315	5,786	5,450	5,804	2.0%
IV							
-Pop.	180	214	242	266	289	291	0.9%
-GDP/PC	2,841	3,945	5,575	6,426	6,878	4,351	0.8%
V							
-Pop.	166	218	286	362	443	524	2.3%
-GDP/PC	2,506	3,133	3,986	5,412	5,053	5,838	1.7%
VI							
-Pop.	1,382	1,687	2,093	2,580	3,103	3,605	1.9%
-GDP/PC	712	1,029	1,530	2,034	2,781	3,817	3.3%
VII							
-Pop.	227	283	361	473	627	803	2.5%
-GDP/PC	894	1,066	1,357	1,536	1,444	1,464	1.0%
World							
-Pop.	**2,524**	**3,039**	**3,3,685**	**4,436**	**5,260**	**6,071**	**1.7%**
-GDP/PC	**2,111**	**2,777**	**3,736**	**4,520**	**5,157**	**6,012**	**2.1%**

[1]GDP/PC is measured in 1990 PPP$ using the Geary-Khamis technique. For more detail, see Maddison, Angus (2003) 228-229.
[2]Annual Compound Growth Rate.
[3]Code: Region I—Western Europe (29), II—Western Offshoots (4), III—Eastern Europe (8), IV—Former USSR (15), V—Latin America (44), VI—Africa (57), World (213). Numbers in parentheses are maximum number of countries per region. Note: Region II—Western Offshoots consists of Australia, Canada, New Zealand, United States of America.
Source: Maddison, Angus (2003) 232, 234.

The majority of the world's poor are women and children, most of whom reside in rural communities. "The situation is especially acute among rural households headed by women whose husbands have migrated to urban centers in search of paid employment."[10] Poverty affects certain other groups disproportionately: persons with disabilities, seniors, indigenous peoples, refugees and internally displaced persons.

Large families and increasing populations place heavy demands on public services like health care and education. If the education system cannot keep pace, the country will end with a pool of unskilled workers, with the effect of pushing down wage rates and savings for investment. Children in large but poor families lack sufficient access to necessities like food and clothing.

The United Nations Fund for Population Affairs is unambiguous in its conclusions. "Long term demographic and economic data from 45 developing countries show that high fertility increases poverty by slowing economic growth and skewing the distribution of consumption against the poor."[11] Since 1970, developing countries with low fertility rates and slower population growth have enjoyed faster economic growth than their counterparts.

Both the United Nations Population Fund and the Commission on Macro-economics and Health, which was established by the World Health Organization and the World Bank, advocate universal access to safe and reliable family planning methods, including contraceptives, within the context of national population policies.[12]

Young, Poor and Resentful

Globally, an estimated one billion new jobs will be required to absorb a projected "youth bulge" over the next decade. Chronically weak economies make it unlikely that the world's least developed countries, mostly concentrated in the Middle East and Sub-Saharan Africa, can meet the challenge. Even with foreign investment and foreign aid, they are unlikely to generate the required level of labor-intensive growth rates.

The world's poorest countries will have the highest proportions of their populations that are young, that is, aged 15 through 29. These countries lack the political, institutional and economic structures needed to integrate this expanding population of young people into the labor force and society.

Massive emigration from developing to developed countries will open up job opportunities for those whose skills are in demand. For unskilled persons, the prospect is bleaker. They will have fewer job opportunities at home and will be unwelcome as immigrants in richer countries.[13]

A case in point. Some nine million people, mostly young, mostly rural, enter Africa's labor market each year. In South Africa alone, half are unemployed. These new job seekers need job opportunities in agriculture and related rural enterprises, entrepreneurial skills, and environments where small businesses and micro-enterprises can flourish. Otherwise, social unrest, even political upheaval, could characterize these youth-dominated societies.

For all regions of the world, youth unemployment rates in 2003 were as least twice as high as the overall unemployment rates. For example, in Sub-Saharan Africa, youth unemployment stood at 21.3 percent compared to 10.9 percent overall. In the politically volatile Middle East and North Africa region, youth unemployment was 25.6 percent—highest in the world—compared to 12.2 percent overall.

Worldwide, despite growth in the global economy, the youth unemployment rate was 14.2 percent compared to 6.2 percent overall. This translated into some 88.2 million unemployed young people.[14]

"By 2010, the global youth population is expected to grow by 116 million, or 11 per cent, reaching almost 1.2 billion....Young people already make up more than 40 per cent of the world's total unemployed."[15] High unemployment rates among this growing population waste the exciting human potential of the young and instead breed frustration and resentment.

The anger of marginalized young people could provoke not only disruption of their own societies but more aggressive assaults on richer nations and international organizations. Youth unemployment and underemployment are associated with crime, vandalism, drug abuse, poverty and social exclusion. Their societies could become seedbeds for revolution and terrorism.

Young revolutionaries will identify western-driven global imperialism as their enemy, one that has left them in poverty and their societies without respect. They will perceive themselves as defenders of their religion, culture and social values.

There need not be a "clash of civilizations." But there could be. And global poverty and unemployment would help fuel it. In short, everyone, not just the poor, has a stake in winning the war on global poverty.

Extreme Poverty around the Globe

While poverty exists throughout the world, the extremely poor are concentrated in developing countries of Asia, Africa, Latin America and the Caribbean. According to World Bank estimates, in 2000 1.1 billion people survived on a dollar a day or less. Three-quarters of them live in rural areas, dependent on agriculture or related activities for survival.[16]

In South and East Asia and the Pacific Region, the number of people in extreme poverty is estimated at close to 700 million or nearly two-thirds of the world's poverty population. South Asia alone has 432 million people in extreme poverty.[17]

There has been progress. Rapid growth, favorable macroeconomic and trade policies and income distribution policies have contributed to the diminution of absolute poverty in South and East Asia over the past thirty years.

Due largely to gains in East Asia, the proportion of people living in extreme poverty in developing countries dropped from 40 percent of the world's population in 1981 to 21 percent in 2001. Impressive gains in average incomes in China have accounted for a significant proportion of this progress. There, more than 150 million people have escaped extreme poverty since 1990.[18]

Elsewhere, the proportion of poor has either grown or fallen slightly in many countries in Africa, Latin America and Eastern Europe and Central Asia.

In Africa, nearly half of the entire population lives in extreme poverty. Some 323 million of these extremely poor people live in Sub-Saharan Africa.[19] The region is plagued by an AIDS epidemic, civil wars, low skill levels and adverse trade relationships.

Consider Ethiopia. The typical worker there must work for a month and a half to earn what a worker in the United States earns in a day. Life expectancy is two-thirds that of the United States and infant mortality twenty times higher. Ethiopians spend 40 percent of their gross domestic product on food compared to seven percent in the United States.[20]

Poor people in Sub-Saharan Africa, who live mainly in rural areas, have less land, less capital, lower levels of education, and lower health status than richer people. Despite the continent's abundant human and natural resources, growth rates of per capita incomes during the 1980s and 1990s were negative in most Sub-Saharan countries.[21]

Middle income Latin American countries have witnessed rising levels of poverty due in part to a debt crisis in the 1980s and subsequent efforts to ameliorate it. The urban poor and the poor in Brazil, Peru and several Central American countries were particularly hard hit.

Throughout Latin America and the Caribbean, the incidence of poverty remained high late into the 1990s, despite a resumption of growth in a number of countries.

The collapse of communism ushered in a period of economic decline and social upheaval among members of the former Soviet Union. Poverty and income inequality increased in almost all countries of Eastern Europe, the Baltic States and the CIS (Commonwealth of Independent States) in the 1990s. Countries of southeastern Europe and the CIS experienced the largest increases in earnings inequality.

Worldwide some 800 million people, a quarter of them children, suffer from chronic malnutrition. The school attendance ratio in the world's fifty least developed countries is 36 percent. Communicable diseases like HIV/AIDS, malaria and tuberculosis are found disproportionately in the poorest countries.

While life expectancy in developing countries reached 65 years in 1998 (up from 55 years in 1970), it still is well below the average of 78 years in the developed countries that make up the Organization for Economic Cooperation and Development.[22]

Because of their own internal problems and priorities (for example the U.S. preoccupation with international terrorism), rich countries devote insufficient attention and resources to the needs of their poorer neighbors. Poverty, however defined and measured, will continue into the foreseeable future as a blot on human progress.

Economic Growth and Disparity

To the extent that global growth is boosted by technologically based productivity gains, the poor, whose main asset is unskilled labor, risk being shunted to the economic sidelines. Investment in human capital, primarily through education and health care, is a proven way to upgrade the skills of poor people and increase their employment opportunities.

Despite encouraging progress in recent decades, this has not happened on the scale that is needed. It is therefore not surprising that growth has been accompanied by increasing disparities within and among countries. Indeed, "between 1960 and 1994, the income ratio between the richest 20 percent and the poorest 20 percent [of the world population] increased from 30:1 to 78:1."[23]

Worldwide, the richest one percent of the world has aggregate income equivalent to the poorest 57 percent. Between 1988 and 1993, inequality increased by five percent. In this period, the real incomes of the world's poorest five percent decreased by a fourth while the real incomes of the top quintile increased by 12.7 percent.[24]

There are some indications that "the long-term trend toward higher inequality [came] to an end" during the 1975-1995 period.[25] However, large inequities persist between rural and urban dwellers, men and women, children and adults, and various ethnic and minority groups.[26]

Some five thousand indigenous and tribal groups are spread among seventy countries. "The world's highest infant mortality rates, lowest income levels, most widespread illiteracy and slimmest access to health and social services are to be found among the world's 300 million indigenous people, half of whom live in Asia."[27]

Urban poverty is keeping pace with urbanization, leading to attendant consequences such as overcrowding, homelessness, contaminated water, inadequate sanitation, crime, substance abuse, domestic violence and other social problems.

The world's poor themselves express feelings of growing insecurity. Poor people are concentrated disproportionately in rural areas and in the informal economies of urban areas. They lack information, skills, access to credit and other ingredients of upward mobility. They must contend with increased crime, corrupt government officials, loss of traditional livelihoods, and breakdowns in social solidarity.[28]

The Many Meanings of Poverty

The concept of poverty has acquired a certain elasticity. Income poverty is the most familiar version of the concept. Below an agreed-on income level, one may be considered poor. For income poverty, a recurring issue is whether poverty should be measured in absolute or relative terms. Most official government poverty lines blend the two.

Absolute measures indicate lack of access to the minimal requirements for human life like food, water, clothing and shelter. Consumption below these minimum levels is assumed to jeopardize the individual's survival.

Apart from adjustments for inflation, an absolute poverty line, which typically is proxied by an income or expenditure measure, remains fixed over time regardless of what else is going on in the economy. The World Bank measures absolute poverty as an income level permitting a nutritionally adequate diet and access to essential non-food needs. The absolute approach facilitates cross-country comparisons but even here a relativistic element is present.

What it takes to survive in one country or culture differs from what it takes in another. Actually, what it takes to survive varies from one person to another and, for that matter, over the course of a given individual's life and circumstances.

Thus any measure of poverty is inherently relative. In developed countries, the lowest incomes tend to be higher than those on which an absolute poverty standard is based. Hence, people in absolute or extreme poverty are found in developing rather than developed countries.

In relative poverty, one tends to focus on the income distribution. If the population were divided into fifths, and the income distribution were equal, the lowest quintile would receive twenty percent of the gross national product, the next lowest quintile twenty percent, on up to the highest quintile.

As represented by the Lorenz curve, in such a case of perfect income equality, the graph would show a straight line at 45 degrees to the right-angled intersection of the X- and Y-axes. Manifestly that does not accord with experience. Typically, the richest (or, in this example, highest) quintile receives far more than twenty percent of the national income and the poorest quintile far less.[29]

Relative measures identify a degree of deprivation compared to an accepted norm in a given society. One's country and one's community establish a minimal standard of living below which one may be considered impoverished. An example of a relative measure of poverty is income below one-half a country's median per capita income.

Poverty and inequality are related but not identical concepts. The well-being of a population depends on the extent of poverty, whether absolute or relative, and the degree of inequality in the income distribution. There is evidence that, for a given rate of economic growth, poverty declines less in countries with higher income inequality.[30]

The most widely used measure of income inequality is the Gini coefficient. The higher the coefficient, the greater the income inequality.[31] Extreme inequality in incomes and assets accentuates poverty, leaving the few very well off and the many either totally excluded from or sharing marginally at best in the benefits of economic growth and development.

If we divide a country's population into the Richest and the Rest, the former will typically have a disproportionate share of a country's total income. Some of the Rest may be in poverty. Redistributing a share of the income of the Richest to the Rest will alleviate poverty.

But that is not the only alternative. If the economy grows, the country's total income will rise. It may rise sufficiently to move an increasing percentage of the Rest above an absolute poverty threshold. If poverty is measured relatively, for example, as less than half the country's median income, the same is true. Hypothetically the proportion of the Rest left with a poverty-level income could decline or even disappear altogether.[32]

In either case, with income poverty reduction measured in absolute terms or in relative terms, the Richest could maintain or even increase their share of the country's total income. It all depends on an expanding economic "pie".

More typical is the case that when inequality increases, so does poverty. In these circumstances, the seeds of social unrest can more easily be sown. What happens under conditions of economic growth? Does income inequality increase or decrease? From the available evidence, no single pattern emerges. Or, to say it more simply, in some cases the income distribution becomes more equal, in some cases less.[33]

When absolute poverty rates have not fallen, it is usually because there has been little or no economic growth. Conversely, and more encouragingly, economic growth usually (but not always) reduces absolute poverty.[34]

For these and other reasons, "the eradication of poverty through sustained and accelerated economic growth continues to remain the overriding priority for developing countries."[35]

Few people deny that economic growth helps to eliminate poverty. Many argue over whether it is sufficient. That argument has a direct bearing on whether to attack poverty directly through targeted interventions or simply to rely on indirect spillovers (or trickle-down) from growth alone.

Poverty in Depth

Determining the number of people in poverty and the proportion of the total population they constitute—a head count ratio—describes the extent of poverty. It does not convey its depth.

For the latter some variant of the poverty gap ratio is often employed.[36] If one takes the income of a poor person and subtracts it from the poverty threshold, one gets an idea of the depth of that person's poverty or, if you prefer, the gap to overcome for the person to escape poverty. Add the results together for all persons in poverty to get the aggregate poverty gap.

If one then divides the result by the poverty threshold, one gets a figure that constitutes a multiplier of the poverty threshold. Use this number as the numerator. The denominator is the total number of persons in the population.

The total population includes poor persons with positive poverty gaps and nonpoor persons with zero poverty gaps. The poverty gap ratio is constructed by dividing the numerator by the denominator. It indicates the average proportionate gap across the entire population. (See Appendix 1 for a simple example.)

A redistributionist scheme takes from the nonpoor and gives to the poor. Eliminating poverty would require overcoming the poverty gap. What would this do to economic incentives? According to the classic neoliberal line, the rich who were forced to share their wealth with the poor would have less motivation and ability to save and invest. The poor would reduce their work effort and rely on redistribution as the easy way out of poverty.

An equally if not more plausible scenario is that, no longer living on the edge of subsistence, poor people would strive to increase their productive capacity and earning power. The risks to family breakdown, environmental stress, human rights abuses and political instability would diminish. Society would be more stable.

Redistribution as a means of ending poverty remains controversial. Many would rely instead on overall economic growth. So far, growth alone strategies appear at best to diminish poverty but fall far short of eliminating it altogether. Whatever one's course of action, one needs a way to estimate the extent and depth of extreme poverty not just nationally but also internationally.

Purchasing Power Parity

To compare poverty income statistics across countries, a common currency must be created. Given price variations among countries, reliance on exchange rates is unsatisfactory. The world community has subscribed to a measure of poverty developed by the World Bank to monitor progress toward this goal.

A consumption-based income standard, however measured and whatever the sources of data, can be applied straightforwardly and universally to all people, poor or not. It reflects the purchasing power of individuals and households to acquire the goods and services needed to escape poverty. Such goods and services include food, clothing, housing and other essentials of daily living.

Hence income is the measure of choice for the World Bank in setting global poverty reduction targets. However an income standard can be misleading. It excludes non-income-producing components of wealth such as real property.

Originally, the World Bank conceived a consumption-based standard built on two elements. One was the expenditure required to buy the minimum in nutrition and other necessities. This was operationalized in the widely used $1 a day standard.

The second element of a global poverty line included the cost of participating in society. This amount was acknowledged to vary from one society to another. It has never been operationalized. Hence by definition any global figures for poverty underestimate the reality.[37]

Gross Domestic Product per capita in U.S. dollars is adjusted using the Purchasing Power Parity index accounts for price differences between countries. It reflects people's living standards better than conventional exchange rates.

The Choice of $1 a Day

The $1 a day standard grew out of a World Bank study of how poor countries view poverty and was designed to be "a poverty line typical of poor countries."[38] Using household survey data from 33 countries, the World Bank selected eight very poor countries and observed that their poverty lines averaged about $1 a day per person.[39]

The choice of $1 a day for a global poverty line resulted from staffers eyeballing scatterplots showing the relationship between poor country poverty lines and mean consumption. In theory, at the Purchasing Power Parity rate, $1 PPP has the same purchasing power in any country's domestic economy as it has in the United States economy.

This international poverty line was converted to country currencies using 1985 Purchasing Power Parity exchange rates for consumption.

With the greater availability of survey and other data from developing countries, the World Bank revised its approach and updated its findings using the 1993 index. Researchers used 265 national surveys from 83 countries covering 1987, 1990, 1993, 1996 and 1998. There were some differences in approach compared to the earlier work.

Earlier estimates were derived using Penn World Tables (with data from 60 countries) as the basis for the 1985 Purchasing Power Parity exchange rates. For 1993, the World Bank developed its own Purchasing Power Parity estimates, using data—which includes better price data—from 110 countries collected under the 1993 International Comparison Project.[40]

To establish an international poverty line for the update, the World Bank took the median (instead of an "eyeball") of the lowest ten (rather than eight) poverty lines within the same set of thirty-three developing countries used for the 1985 figure.

Such methodological modifications and data source differences eliminate analytic equivalency between the earlier and later estimates of global poverty. The 1985 and 1993 indexes are therefore not comparable, even for the same year.

The "new" poverty line, the one that is representative of poverty lines in poor countries but is based on 1993 rather than 1985 Purchasing Power Parities is $1.08 a day, which, for practical purposes is truncated to $1 a day.

Interestingly, despite the differences in their underpinnings, both the new and the old poverty line yield similar global poverty counts for 1993, around 1.2 billion persons. For poverty comparison, PPP-weighted "international" dollars are useful because they value goods and services at a common set of prices, rather than relying simply on exchange rate weighted U.S. dollars.

Pro's and Con's of $1 a Day

The method does not lack for critics on technical grounds. PPP dollars reflect average price levels for a wide range of commodities. However, poor people must focus their spending on necessities like food, clothing and shelter. A PPP dollar may have less purchasing power with respect to such necessities. Hence it would understate the real extent of poverty.[41]

What the poor pay for a bundle of core antipoverty goods and services varies not only among countries but also, as compared to the nonpoor, within countries. The comparability made possible by the PPP measure is rough at best. While the measure can be adjusted for inflation, it fails to reflect any significant changes in relative prices over time (for example, the relative changes in, say, prices for food, housing and cars).

The World Bank's $1 a day poverty line does not indicate whether and to what extent people above or below the line can meet their basic needs or participate meaningfully in society.

For example, it is not possible to tell for any given country what proportion of basic food and shelter needs is covered by the PPP standard. PPP price indices include many items that may be cheap in a developing country but outside the bundle of consumption goods required by the poor.[42]

Some observers question the analytic value and policy relevance of such aggregate measures, since policies affecting poverty reduction must primarily come from within countries and country data are most useful for monitoring progress. Poverty statistics, it is argued, should measure "adequacy not arbitrary thresholds."[43]

For example, the purchasing power parity approach is tied to the strength of a country's currency. If the currency appreciates with respect to the dollar, the number of people in extreme poverty automatically drops.

This appears more like statistical legerdemain than real progress. Hence, for critics, global measures essentially have "limited, essentially propagandistic rather than analytical, value."[44]

Internationally comparable measures of poverty, while admittedly crude and dependent on faulty underlying data, reveal at least to some extent the world's progress in alleviating global poverty. The World Bank's $1 a day standard counts people that by any other definition would be classed as extremely poor. If a country's currency appreciates, some people are "artificially" lifted above that threshold; those who are not remain indisputably poor.

The $1 a day standard is not applied universally. For Latin America it is $2 a day. For Eastern Europe and the former republics of the Soviet Union it is $4 a day. The rationale for these particular adjustments remains obscure.

Data and Measurement Dilemmas

On the heels of poverty measurement comes the question of data. Even when the same poverty measure is used, estimates can vary widely depending on the source and type of data.

The United Nations Conference on Trade and Development has adopted an approach based on national income accounts estimates of private consumption rather than household survey data.[45] Using the $1 a day standard, UNCTAD has determined that household survey data underestimate the incidence and depth of poverty in the least developed countries.[46]

Other researchers, notably Xavier Sala-i-Martin and Surjit Bhalla, have used national income accounts for their analyses. They conclude that the World Bank's figures, which rely solely on survey data, considerably overestimate the number of people living on less than $1 a day.[47] A study by Sala-i-Martin using income data from national accounts puts the number at 350 million, not 1.1 billion.[48]

The Millennium Development Goals adopted by most international organizations call for reducing the proportion of people living on less than $1 a day to half the 1990 level by 2015, that is, from 29 percent of all people in low and middle income economies to 14.5 percent.

Bhalla's analysis, which uses consumption data from national accounts, estimates 650 million poor or 13.1 percent of the world's population in the year 2000. Thus, for Bhalla, the millennium development goal for poverty has been met fifteen years ahead of time. "The past 20 years were golden for poor people."[49]

Advocates of the national accounts approach contend that surveys are capturing less and less of the mean consumption in national accounts and that the downward trend is systematic rather than random.[50] However, the World Bank's Martin Ravallion maintains that analyses of national accounts overestimate consumption by the poor. Combining quintile shares from surveys with national account aggregates biases the consumption expenditure estimates for the poor upwards.

This is because, while surveys typically underestimate income—the extent varies from country to country—this tends to be truer for higher income than lower income respondents.[51] It is unlikely that an underestimate of income by a survey would leave the distribution unaffected. One cannot have it both ways— that is, claim that surveys underestimate consumption of the poor while faithfully reflecting the overall income distribution for national accounts analyses.

Given that consumption-based poverty is the variable of interest, the World Bank opts for person-level microdata as the most direct and reliable way to get at it. Further research is needed to explain and resolve the widening differences in poverty estimation between approaches based on national accounts and household survey-based approaches.[52]

Poverty is not the absence of income so much as the absence of wealth (that is, income *and* assets). Some people may be classified as extremely poor under an income standard but may own or at least control assets like real property. For most poor people, urban and rural, land is the main means to a livelihood.

For instance, "in Uganda, land constitutes between 50 and 60 percent of the asset endowment of the poorest households."[53] The same pattern is found in other developing countries. Since land is so often their key to economic opportunity, issues over property rights and land use policies and practices are vital to the poor.

The poor also benefit from public spending in areas like education, health care, housing, and other services. However, from the standpoint of their value as antipoverty measures, it is hard to allocate this spending appropriately in a national let alone a global context.

Some consumption-based alternatives to the World Bank's approach rely on national budget standards, that is, the baskets of goods and services considered essential by society to satisfy basic needs, participate in societal life or meet some other criteria. Basic needs will vary from culture to culture, country to country, even community to community. A poverty budget standard will vary from one country to another.

So long as a basket's contents are defined in the same way from one country to another, it is possible to gather and aggregate comparable international data. The amount and types of food required to meet basic needs can vary from one society to another but what is meant by "food" is understood universally.

Such approaches are considered more meaningful for policy purposes in that they suggest the types of interventions required at the national level, where action against poverty actually takes place.

Countries can use their own national definitions and standards in their poverty reduction plans. In Tanzania, poverty is measured by a poverty line of $0.65 a day as indicating a state of deprivation preventing a decent human life. Bolivia does not use income in defining poverty, seeing it rather as social exclusion and lack of opportunity to obtain adequate income and needed services.

From a global perspective, the problem is that a person who is designated as poor in a rich country might be redesignated as rich by moving to a poor country. And vice versa. Given increased immigration rates within and among countries, this takes on more than academic significance.

Nonmonetary Aspects of Poverty

Whereas it once could be seen as lack of income or, in some settings, assets, the concept of poverty has been extended in recent decades to cover nonmonetary facets of human existence. What besides income inadequacy is it that the world seeks to eradicate?

A potentially long list could be generated: lack of economic opportunities; illiteracy; malnutrition; disease; disability; shortened life expectancy; inadequate access to social services (education, health care, housing); porous safety nets; social exclusion; and absence of freedom or capability to act according to one's wishes and values.

The United Nations Development Programme defines poverty as the inability to satisfy minimum food and nonfood needs, the lack of minimally adequate income or expenditures, or the lack of essential human capabilities such as literacy, good health, and a long life.

Nobel Prize winning economist Amartya Sen sees poverty as the deprivation of basic capabilities. Thus overcoming poverty means expanding the range of choices available to the poor. Emancipation from poverty for a person, family or community is demonstrated by the capability to make and act on a wider range of choices.[54]

In this broader context, overcoming poverty means acquiring a range of capabilities. These include being able to earn income and acquire assets; gain access to education, health care, adequate nutrition, clean water and shelter; exert influence over public policy choices; command respect as valued members of their community; and withstand shocks like natural disasters, economic adversity and civil conflict.

Human Poverty Indices 1 and 2

The United Nations Development Programme has been in the forefront of efforts to capture the nonmonetary aspects of poverty.

For the United Nations Development Programme, poverty is seen as various forms of deprivation besides unemployment and lack of income. It also includes high levels of morbidity, low life expectancy, illiteracy, substandard housing, lack of safe drinking water, inadequate waste disposal systems, and environmental degradation.

In its 1997 *Human Development Report*, the United Nations Development Programme introduced the concept of human poverty and a means of measuring it, the Human Poverty Index (HPI).[55] There are two versions of the Human Poverty Index, one for developing countries that emphasizes living standards (e.g. access to health services, availability of safe drinking water) and one for industrialized countries that gives greater weight to income and employment.

Thus overcoming poverty begins with making sure that basic human needs are met through the right combination of social services. It goes from there to focus on employment and income generation.

More specifically, for the developing nations, the human poverty index or HPI-1 is measured by deprivation in selected areas. These are the percentages of:

(a) people not expected to survive after age 40;

(b) adults who are illiterate;

(c) people without access to safe drinking water;

(d) people without access to health services; and

(e) very underweight children below five years of age.

For the index, the last three measures are combined into a single composite. For industrialized countries, the index, HPI-2, is modified. Longevity is measured by the percentage of people not expected to survive after age 60.

Knowledge deficits are measured by the percentage of persons who are *functionally* illiterate, that is, cannot read or write well enough to function effectively in society. The standard of living is measured by the percentage of people whose incomes fall below 50 percent of the median disposable household income.

HPI-2 adds a component of poverty not found in HPI-1, namely, social exclusion. It is measured by the rate of long-term (twelve or more months) unemployment.

Composite measures like the United Nations Development Programme's two Human Poverty Indices (one for developing countries and one for members of the Organization for Economic Cooperation and Development and transition countries) capture the broader impact of poverty on individuals and societies.

As composites they do not readily reveal what particular factors account for one's status in the index and, hence, what is required for improvement.

Even if the factors could be disentangled, the lack of comparable data or, in some cases, *any* data creates another set of difficulties. In many countries, there is a shortage of valid and reliable data on infant mortality, life expectancy, health status, nutrition, literacy, access to safe drinking water, discrimination, social exclusion and related characteristics.

Data Collection in Developing Countries

In poor countries, collecting data on the population's well-being through scientifically sound and nationally representative sample surveys can be prohibitively expensive. Compared to investments in more growth-oriented activities, data collection can seem like an unaffordable luxury.

The data on poverty in developing countries tend to be based on the traditional measure of poverty, namely income. Where individual and household surveys are absent, analysts must rely on aggregate data like gross domestic product.

Hence, for global poverty comparisons, an income measure for data collection and analysis is the best available option. This does not prevent each country from establishing its own poverty income line or employing nonmonetary indicators (for example, infant mortality, primary school enrollment, life expectancy) to obtain a more culturally appropriate picture of poverty in its own national context.

The approach to poverty of the United Nations Development Programme is attractive conceptually but can be daunting as the basis for sustained global action against poverty. The $1 a day standard has been widely criticized—and widely used. The criticism is warranted because the measure is flawed. For example, it ignores factors like assets and fails to account fully for purchasing power differentials within and among countries.

Its wide use is also warranted. For all its flaws, it has the advantage of being clear, measurable and capable of being rallied around by a global network. Progress in halving the proportion of people living on $1 a day or less should correlate with progress on other antipoverty fronts.

One can argue that merely halving the proportion of this population leaves an unacceptably large number of the global citizenry in extreme poverty. Furthermore, a $2 a day standard or higher would be more realistic. Such points are unassailable at one level. But one must start somewhere. And that "somewhere" needs to engage the mind and heart of the global community.

At the same time the Human Poverty Index keeps one's attention on non-income aspects of poverty and the complexity of waging an all-out war to eradicate it.

In recent years, there have been efforts to improve data quality and coverage, notably by the United Nations in its National Household Survey Capability Programme and the World Bank through its Living Standards Measurement Study and the Social Dimensions of Adjustment Project in Sub-Saharan Africa.

The Luxembourg Income Study project begun in 1983 contains comparable cross-country household-level microdata from 25 developed countries, including their people whose income falls below official poverty lines.

Monitoring Progress in the War against Poverty

In this book I frequently fall back on income poverty, at times reluctantly. Income is more easily measured than other constructs. Increasing income is a necessary if not sufficient condition for escaping poverty. As a concept, it is limited but, as a measure, it correlates reasonably well with indicators like education, health and housing.

It may well be that a rich person in a society that suppresses freedom of speech is "poor" but I tend to think that a person with minimal income in a freer society qualifies for more immediate assistance.

When measures in addition to income inadequacy are introduced, monitoring global progress against poverty becomes more complicated. For example, a person may be in good health but non-literate.

Or have a high income but a short life expectancy.

Or be non-poor by other standards but live in an area that lacks access to safe drinking water.[56]

Or, if one adopts the range of choice perspective, prosper materially but live in a society that denies freedom of speech or assembly.

The selection of measures of poverty depends on the uses for which they are intended. An income measure may not always correlate with non-economic dimensions, such as access to health care or meaningful participation in political life.

However, a single measure like income is attractive in that it more readily lends itself to cross-country or cross-population comparisons. It becomes a benchmark with which to evaluate a country's development strategy.

Overview of Development Strategies

While global strategies against poverty may be in fashion, policy priorities are subject to change over time. This is particularly true of global institutions with mandates that include but go beyond poverty reduction.

The most prominent examples are the World Bank and the International Monetary Fund. Their priorities are shaped by their richest shareholders that hold a disproportionate share of these institutions' "votes." Better and more systematically gathered data on global poverty can serve as a counterweight to pressures that would downgrade poverty as a global concern.

Development strategies tend to sort themselves into four distinct categories that for convenience we may label structuralism, neoliberalism, interventionism and, for lack of a better term, none-of-the-above-ism.

Structuralism embraces a large if not overriding role for the state to build a modern economy through comprehensive planning and state-sponsored enterprises. It hearkens back to Marxist objections to capitalism as the instrument of class exploitation. It has a frankly redistributionist cast. The 1950s and 1960s emphasized this strategy.

Neoliberalism, the descendant of unfettered free enterprise, sees individual entrepreneurs as the agents of development and supports elimination of obstacles in their way. The trickle down school embraces this theory and scorns all others. Gaining ground in the 1970s, this strategy achieved prominence in the 1980s.

Interventionism tilts in favor of market economies but works to offset the adverse impacts of capitalist progress. This strategy made its presence felt more strongly in the 1990s. Large countries like India and China with very different systems of government have made progress in reducing poverty with this strategy.

Adherents of *None-of-the-above-ism* include skeptics who support vaguer notions of "people-centered" development or reject development altogether as a smoke screen for western, and especially United States, hegemony in world affairs.[57]

The World Bank predicates poverty reduction in developing countries on a trifecta of economic growth, training-and-education and social safety nets. The latter consist of social insurance schemes, means-tested social services and access to health care.

Progress at the margins is hardest to make since by definition the residual poor are least able to tap into the benefits of globalization. The rate of poverty reduction in developing countries will slow insofar as people remain mired in poverty despite increased capital investment and open markets.

Interestingly, countries classified as "developing" can make significant strides toward eliminating poverty through direct approaches. One thinks of Cuba, a lower-middle income country, whose under age five mortality rate and overall life expectancy compare favorably with those of the high income United States.[58] For all its deficiencies, Cuba's socialist system has in some ways worked to the advantage of the country's poorest citizens.

Globalization of the world economy has both positive and negative aspects in the war on global poverty. Globalization can strengthen the ability of institutions within and across countries to coordinate their antipoverty strategies.

In the current international environment, it is hard to visualize significant poverty reduction apart from economic growth. The phenomena are interrelated, even if not neatly correlated. The history of the past six decades suggests the type of risk that comes from concentrating on one to the exclusion of the other.

Global growth and economic integration are necessary but insufficient conditions for the eradication of poverty. They do not by themselves lift people out of poverty. To survive the extremely poor will depend on social services like basic education, primary health care and family planning services, low-cost safe water and sanitation, and nutrition programs.

And an adequate income.

ENDNOTES

1. United Nations (2002(a)) 89. Statement of Michael Moore, director-general, World Trade Organization, at the United Nations International Conference on Financing for Development, Monterrey, Mexico, March 18-22, 2002.

2. Lieberson, Joseph and Jonathan Sleeper (2000) 9.

3. African Development Bank, Asian Development Bank, European Bank for Reconstruction and Development, International Monetary Fund, World Bank (July 2000) i.

4. See www.un.org/millennium.

5. Maddison, Angus (2003) 232-234. My calculations of growth rates.

6. Ibid.

7. Ibid.

8. Ramonet, Ignacio (November 1998) 1.

9. Organization for Economic Cooperation and Development (2001) 31.

10. Estes, Richard, J. (1997).

11. United Nations Population Fund (2002) 22.

12. Ibid.: 53.

13. U.S. Central Intelligence Agency (2001) 36-41.

14. International Labour Organization (2004) 1-5.

15. International Labour Organization, "Ballooning Youth Unemployment May Pose Threat to Stable Development in Asia," press release, 2/27/02. See www.ilo.org/public/english/region/asro/bangkok/newsroom.

16. International Fund for Agricultural Development (2001) iv. Also see the table at www.worldbank.org/research/povmonitor.

17. World Bank (2003) 46.

18. See World Bank, "East Asia & Pacific Region: Global Poverty Down By Half Since 1981 But Progress Uneven As Economic Growth Eludes Many Countries", April 23, 2004. News release no. 2004/309/S.

19. Ibid. Also, see United Nations Development Programme (1998). As a comparison with Sub-Saharan Africa, consider that the entire U.S. population in 2000 is 280 million.

20. Jones, Charles I. (2002) 7.

21. United Nations (1997) chapter 3.

22. African Development Bank, Asian Development Bank, European Bank for Reconstruction and Development, International Monetary Fund, World Bank (July 2000) 2.

23. Food and Agriculture Organization (2000(a)) Foreword.

24. Milanovic, Branko (2002) 88.

25. Dollar, David (2001) 19. He attributes this phenomenon, which does not lack for skeptics, to the acceleration of growth and significant poverty reduction in China and India, both large and both poor, over that period.

26. Data on global income inequalities are improving. In 1997, Klaus Deininger and Lyn Squire of the World Bank released a data set on income inequality. The latest (2000) version has observations from ninety-nine countries. Among its other uses, the Deininger-Squire data set has served as the core for the World Income Inequality Database, developed by the United Nations University's World Institute for Development Economics Research (WIDER). The most recent version of the latter, released September 12, 2000, includes data from 151 countries. The Deininger-Squire database is accessible at www.worldbank.org/research/growth/dddeisqu.htm. The World Income Inequality Database is available at www.wider.unu.edu/wiid/wiid.htm. The Asian Development Bank is reviewing the status of poverty measurement and data availability in each developing member country and is building a database of key poverty indicators.

27. International Labour Organization, Regional Office for Asia and the Pacific, "Indigenous People Still the Poorest of the Poor," press release, 8/8/01. www.ilo.org/public/english/region/asro/bangkok/newsroom.

28. World Bank (1999).

29. Imagine the following distribution of total income: lowest quintile — 5%; next lowest quintile — 10%; middle quintile — 15%; second highest quintile — 20%; and highest quintile — 50%. The curve would be shaped roughly like a bow between the

diagonal 45-degree line (the "bowstring") and the X-axis. A related indicator of income inequality, the Gini coefficient, measures the area between the diagonal and the Lorenz curve. The higher the coefficient, the greater the income inequality.

30. World Bank. 2001(b) 55.

31. To go into a little more detail, the Gini coefficient can be derived from the Lorenz curve. The Lorenz curve plots the cumulative share of the total income held by the cumulative share of the population. It starts with the lowest income group and works upwards, usually in quintiles. The Gini coefficient is the result when the area between the diagonal and the Lorenz curve is divided by the total area under the diagonal. Zero represents maximum equality and one (or 100 percent) maximum inequality.

32. The median income is that amount such that half the population receives more and half less. If poverty is measured in relative terms as half the median income, it is hypothetically possible that no one's income falls below that amount. For example, if the median income is $10,000, half the population could receive less than that amount with no one's income falling below a poverty line of $5,000.

33. Fields, Gary S. (2001) 60. Fields reviews the literature on inequality and growth including his own research over several decades as support for this conclusion. For prior work that suggested the same conclusion, see Ahluwalia, Montek "Income Inequality: Some Dimensions of the Problem" in Chenery, Hollis B., Montek S. Ahluwalia, C.L.G. Bell, John H. Dulloy, and Richard Jolly (1974) 3-27. This body of work essentially provides a review of the Kuznets hypothesis — that income inequality increases in the early stages of economic growth but decreases later — and finds it wanting.

34. Fields, Gary S. (2001) 95-104.

35. Statement from the XIII Ministerial Conference of the Non-Aligned Movement, Cartagena, Columbia, April 8-9, 2000.

36. Because of its sensitivity to distributional effects, a commonly used poverty gap ratio P is the general class of Foster-Greer-Thorbecke (FGT) measures. These can capture both the extent and severity of poverty. Here, $P(\alpha)=1/n[\sum\{(1-(yi/p))\alpha\}]$. For the formula, the population is n, p is the poverty income threshold and yi is the income of the ith poor person. When α is zero, the result is a poverty head count ratio, since each individual measurement takes on a value of 1. When α is 1, it generates a poverty gap ratio indicating the resources needed to eliminate poverty as a function of national income. When α is 2, it yields the squared coefficient of variation in income among the poor (or a variant of the Gini coefficient which measures income inequality). See Foster, James; Joel Greer; and Eric Thorbecke (1984) 761-765. The interpretation of the FGT measure when α is 2 is not straightforward.

37. World Bank (1990) 26.

38. Ravallion, Martin (2002) 2-3 at www.columbia.edu/~sr793/wbreply.pdf. The authors stress that their approach is conservative. With the available data they could neither account for intra-household consumption inequality or individuals' ability to access non-market goods. Much of the groundwork for the approach was laid in prior World Bank research by Ahluwalia, Montek S., Nicholas G. Carter and Hollis Chenery (1979).

39. The eight countries were Bangladesh, Indonesia, Morocco, Nepal, Kenya, Pakistan, the Philippines, and Tanzania.

40. The Penn World Tables provide purchasing power parity and national income accounts converted to international prices for 168 countries for some or all of the years 1950-2000. They were developed as part of the International Comparison Program by the Center for International Comparisons at the University of Pennsylvania. The Penn World Tables break down Gross Domestic Product expenditures into household consumption,

collective government consumption, domestic investment and the net foreign balance. See pwt.econ.upenn.edu. In the 1980s, the International Comparison Program was taken over on a cooperative basis by the United Nations Statistical Office, Eurostat and the Organization for Economic Cooperation and Development.

41. Among the more prominent are Reddy, Sanjay G. and Thomas W. Pogge (2002). These critics favor a standard based on the local cost of a basic set of commodities. This approach is attractive in principle but it is difficult to see how to operationalize it for comparative purposes on a global scale.

42. Wade, Robert Hunter (2002) 6.

43. Gordon, David, "The International Measurement of Poverty and Anti-Poverty Policies" in Townsend, Peter and David Gordon (2002) 66.

44. Srinivasan, T.N. (2000) 15. He adds that only the "somewhat naïve" believe that policies behind bilateral and multilateral aid to developing countries are "driven by [the developing countries'] levels of poverty." While other considerations clearly drive aid levels, poverty reduction is part of the overall political calculus.

45. United Nations Conference on Trade and Development (2002) 50-51. The national-accounts-consistent approach itself is not without its own limitations for household poverty estimation. For example it implicitly includes spending by nonprofit groups, not just households. Private consumption is calculated as a residual from other economic aggregates like output, imports, inventory changes and the like. Relying on national income accounts alone has resulted in overestimation of the rate of poverty reduction. For its poverty reduction forecasts, the World Bank now generally assumes that household consumption growth rates will equal 87 percent of the private consumption growth rates from the national income accounts. See World Bank (2001(a)) 40. Hence national income accounts cannot serve uncritically as a "gold standard" for poverty measurement.

46. Why this should occur is not well understood. UNCTAD speculates that the very poor may be underrepresented in national household surveys and that the value assigned to home-produced consumption is inflated. For less poor developing countries, the opposite is the case — poverty rates are overestimated. See United Nations Conference on Trade and Development (2002) 50-51. However, the World Bank concludes that in household surveys "higher-income groups tend to underreport consumption." (World Bank (2001(a)) 45. The debate goes on.

47. Perhaps further clarification is in order. The World Bank has used reported consumption growth rates from national accounts to align its survey data (which come from different countries in different years) in order to generate global poverty estimates. Also, where survey data on consumption were lacking, consumption was estimated by multiplying survey income data by the share of aggregate private consumption in national income based on national accounts. See World Bank (2001b) 17. Beginning in 2003, based on comparisons of income and consumption from surveys in more than 20 countries where there was data on both variables, the World Bank determined that, where income data were available and consumption data were not, the income data could safely be used to measure poverty directly without further adjustment from national accounts. See World Bank (2004a) 57.

48. Sala-i-Martin, Xavier (2002). The extent to which individual income poverty is grounded in household consumption alone (as highlighted in surveys) or *private consumption* — that is, consumption of households and other entities like non-profit organizations and charities — plus other public spending (as found in national accounts) affects the findings. The latter approach tends to increase mean income per person and therefore drive down the number of people below the $1 a day threshold. This can be defended to the extent that such spending (e.g. on health care or housing) benefits the

poor. But how to separate out such spending from other public spending (e.g. on national defense or, for that matter, corruption) is a dicey proposition. See United Nations Conference on Trade and Development (2002) 50-51.

49. Bhalla, Surjit (2001) 200.

50. Bhalla, Surjit (2002) 104-105.

51. Ravallion, Martin (2003).

52. Apropos of this, in a 1993 report to the government of India, an expert group came out against using an adjustment factor to compensate for the discrepancies in estimates of consumption expenditures between surveys and national accounts statistics. According to their report: "This adjustment is made on the assumption that the difference [in the two estimates] is distributed uniformly across States, and across all sections of the population. We do not find this procedure acceptable because it involves arbitrary pro-rata adjustment in the distribution. Under the circumstances, it is better to rely exclusively on the NSS [quintennial National Sample Survey] for estimating the poverty ratio by State and in rural and urban areas." Unadjusted survey estimates by State would be aggregated to generate national estimates. See Planning Commission, Government of India (1993) 37, 50. Of course, Bhalla would beg to disagree. See Bhalla, Surjit S. (2002).

53. Deininger, Klaus (2003) xx.

54. In this he may be seen as having been foreshadowed by Sir Arthur Lewis who, in *The Theory of Economic Growth*, states the case for economic growth as giving "man greater control over his environment, and thereby [increasing] his freedom." (1955) 421.

55. A precursor was the Capability Poverty Measure, introduced in the 1996 *Human Development Report*.

56. An estimated 3.3 billion cases of illness and 5.3 million deaths in the developing world each year are attributable to unsafe water. See the press release for the 1999 United Nations World Day for Water, which is found at www.unu.edu/hq/rector_office/press-archives/press99/wwaterday.pdf. To take one example, one-third of Asia's population does not have safe drinking water, and one half lacks adequate sanitation.

57. Adapted from Allen, Tim and Alan Thomas, editors (2000). See Alan Thomas, "Meanings and Views of Development" (Chapter 2, 42-48).

58. For both countries, in 1977 the under age five (child) mortality rate was eight deaths per one thousand live births; life expectancy was seventy-six years at birth. See Parker, Melissa and Gordon Wilson, "Diseases of Poverty," Chapter 4 in Allen, Tim and Alan Thomas, editors (2000) 77.

2

Post-War Reconstruction (1941-50)

War and Its Aftermath

Poverty did not preoccupy the world's leaders in 1941-45 period. War did.

Yet, in the midst of war, it is remarkable how much attention world leaders gave to international solidarity and post-war reconstruction. The need for a new international architecture was recognized.

Several permanent international institutions emerged out of the havoc of war. These were the United Nations, the International Bank for Reconstruction and Development, later known as the World Bank, the International Monetary Fund, and the General Agreement on Tariffs and Trade, which evolved in 1994 into the World Trade Organization.

Following the Second World War, the victors focused on reconstructing the war-torn nations in Europe and Asia. Reconstruction plans segued into a vision of long term economic development.

United Nations

On January 1, 1944, more than a year before the end of World War II, 26 nations released a "Declaration by United Nations" in which they pledged to fight the Axis powers.[1] The name "United Nations" was given to the organization by President Franklin D. Roosevelt.

The United Nations is an organization whose member nations have joined together to foster peace and security throughout the world. The forerunner of the

United Nations, the League of Nations, was established in 1919 under the Treaty of Versailles.

Conceived during the First World War, the League of Nations suffered from the lack of participation by the United States and proved incapable of preventing the Second World War. It ceased operations in 1946. However, its experience provided invaluable grounding for the design of its successor.

In 1945, with victory assured, representatives of fifty countries met in San Francisco to draw up the United Nations Charter, which they signed on June 26. Poland, which was not represented at the Conference, signed later and became one of the original fifty-one member states.

The United Nations officially came into existence on October 24, 1945, by which time the Charter had been ratified by China, France, the Soviet Union, United Kingdom, United States and by a majority of other signatories. By late 2002, the United Nations had 191 member states that accepted the obligations set forth in the Charter.[2]

The United Nations was conceived as a conflict-resolution body, a role that could be interpreted quite broadly. As originally signed, the Charter expresses in its Preamble the determination of the peoples of the United Nations "to promote social progress and better standards of life in larger freedom" and "to employ international machinery for the promotion of the economic and social advancement of all peoples...."

Article 1 states that a main purpose is "to achieve international co-operation in solving international problems of an economic, social, cultural, or humanitarian character...." While poverty as a distinct human condition was not mentioned, the "economic and social advancement of all peoples" could be taken as an antipoverty goal.

In Article 55, the United Nations Charter committed the organization to promoting "higher standards of living, full employment, and conditions of economic and social progress and development."

This framed the context for three early publications: *National and International Measures for Full Employment* (1949) followed by *Measures for Economic Development in Under-Developed Countries* (1951) and *Measures for International Economic Stability* (1951). Teams of economists that included future Nobel Laureates Theodore Shultz and Sir Arthur Lewis, prepared these reports with assistance from the UN secretariat.[3]

While a commitment to social justice might be seen as a subtext, Keynesian notions of global economic development drove the thinking embodied in these reports.

They left unresolved (to this day) the question of the degree to which and the point at which economic development alone would achieve substantial reductions in poverty. Any incapacity of pure economic development strategies to bring about real and lasting reductions in national poverty rates within a reasonable time period might dictate leaving room for redistributionist policies.

Among the specialized agencies the World Bank and the International Monetary Fund merit closer attention. These so-called Bretton Woods institutions have come to play a central role in the global war on poverty.

Bretton Woods

Between July 1-22, 1944, about a year before the end of World War II, representatives of forty-four nations met at Bretton Woods, New Hampshire. By then the Allies were anticipating victory.

The immediate impetus was the need to restore the economies of nations devastated by the Depression of the 1930s and the Second World War. Chastened by the worldwide Depression that had preceded the war, the Allies feared a return to protectionist trade policies.

Dominated by the United States and Great Britain, the conferees designed the post-war architecture for international finance, trade, development and security.

The Bretton Woods conferees created the International Bank for Reconstruction and Development and a sister organization, the International Monetary Fund. The first is usually called the World Bank and the two together are referred to as the Bretton Woods Institutions.[4]

The Bretton Woods framework for restructuring the world's economy emphasized as a goal a higher standard of living. Sustained rates of high economic growth were seen as the engine of modernization. Relatively little attention was paid to the question of income distribution, even less to poverty as a distinct social issue.

If anything sentiment swung the other way. Development theory as articulated most masterfully by Sir Arthur Lewis identified two characteristics as critical to growth. One was an adequate share of national income devoted to savings rather than consumption. The other was "adequate [income] differentials [as reward] for skill, for hard work, for education, for risk bearing, and for willingness to take responsibility."[5] The poor, differentially disadvantaged and forced to consume rather than save, fell short on both counts. Economic growth depended on income inequality.[6]

A longer-range vision was incorporated into its purposes as given in Article 1 of the Articles of Agreement. By fostering international trade and equilibrium in the balance of payments, and by making or guaranteeing international loans, the Bank sought to develop the productive resources of its members. It would thereby assist in "raising productivity, the standard of living and conditions of labor in their territories."

In 1946, President Truman appointed Eugene Meyer, publisher of the Washington Post, as first president of the World Bank. Insisting that loans be made only to credit-worthy borrowers, Meyer soon found himself at odds with the Bank's international board of directors who favored a more forgiving approach. Meyer resigned after only six months.

His successor, John McCloy, former assistant secretary of war, stayed for only two years of his five-year term. He succeeded in winning credibility for the

Bank with Wall Street and other large institutional investors. They quickly subscribed to the Bank's first bond sale, a $250 million offering.

Under McCloy, the Bank made its first loan in 1947, to France, followed by others to Denmark, the Netherlands and Luxembourg. The Bank saw its mission as helping reconstruct war-torn economies. A year later, Chile received the first development loan.

The World Bank could not hope to match the scale of U.S. aid to Europe under the Marshall Plan, whose official title was "European Recovery Plan". The Marshall Plan's funds were directed toward strengthening the economies of 16 Western European nations, home to some 270 million people.[7]

The program cost U.S. taxpayers some $11.8 billion to which might be added $1.5 billion in loans that were repaid. Its success was due in no small part to educated and industrialized European nations that used the aid effectively. The Marshall Plan was given a life of four years to assure the American people that it would not become an indefinite commitment.

The World Bank by default turned its attention and resources to the needs of developing nations in Africa, Asia and Latin America. Initially the Bank focused on raising aggregate national incomes, but shifted its attention early on to per capita income as a better reflection of living standards. With experience it gradually acquired better understanding of the issues around growth and income distribution in developing countries.[8]

International Monetary Fund

During World War II, progress was made in designing an open and stable international monetary system. Though limited in comparison to the International Bank for Reconstruction and Development, the Bretton Woods conferees envisioned a significant role for the International Monetary Fund

It was intended as machinery for coping with international monetary problems by promoting orderly exchange arrangements among member countries and making loans to correct balance of payments deficiencies.

An underlying purpose was "to contribute...to the promotion and maintenance of high levels of employment and real income and to the development of the productive resources of all members as primary objectives of economic policy."[9]

Harry Dexter White, chief international economist at the U.S. Treasury from 1942 to 1944, drafted the U.S. blueprint for the International Monetary Fund. It competed with a more ambitious plan prepared for the British Treasury by the internationally renowned economist, John Maynard Keynes.

The compromise adopted at Bretton Woods, New Hampshire in July 1944 defined the International Monetary Fund not as a world central bank but as a promoter of economic growth through international trade and financial stability.

On trade, events unfolded differently.

No to an International Trade Organization

The Bretton Woods conferees envisioned an International Trade Organization as a complement to the International Monetary Fund and International Bank for Reconstruction and Development that would bring discipline to international trade policies.

A Charter was drawn up at a conference in Havana in 1948 but was not approved by the U.S. Congress. As a consequence the International Trade Organization never materialized and emphasis shifted to the General Agreement on Tariffs and Trade (GATT). This was a multilateral treaty that the signatories expected would be overseen by the projected International Trade Organization.

Instead GATT stood alone as principal international trade regulating instrument until 1995 when it was taken over by the newly created World Trade Organization. GATT was based on four themes or principles.

First, by virtue of reciprocity, a country would grant tariff concessions in exchange for similar concessions by a trading partner. Second, under its "most favored nation" clause, any concession granted to one partner would be extended to all other partners in non-discriminatory fashion. Third, countries also agreed not to discriminate between imported and domestically produced goods. Finally, only ordinary tariffs would be used to regulate imports.

Launching an Era of Development

In his inaugural address, January 20, 1949, U.S. President Harry S. Truman set forth his Administration's agenda. In the famous Point Four of his address, the President outlined a vision of a world freeing itself from poverty and progressing in terms of economic development.

> "Fourth...[m]ore than half the people of the world are living in conditions approaching misery....Their poverty is a handicap and a threat both to them and to more prosperous areas. ....[W]e should make available to peace-loving peoples the benefits of our store of technical knowledge in order to help them [achieve] a better life....This should be a cooperative enterprise in which all nations work together through the United Nations and its specialized agencies wherever practicable."

Thus was launched the era of development. It unfolded in the context of a post-war rebuilding period. The period was marked by global competition between the industrialized democracies of the West and the communist societies of Eastern Europe and parts of Asia. It was epitomized by the Cold War rivalry between the United States of America and the Union of Soviet Socialist Republics

"Third world" nations, as they were called, tended to be poor, non-aligned and ripe for development. They represented missionary territory for both capitalist and communist models of development.

Emerging Independent Nations and Poverty

In the developing world, newly independent nations in Asia and Africa emerged from the experience of having been colonized. (The nations of Latin America had preceded them by a century and a half.) For most, their colonial experience was characterized by widespread poverty, whose facets included low income, illiteracy, malnutrition, disease, disability, infant mortality and reduced life expectancy. Their new governments were not unmindful.

The road to development ran through the industrial sector.

Countries like Brazil, Egypt and India had half a century or more of industrial experience, mainly in food processing and textiles. The Republic of Korea and Taiwan had a base of education and industrial experience. At the opposite extreme, the newly freed nations of Sub-Saharan Africa lacked both an educational base and industrial experience.[10]

India's Plans for Development

As a developing country with a history of being colonized, India has an impressive track record of documenting its planning experience and evaluating its progress in fostering growth and alleviating poverty. India could be described as the "poster child" of government-led development, since it mixed state planning with emphasis on self-help.

Since the 1950s, the country also has regularly conducted the National Sample Survey, which monitors consumption by a representative sample of the population.[11] These extensive and high quality surveys provide a reasonably clear picture over time of national and sub-national poverty trends.

India was one of the seventeen countries meeting in Atlantic City, New Jersey during June 1944 to prepare an agenda for the Bretton Woods conference. The Indian delegation suggested the name International Bank for Reconstruction and Development to the agenda drafting committee. And India was one of the forty-four nations that signed the agreement establishing the World Bank.[12]

In the planning leading up to India's independence in 1948, groups like the National Planning Committee of Indian National Congress viewed the eradication of poverty as an indispensable element of future development. Most of these groups saw rapid economic growth through industrialization as the main pathway out of poverty.

But not just growth for the sake of growth. Independence, economic growth and poverty reduction were linked from the start.[13]

In March 1950, India established a Planning Commission with Jawaharlal Nehru as the first Chairman. The following year it published the first of a series of five-year plans geared to the country's development. Under its first five-year plan (1950-55), the government intervened at strategic points to make sure that development was proceeding in line with the stated objectives.

The first five-year plan was followed in succession by two others. In 1965, there was a break due to war between India and Pakistan. Drought, currency devaluation and price increases disrupted the planning process; annual plans were published for 1966, 1967 and 1968. The fourth five-year plan began in 1969. Plans five, six and seven followed on course. Because of political events, the eighth plan released in 1990 was not implemented until 1992. It featured the initiation of structural adjustment policies.

India's first eight plans emphasized public sector support for heavy industries. Plans nine and ten have shifted the emphasis with the public sector setting broad goals and the private sector given more scope in the development process.

Disappointment with subsidies for the poor and the performance of approaches like the Integrated Rural Development Programme have led the Commission to consider alternatives. One of these is the redirection of resources toward "various types of basic infrastructural asset creation programmes in rural areas."[14]

Table 2. Poverty in India: 1974-2000 (Selected Years)

YEAR	1973/ 1974	1977/ 1978	1983	1987/ 1988	1993/ 1994	1999/ 2000
Number (in Millions)	321	329	323	307	320	260
Percent of Population	54.9	51.3	44.5	38.9	36.0	26.1

Source: Indian Economic Survey, 2001-2002, as summarized in Nathan Associates, Inc. (2002) 4.

Despite nagging problems with implementation, participation rates and the overall pace of progress, India's Planning Commission sees antipoverty programs as a valid component of national growth efforts. In recent years the Commission has adopted a more market-oriented and less state-dominated approach to overall economic development.

During the 1990s, India emerged as one of the ten fastest growing countries in the world. While poverty rates and the absolute numbers both declined, the country nonetheless remained home to nearly 260 million poor people, as measured by the government's official poverty line. The persistence of widespread poverty is disheartening since the alleviation of poverty has guided development planning from the beginning.

At the same time, there have been notable successes in India's antipoverty strategies. States like Kerala, Haryana, Bihar, Himachal Pradesh, Karnataka and Rajasthan have witnessed sharp declines in their poverty levels. Other states like Orissa and Madyha Pradesh have been unable to reduce their poverty rates.

Through a sustained systematic approach to development and poverty reduction, as formulated in its five-year plans, and an impressive body of research on the effects of its initiatives, India provides a unique opportunity to assess what works in alleviating poverty, what does not, and why.[15]

International Relief Organizations

Concern with post-war reconstruction and development was not limited to governments. Private nonprofit entities, both religious and secular, stepped in to provide relief and to combat poverty.

In 1943, during World War II, for example, the Roman Catholic Bishops of the United States established Catholic Relief Services to aid in the resettlement of Europe's war refugees. Other prominent examples of humanitarian work were Oxfam, CARE, Caritas Internationalis, Christian Aid and World Vision.

In some respects, they served as the vanguard of what developed in the succeeding decades into an impressively large network of international non-governmental organizations aimed at eliminating poverty, safeguarding the environment and promoting human rights. Their organizational structures (as reflected in their boards of directors, advisory committees and staffs) have become decidedly more multinational.

Oxfam's Origins[16]

During World War II, the Allied nations imposed a naval blockade on Greece, which had been occupied by German forces. Lacking access to food and medicines, Greece experienced famine. In May 1942, a Famine Relief Committee was established in Britain. One of the local affiliates was the Oxford Committee for Famine Relief, which first convened in October 1942.

Its founding members included Canon T. R. Milford of the University Church and Professor Gilbert Murray, a member of the national Committee and former Regius Professor of Greek at Oxford. Cecil Jackson-Cole, a London businessman appointed Honorary Secretary in December managed the Committee's work for many years.

The Oxford Committee continued on after the war, providing food and clothing to refugees and other persons in war-ravaged European countries. In 1949 the Committee expanded its mission to assist people suffering from war or other causes anywhere.

In 1951 the Oxford Committee for Famine Relief in Great Britain raised funds to combat famine in Bihar, India. In 1953, its fundraising assisted persons orphaned or made homeless or hungry by the Korean War. The Committee gradually became known by its abbreviated telegraph address, Oxfam, and formally adopted this name in 1965.

Over the succeeding decades, it emerged as a significant non-governmental force in global antipoverty efforts through its humanitarian relief work, community-based development projects, research, advocacy and campaigns on issues like crippling debt burdens and unfair trade practices.

CARE[17]

In the United States, CARE, headquartered in Atlanta, Georgia, is one of the world's largest private humanitarian organizations.

In 1945, as World War II ended, twenty-two United States organizations joined in an effort to send lifesaving CARE packages to the war's survivors. The first CARE Packages were U.S. Army surplus "10-in-1" food parcels intended to provide one meal for ten soldiers during the planned invasion of Japan. When these ran out CARE assembled its own packages with assistance from American companies.

Approximately twenty thousand packages reached Le Havre, France on May 11, 1946. They were the first of some one hundred million more CARE Packages sent over the next two decades to people in need in Europe, Asia and many developing countries elsewhere.

In 1948, CARE airlifted food to Berlin when troops of the Soviet Union set up a blockade. The first vehicle to enter Berlin after the lifting of the blockade was a CARE food truck. A year later CARE began its work in the developing world by starting a project in the Philippines.

Caritas Internationalis

Caritas Internationalis is a confederation of 162 Catholic relief, development and social service organizations. The first Caritas organization was started in Freiburg, Germany, in 1897. Other national Caritas organizations were formed in Switzerland in 1901 and in the United States as Catholic Charities in 1910.

In the United States, the demand for charitable assistance from the Catholic Church had risen with increased immigration during the 1800s. A network of Catholic Charities agencies grew up to provide social services and health care while advocating on behalf of the poor.

In July 1924, during the Eucharistic World Congress in Amsterdam, sixty delegates from twenty-two countries formed a conference, with headquarters at Caritas Switzerland in Lucerne. In 1928, the conference became known as Caritas Catholica. The delegates met every two years until World War II.

Work resumed in 1947 with the approval of the Vatican's Secretariat of State. Caritas was designated by the Secretariat of State to represent all international Catholic welfare organizations especially at the United Nations.

In the United States, Catholic Relief Services, a member of the Caritas federation, was established in 1943 as a private, nonprofit corporation.[18] It serves as the global humanitarian aid and development agency of the U.S. Conference of Catholic Bishops. Its board consists of members elected from the USCCB.

The Caritas approach, which is based on the social teachings of the Catholic Church, emphasizes the dignity of the human person and the need to overcome poverty, dehumanizing working conditions and unjust social structures.

Christian Aid[19]

Christian Aid began in 1945 as Christian Reconciliation in Europe, following the devastation of World War II. In 1949 it became the Department for the Inter-Church Aid and Refugee Service within the British Council of Churches where it focused on world refugee settlement and justice issues. It collaborated with the World Council of Churches and churches in the newly independent countries of the South.

In 1964 the organization changed its name to Christian Aid. In 1991, Christian Aid became a separate legal entity, but retains close ties to the British Council of Churches.

Every year during Christian Aid Week, over three hundred thousand volunteers in the United Kingdom and Ireland collect money to help the world's poorest communities. Christian Aid is not a missionary society but an overseas development agency, sponsored by forty British and Irish Churches. It works in over sixty of the world's poorest countries.

World Vision

World Vision International is a Christian relief and development organization. The organization was founded by American missionary Bob Pierce following a trip to China and Korea in 1947. In one encounter Pierce met White Jade, a young Christian girl too poor to attend her local school. Challenged by White Jade's teacher, he began sending $5 a month towards the school's fees. It was the beginning of a child sponsorship program.

In 1950, World Vision was legally incorporated as an organization and national offices soon appeared in Canada, Australia and New Zealand. By 1966 the ministry had a worldwide scope. Though established to care for orphans in Asia, World Vision has come to focus on broader approaches to community development and advocacy for the poor.

A New Global Architecture

By the end of a tumultuous, war-torn decade that saw loss of life and destruction on an unprecedented scale, there had been put in place a new global architecture. It included newly independent states, many of which emerged from colonial status, organizations of nation-states, and non-governmental relief organizations.

The United Nations sought to preserve the peace, the Bretton Woods institutions aided in economic reconstruction and the non-governmental organizations provided emergency relief services.

Gradually poverty as a global issue began to work its way into their missions.

ENDNOTES

1. The name Axis was applied first to Germany and Italy, whose governments signed the Rome-Berlin Axis agreement in October 1936. Japan was added to the Axis when it signed the Tripartite Pact on September 27, 1940. The term later came to include Hungary, Romania, and Bulgaria.

2. www.un.org/Overview/unmember.html.

3. Emmerij, Louis; Richard Jolly; and Thomas G. Weiss (2001) 26-39.

4. Later, as more entities were added, the whole complex became known as the World Bank Group.

5. Lewis, W. Arthur (1955) 379. An extreme version of this view was that, in order to foster greater differentials and more savings on behalf of growth, the incomes of the poor, relative to other classes, should be *depressed*.

6. Sir Arthur Lewis' *The Theory of Economic Growth* remains a classic in the field. It was the first comprehensive treatment of the topic of growth since John Stuart Mills' *Principles of Political Economy* (1848). Sir Arthur was explicit that his focus is on growth, not distribution. (See his Introduction.) Hence it is misleading at best to infer that he is indifferent to the question of poverty. Rather, in this book, growth or wealth creation (not income distribution) was the primary unit of analysis.

7. The 16 countries were Austria, Belgium-Luxembourg, Denmark, France, Federal Republic of Germany, Greece, Iceland, Ireland, Italy, Netherlands, Norway, Portugal, Sweden, Turkey, United Kingdom and "Regional". For more detail, see www.marshallfoundation.org.

8. Goldin, Ian; Halsey Rogers; and Nicholas Stern (2001) 5.

9. Articles of Agreement of the International Monetary Fund, Article 1.

10. As noted by Pack, Howard, "Industrialization and Trade," Chapter 9 in Hollis Chenery and T.N. Srinivasan (1988) I:337.

11. "Often conducted annually, the survey has used consistent poverty lines (49 rupees for rural areas, and 57 rupees, both in terms of 1973-1974 prices.)" See Nathan Associates, Inc. (2002) 2.

12. www.ieo.org/world-c2-p1.html

13. Srinivasan, T.N. (2000) 1-3

14. Planning Commission, Government of India (2001) 29.

15. United Nations, Executive Board of the United Nations Development Programme and of the United Nations Population Fund (2002) 12. Also see Planning Commission, Government of India (2002(a)) 293.

16. The main source for this section is www.oxfam.org.

17. CARE originally stood for "Cooperative for American Remittances to Europe." That was later changed to "Cooperative for Assistance and Relief Everywhere, Inc."

18. Officially, Catholic Relief Services — United States Catholic Conference, Incorporated.

19. Information drawn from www.christian-aid.org.uk.

3

Trickle-Down Triumphant (1951-60)

The Mantra of Industrialization

Economic thinking in the 1950s and 1960s viewed capital as the engine of growth. There was worldwide expectation that, through policies on interest rates, currency exchange rates and trade, developing countries would expand their economies beyond agriculture to include industrialization.

For our purposes, economic growth refers to the increase in the real per capita gross domestic product over time. It is distinguished from economic development, which combines growth with improved living standards and poverty reduction rates.

It was widely accepted that economic growth in the developing world was predicated on rapid industrialization. An unemployed rural labor force would gain access to higher productivity and decently paying jobs in industry. Thus international aid incorporated an anti-rural bias.

Furthermore, chastened by the Great Depression of the 1930s and the ensuing collapse of world markets, aid agencies assumed the need for a strong state role in development strategies. The state would take the lead in planning production targets, allocating resources and marketing outputs.

Post-colonial governments were trusted to have the best interests of citizens at heart and the capacity to make economic progress possible. Many developing countries dependent on single commodities were eager to take advantage of advances in agriculture, to improve education and health care and to reduce poverty.

Poverty declined in Eastern Europe among nations that were part of the Union of Soviet Socialist Republics. In Hungary, for example, the proportion of people living under the poverty line dropped from 60 percent in the early 1950s to 14 percent by 1972.[1]

The World Bank as a Development Organization

During the 1950s, the World Bank slowly came to grips with its role as a development organization. The needs of the developing world were great but the World Bank proceeded cautiously. Under its president Eugene Black, who served from 1949 to 1963, the World Bank financed projects to build infrastructure—roads, power plants, irrigation systems, dams, ports and related facilities.

Lacking confidence in market incentives as an engine of growth, the Bank believed that the government should play the dominant role in planning and resource allocation.

In the Bank's view infrastructure was the *sine qua non* of industrial development. The Banks made such loans only after careful deliberation of the borrowers' creditworthiness. This worked to the disadvantage of poor countries like India and Pakistan that could not meet the Bank's standards. During the 1950s, the World Bank's lending was directed away from the poorer countries.

With a triple-A bond rating from Wall Street, the Bank nurtured an image of financial soundness. In advancing its agenda, the World Bank enjoyed a signal advantage over the other development organizations—a large supply of hard cash.

While "development" was prominent in the World Bank's lexicon, "poverty" was not. It did not direct its lending toward underdeveloped regions of the world, poor countries within those regions and specific sectors like health, education and agriculture where the poor stood to benefit more directly. Rather its lending was dominated by large investments in specific projects that met the Bank's standards for creditworthiness and contributed to building a country's economic infrastructure.

The richer economies benefited from these policies. The Bank's charter did not distinguish among more or less developed countries. "Of the $5.1 billion in total lending commitments for development purposes, one-third ($1.7 billion) went to European and other more developed countries, such as Australia, Japan and South Africa."[2]

With decolonization, a number of new and generally poor counties appeared and gained a voice at the United Nations. The concepts of "poverty" and "under-development" began to take hold in international discourse. As a result, "the number of poor borrowing countries rose from eight in 1950 to thirty in 1960..."[3] By 1958, India had emerged as the Bank's largest and most frequent borrower.

Community Development Movement[4]

As opposed to top-down or "vertical" assistance for projects designed elsewhere, community development emphasized a comprehensive or "horizontal" approach that highlighted the role and felt needs of rural residents in local area planning.

In 1952, India officially inaugurated a nationwide Community Development Program as a growth strategy for rural areas. The program received major support from the Ford Foundation and the United States government.

Community development agencies set up within the national government trained local leaders and village workers in identifying needs, assessing available resources, and setting priorities. Community-based projects covered a wide range, including increased food production, industrial development, health care, sanitation, schooling and expanded infrastructure (roads, power generation, public facilities).

With support from the United States and various United Nations agencies, the community development movement expanded well beyond India. For the United States, it represented a democratic alternative to communist agitation among desperately poor and disenfranchised rural areas.

Countries receiving assistance from the United States in the early to middle 1950s for community development included Afghanistan, Ceylon (now Sri Lanka), Egypt, Indonesia, Iran, Jordan, Nepal, Pakistan, and the Philippines. The community development movement peaked in 1960, by which time there were over sixty regional or national projects in Africa, Asia and Latin America.

By then, the movement had begun to decline due to lack of satisfaction with its results on the part of developing country governments. The pace of real and lasting change was judged to be unacceptably slow. It took time, too much time, in the eyes of impatient national officials, for communities to develop indigenous leadership, gain experience in planning and managing projects and achieve growth with equity.

The movement was often a victim of national politics. Projects begun under one national administration were often downgraded following a change in the country's political leadership. Originally lodged within the office of the president or prime minister, the government's community development bureaucracy would be buried deep within one of its ministries. Community-based rural organizations that were identified with the previous regime were held suspect.[5]

With the loss of national government support, international assistance for community development diminished soon thereafter. The success of the Green Revolution in combating food shortages and malnutrition, especially in Asia, contributed to lowering the importance given to rural community development schemes.

In the 1970s, community development principles reasserted themselves in the emphasis on integrated rural development projects, which enjoyed considerable U.S. support.

Other State-led Approaches

Under China's first five-year plan (1953-1957), government investment in agriculture and industrial planning had reportedly increased gross domestic product by 12 percent. In 1958, under the new "Great Leap Forward" strategy, new technologies for rural areas were promoted as was development of rural light industry. The strategy called for elimination of private property and forced collectivization of farms.

Under a relatively closed import-substitution-industrialization (ISI) model, combined with a mixture of state management and private sector initiative, a number of Latin American economies (Chile, for instance) experienced growth. Governments employed restrictive licensing systems, protective tariffs, and multiple exchange rates among other devices to build up domestic manufacturing.[6]

In some Asian and Latin American countries, effective economic management offset the effects of high trade barriers.[7] On the contrary, Africa's economic performance proved less than stellar, due at least in part to inadequate governmental infrastructure.

Overall the state-led approach to development was disappointing. Governments proved less than omniscient in planning and less than disinterested in the distribution of benefits. On the contrary, government planners worked with limited data and inadequate models. Government structures were viewed as more responsive to special interests than the general welfare.

Government control of the economy discouraged private entrepreneurship and market-oriented reforms. Consequently, firms tended to seek government subsidies rather than improve productivity and competitiveness in world markets.[8]

Widespread household poverty made it impossible to promote savings rates in developing countries that would free up capital for investment and growth. Foreign aid was directed to national governments as support for government planning and infrastructure building.

In the case of the United States, aid was delivered more on national security than humanitarian grounds. It was seen as a weapon in the Cold War waged against the spread of Soviet communism. Aid also served domestic commercial interests insofar as it was tied to the import of U.S. goods and services by developing countries.

Resisting Redistribution

To oversimplify, the pathways out of poverty boiled down to two: growth or redistribution. In line with the prevailing orthodoxy in development economics, the World Bank was wary of redistributionist programs such as propounded by the governments of Guatemala and Ceylon. They would reduce savings and hamper investment. No, the poor would simply have to be patient until the benefits of growth trickled down to them.[9]

In *The Theory of Economic Growth*, Sir Arthur Lewis postulated that growth demands a wide range of skills and "the 'middle' classes thus grow rapidly...[thereby] widening the differentials between skilled and unskilled, literate and illiterate, supervisory and supervised..."[10]

It was widely accepted that the benefits of growth would trickle down to the poor. According to Simon Kuznets, with economic growth came greater income inequalityfor a time. Gradually the benefits of growth would expand more widely.

The pattern would arise from the shift from a slow growth agricultural economy where incomes were low across the board to a rapidly growing and technologically charged urban industrial economy that exacerbated income disparities. Over time income inequality within the urbanized industrial sector would decrease. This process was illustrated by an inverted U curve.[11]

This theory stimulated a body of research throughout the 1950s, 1960s and 1970s in pursuit of a per capita income level that once reached would mark the turning point in the curve. This "holy grail" of development economics has not been found and increasingly skepticism has arisen about the validity of the hypothesis itself. The goal of unalloyed growth slowly gave way to the goal of economic development that reduced poverty and raised living standards.

Competition from SUNFED

In 1959 there was established the Special United Nations Fund for Economic Development (SUNFED) to provide soft loans on concessional (that is, below market rate) terms to developing nations.[12]

Wealthier northern countries (most notably the United States) saw SUNFED as a South-dominated competitor. At their urging, World Bank president Eugene Black established the International Development Association. Like SUNFED, but with much more money, the International Development Association became a soft lender to developing nations.

This was seen as a way for wealthier nations to assist the world's "have-nots," while maintaining the discipline and accountability of a bank. More practically, it served as the Bank's counter to the growing prominence of SUNFED.

President Dwight D. Eisenhower proposed that the International Development Association should become part of the World Bank. The Association's Articles of Agreement became effective in 1960. The first IDA loans or credits were made in 1961 to Honduras, India, Sudan and Chile.

By making softer concessional loans, the International Development Association accomplished three things. It made credit available to poor countries that could not afford to borrow at market rates. It expanded the Bank's clientele and the scope of its lending beyond large-scale infrastructure projects to include education, water and agriculture. And it preserved the creditworthiness of the International Bank for Reconstruction and Development.

In 1959, the United States and nineteen Latin American countries established the Inter-American Development Bank; it included a Social Progress Trust Fund designed to make soft or concessional loans for development.

Eugene Black, who had resisted the creation of the International Development Association, gradually became a convert and in his final years as president began to push for higher rates of IDA financing. The competition from SUNFED had moved the Bank toward a more explicit antipoverty agenda.

Humanitarian Relief

During the decade, international relief organizations began to shift their focus from post-war reconstruction to meeting critical needs in the developing world.

In 1951, CARE initiated relief operations in Korea as war there expanded. In 1954, the U.S. Congress passed Public Law 480, which permitted the use of America's surplus food to fight hunger overseas. Under the Marshall Plan, a quarter of the assistance had consisted of food, feed and fertilizer.

With the phaseout of the Marshall Plan, U.S. farm interests lobbied for the continuation of food aid. CARE made extensive use of this new resource. In 1956, CARE shipped food to Hungarian refugees after their country's failed revolt against the Soviet Union.

In December 1951, upon approval of its proposed statutes by the Holy See, the first constitutive General Assembly of Caritas Internationalis took place. Founding members came from Caritas organizations in 13 countries: Austria, Belgium, Canada, Denmark, France, Germany, Holland, Italy, Luxembourg, Portugal, Spain, Switzerland, and the United States.

In 1957, the Confederation changed its name to Caritas Internationalis to reflect the presence of Caritas members on every continent. In the United States, both Catholic Relief Services and Catholic Charities are members of Caritas North America.

In 1960, the Oxford Committee for Famine Relief took a lead role in the international Freedom from Hunger campaign launched by the United Nations Food and Agriculture Organization.

A Banner Year

1960 proved to be a banner year for the world's development agenda. In that year no fewer than seventeen countries of Africa threw off their status as colonies and emerged as independent nations. They and other former colonies of the "third world" now sought escape not from colonization but from poverty.

For this they needed the know-how and financial assistance of the world's richer nations. This created a push not only for traditional economic investment but also for the broader notion of human development.

Also in 1960, several major new international entities were created: the Development Assistance Group (January), the International Development Association as part of the World Bank Group (September) and the Organization for Economic Cooperation and Development (OECD) (December).

The Development Assistance Group was established at the initiative of Douglas Dillon, U.S. undersecretary of state (1959-61) and secretary of the treasury (1961-65). The idea was to provide a forum for consultation among donor countries. The original members were Belgium, Canada, France, Germany, Italy, Portugal, United Kingdom, United States and the Commission of European Economic Unity. Japan was invited immediately to participate and the Netherlands joined the Group in July 1960.

The OECD began formal operation in September 1961; its secretariat included a Development Department. In December, the Development Assistance Group was reconstituted as the Development Assistance Committee and held its first meeting as an integral part of the OECD in October 1961.

In 1960, under World Bank auspices, there was established the Aid-to-Pakistan Consortium to foster coordination among the major donors of aid to the country. The original members were Canada, Germany, Japan, United Kingdom, United States, and the World Bank.

At a conference in Baghdad in September 1960, the five nations of Iran, Iraq, Kuwait, Saudi Arabia and Venezuela established the Organization of Petroleum Exporting Countries (OPEC).[13] It began as a counterweight to the main transnational corporations known as the Seven Sisters that dominated the international oil market.[14]

The Organization sought to coordinate petroleum supply and prices for the benefit of its members as well as consuming nations. After five years in Geneva, OPEC moved its headquarters to Vienna in 1965.

Theories, Statistics, Models and Computers

Theorizing about the growth process became a growth industry itself. In the 1950s, new theories were subjected to ever quicker and more rigorous testing, due to improvements in statistical estimation, economic modeling and computerization.

At the end of the 1930s, economist Alan Fisher had formulated and fellow economist Colin Clark had further elaborated a three-stage model of production. Primary production involves agriculture, mining, fishing, and forestry. Secondary production advances to industrial production through manufacturing and construction. Tertiary production emphasizes services like education and tourism. The three stages are associated with low, middle and high-income countries, respectively.[15]

The Harrod-Domar model, which was developed independently by Roy F. Harrod and Evsey Domar, was originally created to describe business cycles.[16] Following World War II, economists in the emerging field of development economics adapted this ready-made theory to the problems of reconstruction in war-torn Europe and subsequently to growth in developing countries.

The model describes growth as a function of the level of savings and the productivity of capital investment. Production was assumed to be proportional to capital stock.[17] Savings provide the funds that are borrowed for investment purposes. Productivity is measured by the ratio of capital to output. Advances in technology enable firms to produce more output with less capital and thereby lower the ratio of capital to output.

Applying this elegantly simple but ultimately unsatisfactory theory, if we assume a four-to-one capital output ratio, a three percent growth rate in gross domestic product would require a 12 percent savings rate. If poor countries could not manage the required savings rate, the financing gap might need to be filled by donor assistance.[18] The model has been criticized for its limitations in handling debt dynamics.[19]

The Two-Gap Model

The two-gap model was designed to address the problems of what was perceived as "structural disequilibrium" (price rigidities, for example) in developing countries. It extended the Harrod-Domar model under the assumption that domestic and foreign savings would not for the most part substitute for one another; they were instead complementary.

If domestic savings for investment faltered, foreign "savings" or foreign exchange earnings could fill the gap. These could come in the form of export revenue or official development assistance. If the latter faltered as well, two gaps resulted, investment declined and projected growth rates would have to be revised downward.

The model has attracted critics but nonetheless remained in wide use, notably within the World Bank.[20]

In 1954, Arthur Lewis proposed a dual sector development model. Developing countries were seen as having traditional subsistence-based agriculture side by side with a nascent but more technologically advanced industrial sector. Rural areas would provide both food surpluses and a relatively permanent labor supply for emerging industries.

The latter would over time draw people away from rural and into urban settings due to the attraction of higher incomes and a more desirable quality of life. This would benefit farmers who would be freed from subsistence agriculture. Higher incomes would foster savings and an expansion of funds for investment.[21]

Lewis also devised a basic model to describe the development of the terms of trade between poor countries with raw materials and tropical products and rich countries with industrial goods.

Imagine conditions where poor and rich countries trade different types of products (say, "coffee" for "cars"), but also compete with the same products (say, a food product like "corn"). The terms of trade between the two sets of countries are determined by the differences in productivity (agricultural work productivity in this example).

Low agricultural productivity in developing countries prevents them from competing effectively, particularly when richer countries subsidize their domestic producers.

Developing countries cannot provide equivalent subsidies or match the technological and organizational advantages of the richer countries. Unfavorable terms of trade constrict growth in developing countries and exacerbate poverty, which is found disproportionately in rural areas.

Taxiing Toward Take-off

American economic historian Walter W. Rostow propounded a theory of development that proved quite popular. It posited several stages of growth. Stage one described an economy dependent on subsistence agriculture and barter trade. In stage two, trade expanded due to surpluses arising from more specialized activities. This in turn fostered new transport systems and entrepreneurship. Stage three saw workers shifting from agriculture to industry.

Growth was limited to a few economic sectors and geographic regions; still it increased the capital pool and stimulated further investment. In stage four, technological innovation expanded the size and scope of goods, services and investment opportunities. The economy reached "take-off" in stage five with mass consumption, stable durable goods industries and an increasing role for services.

Outside assistance could help developing countries compensate for their initially low savings rates and inadequate investment levels. They could thereby achieve the preconditions for sustained development.

The Rostow scenario has been faulted for ignoring various structural factors responsible for low savings and investment. Such factors included insufficient skilled labor, limited managerial expertise, and inadequate legal and regulatory systems.

Technology as the Key to Growth

To better characterize the observed growth rates in developing countries—as distinct from short-term business cycles—Robert Solow significantly modified and enriched the Harrod-Domar model. Solow's neoclassical growth model showed how increased capital stock generates greater per capita production.

Under the theory, increasing capital intensity will contribute less and less to production due to declining yields per unit of capital investment. In other words, a marginal dollar invested produces less than the first dollar invested as the law of diminishing returns kicks in.

Thus, the long-run rate of growth of output per unit of labor input is independent of the savings (or investment) rate. Over time, the elements of an economy will converge to a steady-state condition with identical growth rates for capital, labor and total production. In neoclassical theory, investment does not determine the growth rate, only the level of per capita income.

The factor that can change this scenario and is therefore key to long run growth is technological progress.[22] The Solow extension of the Harrod-Domar model and two-gap analyses captures more realistically the relationships among foreign debt, domestic saving and capital intensity. It has exerted immense influence in the development community in the last four decades.

Subsequent work by others has emphasized distinctions between human and physical capital, and what each contributes to growth. Human capital in particular is seen as a factor in technological innovation.[23]

Endogenous Growth Theory

More recently, there has emerged endogenous growth theory, which, as the name implies, stresses the significance of intranational factors. It is concerned with the economic and social forces within a country that undergird technological progress. It places a high priority on human capital development. The theory to some degree reacts to the heavy emphasis in economic growth literature on exogenous factors like the globalization of trade, capital flows and technological advances.

From the endogenous perspective, growth can be fostered by, and indeed may depend on, a country's investment in domestic research and development and the expansion of knowledge. Exponential growth is a function of the increasing generation and dissemination of new ideas and inventions.

As economic goods, ideas like just-in-time inventory control are "nonrivalrous", that is, a single idea (unlike, say, a single automobile) can be used by many people at the same time.[24]

Thus new knowledge is viewed not only as a form of capital but one that, under some versions of the theory, is even more important than physical capital.[25] Consequently intellectual property rights as codified in patent and copyright law have become more critical in global trade negotiations and a source of recurring disputes between rich and poor countries.

Richer countries led by the United States have sought to protect their interests (and financial returns) in the new technologies they have marketed while poorer countries have protested unfair pricing and technology transfer restrictions.

Mathematical Modeling

For developing countries, mathematical models are used to analyze growth, structural change, investment, income distribution, trade and adjustment to external shocks. In the 1950s, economists relied on linear input-output models. The wider use of linear programming in the 1960s thanks to advances in computing power introduced choice, pricing and optimization into modeling. The inability to adjust for unrealistic assumptions detracted from the popularity of these models in development economics.

In the 1970s, as an outgrowth of the prior work, there emerged non-linear, multisectoral models that simulated market economies. Called computable general equilibrium (CGE) models, they found an application in developing countries.[26]

These models have their origin in the general equilibrium theory of the great French economist, Leon Walras (1834-1910). The underlying statistical structure relies on social accounting matrices, a general macroeconomic accounting framework used for the United Nations System of National Accounts.[27]

Among other uses, CGE models have been employed to analyze the impact of structural adjustment policies on the income distribution as well as the likely effects of alternative development strategies. Advances in techniques for solving the equations in CGE models "routinely and cheaply" have contributed to their widespread popularity.[28]

A Decade of Development(s)

The decade of the 1950s was characterized by advances in development theory, the creation of new international institutions designed to foster growth in developing nations and the expansion of non-governmental relief organizations from their post-war focus on Europe to other parts of the world.

Despite the progress in economic theory, data collection and mathematical modeling, no universally accepted model of development has emerged. Nor is economics enough. The relationships among economics, social structures and political power affect the ways policy is developed and implemented in poor countries. Yet these relationships are not well understood. History remains the best available guide to what does and does not work to foster growth and alleviate poverty.[29]

The prevailing notion of "development" as distinct from "relief" and "reconstruction" and the awareness of the needs (and political importance in the Cold War) of developing nations signified a shift of emphasis from crisis conditions in war-torn areas to a long-range agenda embracing the entire globe. As newly independent nations found their voice, poverty became a more prominent topic in international discourse.

A period of heady, but overblown, optimism was to follow.

ENDNOTES

1. United Nations Development Programme (1997) 25.
2. Kapur, Devesh, John P. Lewis and Richard Webb, editors (1998) 93.
3. Op. cit. 98.
4. Voth, Donald E. (2002) 45-50.
5. As astutely noted by Donald E. Voth (2002) 49n, a similar pattern occurred subsequently in the United States. In 1964, the Office of Economic Opportunity, the lead organization for the Johnson Administration's War on Poverty, was placed within the Executive Office of the President. In 1975, under the Ford Administration, it was superseded by an independent agency, the U.S. Community Services Administration. The latter was abolished altogether in 1981 under the Reagan Administration. Its residual programs and administrative functions were transferred to a large cabinet agency, the U.S. Department of Health and Human Services. See Clark, Robert F. (2002).
6. Thorbecke, Erik, "The Evolution of the Development Doctrine and the Role of Foreign Aid," in Tarp, Finn, editor (2002) 22.
7. Under import-substitution, a region or a nation begins to produce what formerly it purchased from outside parties. For developing countries it may be adopted as a form of economic protectionism in order to protect infant industries and stimulate job growth.
8. Goldin, Ian; Halsey Rogers; and Nicholas Stern (2002) 6-7.
9. Kapur, Devesh; John P. Lewis; and Richard Webb, editors (1998) 135.
10. Lewis, W. Arthur (1955) 180.
11. Kuznets, Simon (1955). For evidence of the lack of a consistent relationship over time among poverty, inequality and growth, see Ferreira, Francisco (1999).
12. Originally it was called simply the United Nations Fund for Economic Development, but the acronym would have provided fodder to critics like the World Bank. See Singer, Hans W. (1986) 301.
13. Eight other countries joined later: Qatar (1961); Indonesia (1962); Socialist Peoples Libyan Arab Jamahiriya (1962); United Arab Emirates (1967); Algeria (1969); Nigeria (1971); Ecuador (1973); and Gabon (1975). The latter two withdrew in 1992 and 1994, respectively.
14. The Seven Sisters were Exxon, Gulf, Texaco, Mobil, Socal, BP and Shell.
15. See Fisher, Alan G.B. (1935) and Clark, Colin (1940).
16. See Harrod, Roy W. (March 1939) and Domar, Evsey (April 1946).
17. Production is often measured with the Cobb-Douglas production function, $Q=AK\alpha B\beta$ where Q is output, K is capital, L is labor and A, α, and β are constants. A specialized case occurs for $\alpha+\beta=1$. The equation also appears in its logarithmic form, $\ln Q=\ln A+\alpha \ln K+\beta \ln L$. The function, popular in empirical economics since the 1920s, is named for mathematician Charles W. Cobb and economist (at one time, lumberjack, later U.S. senator) Paul H. Douglas. The function has been used not only for economic output but also for the "production" of social goods like educational services and household food intake (proxied by calories, for example). See Pemberton, Malcolm and Nicholas Rau (2001) 258.
18. Easterly, William (1997).
19. For example, see Eaton, Jonathan, "Foreign Public Capital Flows", Chapter 25 in Chenery, Hollis and T.N. Srinivansa, editors (1989) 1328-29.
20. See Bruton, H.M. (1969) 66:566-577.

21. Lewis, W. Arthur (1954).

22. Solow, Robert M. (1956).

23. For more, see Aghion, Philippe and Peter Howitt (1998).

24. Jones, Charles I. (2002) 80-81.

25. See Romer, Paul M. (1986) and, for an excellent review of the literature on this theory, Aghion, Philippe and Peter Howitt (1998).

26. Starting with a study by Adelman, Irma and Sherman Robinson (1978) of Korea.

27. A Structural Accounting Matrix for a country (or other entity) is designed to maintain a consistent framework for production, institutional and household income and consumption. A stylized Social Accounting Matrix shows expenditures and receipts in matrix format for activities (e.g. domestic sales and imports), commodities, payments, enterprises, households, governments, capital accounts and the "rest of the world" (i.e. external transactions) plus column and row totals.

28. See Robinson, Sherman, "Multisectoral Models", Chapter 18 in Chenery, Hollis and T.N. Srinivasan (1989) II: 889.

29. Bird, Richard M. and Susan Horton, editors (1989) 15-22.

4

Structuralism Supreme (1961-70)

Government in the Forefront

In the 1960s, it continued to be assumed that significant public sector involvement in the economy was required to accelerate industrialization in developing nations. Industrialization was considered the key to development but developing countries were seen as lacking sufficient numbers of private entrepreneurs willing or able to undertake large industrial projects.

Government-sponsored enterprises would fill the gap. This in turn would lead to lower unemployment and higher incomes for poor people. The state assisted the poor directly in a variety of ways. It subsidized credit for the rural poor and others by operating state-run banks or by providing incentives or even mandates to private lenders.

Upsurge in Development Activities

Over the decade from 1961 to 1970, the volume of world trade grew on average more than eight percent a year. Production became more and more globalized and the transnational corporation appeared as a new topic in international economics.[1]

While the curve was by no means consistently smooth and positive, economic growth occurred in many low-income and middle-income countries over the four decades starting in 1960.

The share of gross development product accounted for by agriculture halved from 32 percent to 16 percent, while industry's share grew from 21 percent to 36 percent.[2] Despite rising rates of economic growth, millions of people were mired in poverty. The gap between the haves and have-nots widened.

First United Nations Development Decade

In 1962 the United Nations, at the urging of U.S. President John F. Kennedy, launched the first United Nations Development Decade. Earlier, in his inaugural address, President Kennedy had signaled a new sense of purpose in international affairs:

> "To those peoples in the huts and villages of half the globe struggling to break the bonds of mass misery, we pledge our best efforts to help them help themselves.... If a free society cannot help the many who are poor, it cannot save the few who are rich."[3]

The first objective of the first Development Decade, according to the General Assembly resolution 1710 (XVI) of 19 December 1961, was to attain "a minimum annual rate of growth of aggregate national income of 5 per cent at the end of the Decade."[4]

A second was to increase the flow of capital and official development assistance so that it reached approximately one percent of the combined national incomes of the developed countries. The resolution focused its attention on the country level, not individuals within countries.

Inaugurating themes to be reiterated in the succeeding development decades, the General Assembly highlighted the needs of less developed countries dependent on "a small range of primary commodities." International arrangements were required whereby these countries could expand their sales of products at stable and remunerative prices. This would enable them to help finance their own development through foreign exchange earnings and domestic savings.

At the same time the resolution called for increases in the flow of public and private resources from external bodies (private investors, donor countries, specialized international agencies) to developing countries.

Development enjoyed a prominent place on the international agenda. With the Cold War in full swing, and the political leanings of developing nations in Asia, Africa and Latin America in play, the western industrialized nations were motivated to foster development.

Planning for Development

The United States and some major western European countries sought to demonstrate that capital-intensive free market approaches trumped communism as the route to economic self-sufficiency. The promise of poverty alleviation served as a weapon in the building of alliances.

The OECD's Development Assistance Committee had a mandate to develop guidelines for aid programs and increase the flow of financial resources to developing countries. At its inception, members provided 94 percent of such assistance, with the United States alone accounting for over half.[5]

In the two-sector development model propounded by Arthur Lewis, agriculture was relegated to a passive role while industrialization took hold. In the latter half of the 1960s, agriculture regained respectability as at least a junior partner with industrialization. Thus "an increase in agricultural output and productivity...would facilitate the extraction of a new transfer out of agriculture and into the modern sector."[6]

Successful development was seen as dependent on adequate savings for investment, and relative equilibrium in the developing countries' balance of payments. Toward the end of the decade, the focus shifted somewhat from concentration on gross national product as the key growth indicator to the problems of structural unemployment and underemployment.

The development of appropriate skills among the population through education and training and the expansion of the jobs base became core objectives in and of themselves. Foreign aid began to emphasize investment in human capital.

A United Nations Committee on Development Planning was established and chaired by Dutch economist Jan Tinbergen, who in 1969 received the Nobel Prize for economics; the Committee monitored progress over the First Development Decade and generated recommendations for the one to follow.

The Committee pressed for the reduction of poverty through growth, distribution and improvements in employment, health, education, housing and related social services. It characterized its approach as "the necessary 'war on poverty.'"[7]

The United Nations, which operated on a one country-one vote basis, served as a counterweight to the Bretton Woods institutions, which were seen by developing countries as dominated by western industrialized interests.

A Third Way Emerges

If the United States and its allies were the first world, and the Soviet bloc in Eastern Europe the second, the third world lumped together a diverse group of nonaligned nations, including those that gained independence from colonial rule starting after World War II.

Over time the phrase came to refer to developing countries of Asia, Africa, Oceania, and Latin America that were characterized in large part by widespread poverty, high birthrates, and economic dependence on the advanced countries.[8]

In 1955, representatives from twenty-nine Asian and African nations met in Bandung, Indonesia. They agreed to promote economic and cultural cooperation and to resist colonialism. China played a prominent role. Several countries were not invited: North Korea, South Korea, South Africa and Israel.

At the opening of the conference, April 18, 1955, President Sukarno of Indonesia asserted that the participants were "united...by a common detestation of colonialism...of racialism...and...by a common determination to preserve and stabilise peace in the world..."[9]

The conference triggered the Non-Aligned Movement, which was launched in 1961. Its founders included Jawaharlal Nehru, Prime Minister of India; Kwame Nkrumah, Prime Minister of Ghana; Gamal Abdel Nasser, President of Egypt; Achmed Sukarno, President of Indonesia; and Josip Broz, better known as Tito, President of Yugoslavia.

Following a June preparatory meeting in Cairo, the first Conference of Non-Aligned Heads of State or Government was convened in Belgrade, September 1-6, 1961, largely through the initiative of Yugoslavian President Tito. Twenty-five countries were represented. The nonaligned movement's members came from Asia, Africa and Latin America and covered over half the world's population.

These third world nations strove to stay neutral in the Cold War between the United States and the Soviet Union. Today, the group includes oil rich nations like Saudi Arabia, newly industrialized nations like South Korea and very poor nations like Haiti. Numerically it dominates the United Nations General Assembly but, due to its economic and cultural diversity, does not vote as a bloc on all issues. By the end of the twentieth century, the movement had 115 members and seventeen observer states. By then they faced the task of redefining themselves in light of the end of the Cold War.

With the end of the Cold War, regional and ethnic conflicts have broken out in many parts of the world. Conditions of poverty and inequality often trigger these conflicts, which tend to create even more poverty and social upheaval. Hence, the focus in third world nations has shifted to cooperative international action against poverty, environmental degradation, and drug trafficking.

Non-governmental Organizations

International non-governmental organizations continued to adapt their missions to changing global realities. They shifted from crisis intervention to longer-range development strategies. Besides providing services to local communities, they expanded their advocacy activities at the national and international level to include human rights, women's rights, environmental issues and poverty.

Government-sponsored bodies like the United Nations granted them more formal recognition but genuine cooperation was lacking. While national governments were seen as the engine of growth and received the lion's share of foreign aid, non-governmental organizations grew quietly in their numbers and influence.

During the 1960s, Oxfam began to stress poverty alleviation. The development of local water and sanitation facilities became one of the

Committee's special areas of expertise. In the late 1960s, to raise funds, Oxfam started what has become a network of some 830 shops throughout the United Kingdom. Staffed by volunteers, the shops sell donated goods and handicrafts from overseas.

In 1966, CARE began to phase out its famous CARE Package in favor of self-help projects. It involved governments in sharing project costs in their own countries.

Throughout the 1960s and 1970s, Caritas Internationalis gained membership and expanded its global operations. Catholic Relief Services, the U.S. member of Caritas North America, opened offices in Africa, Asia, and Latin America. While providing relief in emergency situations, the agency sought ways to help people in the developing world to break the grip of poverty.

Like other international organizations, it opted to support sustainable, community-based initiatives. These included agricultural improvements, community banks, health education, and clean water projects among others.

The scale of these efforts was insufficient to make a statistical dent in global poverty. But these private non-governmental organizations operated with a high degree of flexibility and innovativeness. Frequently they bypassed official government channels and partnered directly with community-based organizations.

Through their work, the international humanitarian groups pioneered new approaches to poverty alleviation and local community development that in some cases were later adopted on a larger scale by government-supported institutions.

In their aid projects, they have reinforced the values of participation, decentralization and community-based development. They have helped empower local people by giving them roles and responsibilities in the management of local projects.

They have provided a forum through which the poor made known their needs and aspirations. They have attacked gender inequities and opened new avenues for meaningful involvement by women in the development process.

More broadly, they have fostered partnerships and linkages among various antipoverty groups, thereby building up their collective impact or what is often described as "social capital". They have lobbied at national and international levels for good governance, accountability and the effective use of anti-poverty resources.

Oxfam, CARE, and Caritas Internationalis, along with a vast array of other non-governmental organizations, both local and international, have gained recognition as key instruments in development and poverty reduction. It is widely accepted that government-to-government assistance alone is inadequate for achieving sustainable development and world without poverty.[10]

Non-governmental organizations are seen as being in touch with poor people and their issues at the grassroots. Besides delivering needed services and support at the community level, they are recognized as credible advocates for change in national and international forums.

Banking on Poverty

At the start of the 1960s, it was widely assumed that large public infrastructure projects were a precondition for overall economic growth. The World Bank concurred. "Between fiscal years 1961 and 1965, 76.8 percent of all Bank lending was for electric power or transportation."[11]

Eugene Black's successor, George Woods, a New York Investment banker with an abrasive management style, pushed the World Bank's loan portfolio beyond large infrastructure projects to include other aspects of development, such as education, health and sanitation. This departed from the Bank's prior focus on strictly defined economic activity with a higher probability of return on investment than the riskier realm of social lending.

Woods was willing to tolerate less rigorous standards of borrower country creditworthiness, which had become an obstacle to expanding the World Bank's loan portfolio, in favor of social lending that could accelerate the development process.

The International Development Association provided a significant share of the Bank's grants and concessionary loans (or "credits") to countries with poor creditworthiness. From concentrating on financing for large infrastructure projects in creditworthy nations, the Bank had come to support riskier social lending in very poor countries.

This created a predicament. Whereas the Bank had previously boasted of high repayment rates among its borrowers, it now faced the prospect of defaults. While not acknowledged officially, the Bank's response was to engage in rollover financing, that is, making new loans to enable borrowers to make payments on old loans.

Lending as an instrument of growth dominated concerns about the borrowers' creditworthiness. Defaults by borrowing countries tended to be seen as a liquidity problem caused by slow growth rather than indicators of structural weakness in governance. More and more of the developing countries' resources went into debt servicing rather than meeting social and economic needs.

At the Bank, the International Development Association required replenishment of its resources every three or four years. During the mid-1960s the United States refused to continue leading the effort but instead called on the Bank to do its own fundraising. The replenishment exercises have proven to be a recurring trauma for the Bank.

During the 1960s the International Development Association's lending commitments were increasingly weighted toward the poorest countries. The International Development Association provided not only soft loans but loans for sectors not previously addressed by the World Bank. It began to support projects in agriculture, water supplies, and education.

In such unfamiliar territory, the Bank sought out experts in other specialized agencies of the United Nations. These included the Food and Agriculture

Organization; United Nations Educational, Scientific, and Cultural Organization; World Health Organization and the United Nations Conference on Trade and Development.[12]

In 1963, the International Monetary Fund established the compensatory financing facility. It was geared to the needs of developing countries whose economies depended on the export of primary products like coffee, cotton and minerals.

Current account receipts in these countries can fluctuate considerably due to movements in prices. Pricing in turn is a function of production factors like drought and cold and changes in demand from industrialized countries. The compensatory financing facility covered shortfalls in the current account receipts for these products.[13]

McNamara's Bank

Woods' successor, Robert S. McNamara, former U.S. secretary of defense, inaugurated a crusade against poverty with missionary zeal. Prior to his tenure, the World Bank essentially lent money to finance discrete projects in nations it deemed creditworthy and capable of performing effectively.

McNamara greatly expanded the lending for social programs begun by Woods. Under the trickle-down theory, he contended, benefits will accrue to the few and "disparities in income will simply widen."[14]

Despite opposition by some World Bank staffers, who believed in lending to countries solely for "productive" purposes, McNamara mounted a frontal assault on poverty. He was fortunate in that his predecessor Woods had moved the Bank closer to becoming a development agency.

McNamara was skeptical that the benefits of growth would be disseminated widely among low-income people in developing countries, at least within any reasonable time frame. Having served as the U.S. secretary of defense for six years, he saw the limitations of a purely military approach to national security (the Vietnam War serving as exhibit A).

Security, he argued, depended as well on poverty reduction and economic growth in the world's poorer nations.[15] As a member of the Kennedy and Johnson administrations, he was exposed to the liberal thinking that led to the U.S. "War on Poverty" in the 1960s..

McNamara pursued his agenda not through income distribution schemes but by fostering productivity growth among the poor. He did not identify poverty reduction with an expansion of welfare. Rather he was persuaded that long-term economic growth was the key to poverty reduction and employment. He sought ways of enabling the poor to participate in growth-oriented activities.

At the same time the emphasis on poverty seemed to imply that the dissemination as well as the creation of wealth needed to be part of any Bank-supported scheme. McNamara and his advisers struggled for several years to devise the appropriate operational formula. His approach seemed to require tradeoffs between maximal growth and dissemination of its benefits.

He began shifting some of the Bank's loans (and consequently recipient country expenditures) away from large infrastructure projects and urban industrial expansion toward agriculture, rural development and social services. He also greatly increased financial support for research on poverty and development within the Bank.

McNamara spelled out his vision in annual speeches; in a particularly famous 1973 speech in Nairobi, he noted that 40 percent of the world's population lived in absolute poverty and that the poor were concentrated heavily in rural areas. He committed the Bank to land reform and large-scale rural works projects

Rural Development

This promotion of rural development was a decided shift for an institution biased toward urban industrialization as the key to growth.[16] As a new area of emphasis, Bank-assisted rural development experienced difficulties in project design and implementation.

Historically, and particularly in colonized nations, tenants obtained usufruct rights to some plots in exchange for their corvée (unpaid) labor elsewhere on the estate. The conversion of large tenanted landholdings to smaller, owner-operated family farms proved daunting.[17]

Large landholding systems, which served as an instrument of social control (for example, by limiting tenant mobility), often left much of the land uncultivated and constrained market expansion. Rising population densities, decreased land availability and food shortages undermined the arrangement.

Conflict ensued between rich, often absentee, landlords and their poor but ever more restive tenants. In some cases, landlords substituted capital for tenant labor, thereby mechanizing and commercializing their agricultural holdings. Tenants lost their usufruct or sharecropping rights and sank deeper into poverty.

The laws governing production relations and property rights proved inadequate. In Latin America especially, projects aimed at increasing food production among small farmers ran into obstacles over land tenure and titling.[18]

In the agricultural credit component of projects, repayment rates in Brazil, Colombia, and Haiti among others were low. Because of inadequate infrastructure, the maintenance of newly completed public works like roads and wells lagged.

Irrigation systems in countries like Brazil, Indonesia and the Philippines led to dislocation in local communities, flooding of lands and relocation of residents.

Still, with World Bank assistance, modest increases in food production were achieved in Paraguay, Brazil's Rio Grande do Norte area, Mexico, Bolivia, Nigeria, Tanzania, Nepal, and the Philippines. Benefits sometimes accrued more to wealthier landowners and market intermediaries than small farmers.

The Bank had to learn patience and flexibility in its lending for rural development projects. Rather than bail out of failing projects, the Bank leaned toward redesign. When successful, the projects helped legitimize rural development on behalf of the poor as a governmental priority. They served to underpin and strengthen national institutions like Tanzania's Rural Development Bank and Brazil's agricultural research agency.[19]

McNamara on Other Social Issues

McNamara also took a close interest in education, nutrition, health and population issues. He created a nutrition unit within the Bank in 1972, sponsored a successful international consortium to eradicate river blindness in West Africa and incorporated health components in the Bank's agriculture, population and education projects.[20]

Other developmental issues that the Bank began to address more systematically at McNamara's prodding included urbanization, water and sewer systems, education, and basic needs.

The Bank supported slum-upgrading projects in a number of countries to improve road paving, footpaths, drainage canals, and community facilities. This work often necessitated some relocation and resettlement, generally around seven percent of residents (but reaching a high of 30 percent in Morocco). Such disruption bred tensions around issues like compensation and the adequacy of alternative housing arrangements.

At the same time, according to World Bank officials, successful projects in Indonesia and the Tondo area in the Philippines helped make slum-upgrading a higher long-range priority for the national governments of those countries.[21]

Under McNamara, the World Bank's annual lending went "from less than $1 billion in 1968 to more than $12 billion in 1981."[22] While ethically praiseworthy, McNamara's approach had a severe downside. Within the World Bank, staff labored to meet lending targets. Loans were pushed through without adequate preparation and management oversight.

Developing countries held the upper hand in negotiations with the Bank. Hence they often successfully resisted the imposition of stringent loan conditions and violated actual loan conditions with impunity. In short, his approach fostered the indebtedness of developing countries.

Of Default Rates and Development

McNamara's crusade against world poverty exposed contradictory pressures in the World Bank's mission. As a bank, it made loans that it determined were repayable. Default rates were a matter of grave concern. Grants were the exception, not the rule. Yet soft social lending loans to developing countries raised the risk of default.

World Bank lending was designed to promote economic growth. Many economists argued that putting loaned money into the hands of the wealthy few, who could thereby make large-scale economic investments, made more sense than dispersing it among the many poor.

Consistent with its free market and capitalist origins, the Bank viewed with horror any suggestion that its resources be used to foster income redistribution. Yet income redistribution was the surest and shortest road to reducing income disparities.

United Nations Conferences on Trade and Development

Within the United Nations Economic Commission for Latin America, the Argentine economist Raoul Prebisch (1901-86) and others highlighted the imbalance in economic power relations between the wealthy industrialized nations of the North and the poorer, often newly independent nations of the South.

Beginning in the 1930s, Prebisch, a professor of political economy in Buenos Aires and economic adviser to the Argentine government, contended that Latin America had become too dependent on exports of its natural resources.[23] In essence, the nations of the South (the Periphery) had to export an increasing amount of their raw materials and commodities to obtain a decreasing amount of finished industrial goods from the North (the Center).

There are indications that Prebisch relied to some degree at least on previously (albeit anonymously) published work on the declining terms of trade by Hans Singer, the third economist appointed to the UN secretariat. In any event, the Prebisch-Singer thesis helped explain why developing countries tended to face persistent balance of payments problems.[24]

The industrialized importing nations, most notably, "El Gigante del Norte", the United States, converted the South's resources into more manufactured goods. These were then sold back to the very countries that provided the resources.

The gap between Latin American revenues from exports of its natural resources and expenditures for imported finished goods grew wider. Under ever worsening terms of trade, Latin American nations fell further and further behind the developed nations.

The solution for economists like Prebisch was to curtail exports of natural resources in order to stimulate domestic industrial production. In policy terms this often meant restrictions on foreign investors and imposition of trade barriers. The approach was labeled import-substitution-industrialization (ISI).

At the United Nations, Prebisch served as executive secretary for the Economic Commission for Latin America from 1950 to 1964. Prebisch's structuralism theory provided the impetus behind the creation of Third World organizations like the Organization of Petroleum Exporting Countries (OPEC) and the United Nations Conference on Trade and Development (UNCTAD).

In 1964 Prebisch served as secretary-general for the first United Nations Conference on Trade and Development, which underscored the North-South dichotomy. His report, *Search for a New Trade Policy for Development*, set parameters for the conference agenda.

The Conference marked a shift toward pro-South perspectives on development issues within many United Nations agencies. UNCTAD pursued strategies on behalf of developing countries aimed at more favorable arrangements for commodities and increased access to the markets of developed countries.[25]

A Second United Nations Development Decade

Under UN resolution 2626 (XXV) of October 24, 1970, the General Assembly proclaimed the Second United Nations Development Decade. It noted that while "a part of the world lives in great comfort and even affluence, much of the larger part suffers from abject poverty, a condition that contributed to the aggravation of world tensions. The signatories committed themselves to an international development strategy "designed to create a more just and rational world economic and social order...."

The International Development Strategy for the Second Development Decade included special measures on behalf of the least developed countries. The strategy for development focused on nine areas:

♦ trade arrangements more favorable to developing countries;
♦ regional and subregional integration and trade expansion;
♦ greater financial resource transfers from developed countries;
♦ reductions in maritime transport costs;
♦ special assistance for the least developed countries;
♦ special assistance for land-locked countries;
♦ application of science and technology to developing economies;
♦ human development through education, health care, etc; and
♦ augmented production and improved productivity.

The 0.7 Percent Target

In its resolution on the first United Nations Development Decade, the United Nations established an official development assistance target of 0.7 percent of the Gross National Product of the developed countries.

The 0.7 percent target level was derived from the work of the Committee on Development Progress over the course of the First Development Decade and more particularly from calculations made by the Committee's chair, Jan Tinbergen.[26]

Official development assistance referred to aid from the public sector of developed countries; it was designed to augment private investment, which the Committee projected at approximately 30 percent of total inflows to developing countries.

During this period, international concerns over lagging development of developing countries mounted, as underscored by the Pearson Report of 1969 and the Tinbergen Report of 1970.

For example, in 1969 the Pearson Commission warned that some countries resisted committing "a fixed amount or share of national product" for any particular purpose.[27] In fact, as a share of the aggregate gross national product of the developed countries, the 0.7 percent target has never been met.

Two years later, in the same month the OECD's Development Assistance Committee published recommended terms and conditions of official development assistance.

The United Nations Second Development Decade emphasized rural development as a key to combating poverty and narrowing the income gap between rural and urban families. The United Nations promoted the establishment of employment targets and absorption of more of the labor force into modern non-agricultural jobs.

New International Economic Order

On May 1, 1974, the Sixth Special General Assembly of the United Nations adopted the *Declaration to Establish a New International Economic Order and Special Project to Support Most Seriously Affected Countries.* In December the UN adopted a "Charter of Economic Rights and Duties of States." Article 8 called for "structural changes in the context of a balanced world economy in harmony with the needs and interests of all countries, especially developing countries...."[28]

A goal of this initiative was to foster the transfer of real resources from developed to developing countries on a continuous and predictable basis. It introduced notions of "equity" and "interdependence" among nations, not just within them. Thus not only did developing nations have the responsibility to assure equitable distribution of resources within their borders, but developed nations also had a responsibility to distribute their resources across borders to the developing nations.

Such redistributionist underpinnings coupled with "abrasive rhetoric and confrontational tactics" triggered resistance among world powers like the United States and led to the initiative's demise.[29] At the same time, the World Bank published *Redistribution with Growth*, a volume whose thesis was that policies on the distribution of wealth actually fostered growth.[30]

The World Bank and other international aid institutions attempted to attack poverty directly by increased financing of rural projects, education and overall human development. For example, lending by the International Development Association "increased from an average annual level of commitments of $229 million in 1961-68 to $3.8 billion in 1980."[31]

Global, Regional and Bilateral Aid Agencies

A number of specialized agencies devoted to reducing poverty and promoting development have emerged within and in tandem with the UN system. Many are funded not from the United Nations but by donor countries directly in the form of official development assistance.

The United Nations, at the instigation of Nobel Prize winning economist Simon Kuznets, established a system of national accounts. Richard Stone, who helped draft the initial system in 1952 and oversaw most of the 1968 revisions, also received the Nobel Prize in 1984.

The system of national accounts has become the standard statistical resource for describing countries' economic affairs. Most members of the United Nations make regular entries in the system.

In 1968, the United Nations initiated the International Comparison Program, which created the first systematic multilateral set of purchasing power comparisons. The World Bank provided significant support for the project.

On June 15, 1964, at the end of the first session of the United Nations Conference on Trade and Development, there was signed the "Joint Declaration of the Seventy-Seven Countries."

At the first ministerial meeting of the G-77 in Algiers in 1967, the G-77 adopted the Charter of Algiers that created a permanent institutional structure. Although the membership has grown to 132 countries, the G-77 has retained its original name. It is the largest coalition of developing nations in the United Nations system.

In November 1964, the African Development Bank came into being; it was followed almost two years later by the Asian Development Bank, of which Japan was one of the founding members.

The United Nations Development Programme was established in 1965, twenty years after the creation of the United Nations. The UN General Assemblyestablished the United Nations Capital Development Fund in 1966 primarily for small-scale investment in the poorest countries.

Other important entities emerged in 1967: United Nations Industrial Development Organization (July), European Community (July), and the Association of Southeast Asian Nations (August).

With increased industrialization and a declining agricultural sector, rural residents migrated to urban areas in search of work. Economic growth was accompanied by high unemployment, low wages and an ever more unequal distribution of income.

Economists came to see that higher rates of growth did not always correlate with a rising standard of living across the board. The International Labour Organization advocated growth with employment as a means of reducing poverty and alleviating societal tensions.

During the administration of President John F. Kennedy, the United States enacted the Foreign Assistance Act, established the Agency for International Development to handle bilateral economic aid, created the Peace Corps and launched a ten-year program of aid to Latin America called the Alliance for Progress. Similar bilateral aid institution-building occurred in other nations, for example Canada, France, Germany, Japan, Sweden, and the United Kingdom. (See Appendices 3 and 4.)

In 1970, OECD's Development Assistance Committee wrestled unsuccessfully with the practice of tying aid to the purchase of donor country goods and services. While the majority of the committee's members favored untying bilateral loans, there was reluctance by some to commit themselves in principle to such an arrangement. Members like France, Italy and Canada cited their own special circumstances and the United States found itself with a growing balance of payments problem.

Such issues appeared esoteric in the light of appalling poverty conditions in much of the globe.

Environmental Issues Related to Poverty Reduction

The world's poorest people are found predominantly in rural areas, where they tend to rely on renewable natural resources like soil, forests, water and pastures. Population pressures and inadequate national policies are leading to deterioration of these resources.

The degradation of natural resources in developing countries in pursuit of rapid economic growth may prove counterproductive. A degraded environment could undermine efforts to meet long-term basic human needs. The world faces significant problems in the management of its natural resources. Overplanting, overfishing and overgrazing threaten the renewability of soil, fish stocks and pasture.

Despite proliferating international efforts to conserve forest resources, the rapid rate of tropical deforestation proceeds unabated. Developing countries with urgent needs for investment and capital have allocated a significant amount of their forests to logging concessions.

Poverty alleviation strategies have included converting large areas of forest to agriculture. However, agriculture in these conditions is often unsustainable due to poor soils underlying tropical forests. Tropical forest destruction leads to shortages of wood and biologically productive wetlands. Lakes, reservoirs, and irrigation systems become more subject to silting. There is loss of plant and animal species. Over time, indigenous peoples are deprived of their resource base.

At the extreme, deforestation can result in desertification and destabilization of the earth's climate. Conversely, advocates contend, properly managed tropical forests provide resources essential to the economic growth as well as genetic resources of value to developed and developing countries alike.

To increase incentives in developing countries to protect tropical forests, environmentalists lean toward positive approaches like increased foreign aid and debt relief rather than punitive economic measures.

Both developed and developing countries have an interest in cooperating to achieve environmentally economic policies. International cooperation is needed to maintain and where possible to restore the land, vegetation, water, wildlife, and other resources upon which economic growth and human well being are ultimately dependent.

The Green Revolution

In 1970, over 900 million people around the world suffered from malnutrition. That figure began to drop thereafter, thanks in no small part to the "Green Revolution". The Green Revolution refers to spectacularly improved yields of major food crops (rice, wheat, maize) that occurred particularly during the late 1960s and early 1970s.

Over a ten-year period beginning in 1943, a research program funded by the Rockefeller Foundation and the government of Mexico led to the development of new varieties of wheat that enabled Mexico to become self-sufficient by 1956.

In 1960, buoyed by this success, the Rockefeller and Ford Foundations established the International Rice Research Institute at Los Banos in the Phillippines. The Institute's research produced a new rice plant hybrid, the famous IR8, whose high yield launched the Green Revolution. This was followed by other new high-yielding seed varieties whose value was recognized by the governments of developing countries.[32]

The revolution consisted of a package of agricultural reforms, including rapid dissemination of the new seed varieties, better use of moisture through irrigation and controlled water supplies, more widespread use of fertilizers and pesticides, and the development of related management skills. It was made possible by large public investments in rural infrastructure projects, reforms in national agricultural research systems and cooperation with international agricultural institutes.[33]

The impact of the Green Revolution was greatest in Asia. Rice production in countries like Sri Lanka and Pakistan soared. Within a few years a heavily populated country like India changed from food-deficit status to agricultural exporter. New agricultural technologies improved production and reduced the country's vulnerability to fluctuations in monsoon rains.

The Green Revolution forestalled a food crisis and became the foundation for significant economic growth in China and elsewhere in South and Southeast Asia. Over the past thirty years, consumers have benefited as real food prices in Asia and elsewhere in the world have declined while rural incomes have increased.[34] However, the blessings were not unmixed.

The Green Revolution required significant use of agrochemical-based pest and weed control in some crops, thereby raising environmental and health concerns. Water management required skills that were not always available.

And the Green Revolution did not end world hunger. In the short- and medium-term, it led to an oversupply of food, which drove down prices. This adversely affected the incomes of small farmers who were faced with paying off the high initial and ongoing costs of seed, pesticides and equipment.

The Green Revolution transformed third world farming as farmers abandoned traditional practices in favor of new seed varieties, chemical fertilizers, pesticides and irrigation. The use of tractors and other forms of mechanization that came with the Green Revolution benefited richer and more "progressive" landowners but also led to job losses among tenants and sharecroppers.

Food surpluses were often exported to richer countries instead of being distributed to the producer country's own poor. Low pay in the producer countries meant that workers could not afford to buy the very foods they were exporting.

Biotechnology

Whereas the Green Revolution took advantage of chemically-intensive methods, advances in biotechnology in recent decades have led to the production of new crops and crop strains through genetic modifications at the molecular, cellular or tissue levels. These advances have the potential on an industrial scale to increase crop productivity and reduce global poverty and hunger. They can also serve to diminish the exposure of poor farmers to toxic agricultural chemicals.[35]

Some critics observe that the existence of 800 million malnourished persons worldwide is due not to lack of food but lack of adequate food distribution systems. They worry that the expansion of biotechnology industries will bring profits to a few global corporations while destroying the livelihoods of poor farmers.

Among other factors, issues around intellectual property rights and weak plant breeding capacity hinder the ability of poor farmers to access modern methods of biotechnology.[36]

More broadly, there are fears that genetically modified food products may threaten the traditional diversity of agricultural output and have undesirable (though as yet undiscovered) biological effects. The impact of gene-based technologies on food safety, environment, health and socio-economic conditions in developing countries is not well understood. There are concerns about proper labeling and the ability to trace back to the origin of modified organisms.

Such factors, critics contend, argue for a less headlong and more regulated approach to the development and dissemination of gene technologies. The United States and Canada among others have advocated an approach based more on risk-reward analyses and information-sharing rather than regulation.

Whether it proceeds on a fast track or a slower one, if world food security is the overriding priority, it seems self-evident that biotechnology could play a crucial role. The more fundamental question is whether and, if so, how participants in the biotechnology revolution, who are based largely in the private sector, will shape their industry to benefit the world's malnourished.[37] At present, the prospect of the Green Revolution being succeeded any time soon by a Gene Revolution remains uncertain at best.

Reasons for Optimism

By the end of the 1960s, global poverty had emerged as both a multifaceted problem and an international priority. Poverty had become entwined with a number of old and familiar themes like growth as well as new and emerging global interests like gender equity and environmental protection.

International bodies devoted more and more resources to poverty reduction. Developing nations seemed to be on the path to sustainable growth. The spread of the Green Revolution and new advances in biotechnology meant that food security had become more a problem of distribution than production.

Optimists could be excused for thinking that global prosperity and the eradication of poverty were foreseeable. The heavy conceptual work was viewed as virtually complete. Globally many key interest groups had coalesced around the issue of poverty.

However, new realities were setting in.

ENDNOTES

1. De Vries, Margaret Garritsen (1986) 96.
2. Hewitt, Tom in Tim Allen and Alan Thomas, editors (2000) 295.
3. Inaugural Address, President John F. Kennedy, January 20, 1961.
4. The quote is taken from the resolution itself. Also, see Emmerij, Louis; Richard Jolly; and Thomas G. Weiss (2000) 44 and United Nations (1962) 6.
5. U.S. General Accounting Office (1983) 1.
6. Thorbecke, Erik, "The Evolution of the Development Doctrine and the Role of Foreign Aid," in Tarp, Finn, editor (2002) 25.
7. United Nations (1970).
8. The French demographer Alfred Sauvy coined the phrase "third world" in a 1952 article in the *France-Observateur* titled "Three Worlds, One Planet." The phrase "third world" was used at a 1955 conference of African and Asian nations in Bandung, Indonesia. In 1956 Georges Balandier at the National Institute of Demographic Studies in Paris edited a book titled *Le Tiers du Monde: Sous-développement et Développement*. In 1959, French economist François Perroux put out a new journal called *Le Tiers du Monde*. By the end of the 1950s the term was widely used in the French media.
9. The quotation is drawn from the Internet version of the Modern History Sourcebook at Fordham University, Paul Hallsall, editor. www.fordham.edu/halsall/mod/1955sukarno-bandong.html.
10. Creative Associates International, Inc. (2002) 108.
11. Ayres, Robert L. (1983) 2.
12. Kapur, Devesh, John P. Lewis and Richard Webb, editors (1998) 1:190-191, 549.
13. In August 1979 the facility was expanded beyond merchandise exports to include receipts for travel and workers' remittances. In May 1981, an integrated facility scheme

was introduced, under which financial support was made available to countries whose balance of payments was adversely affected by imports as well. Specifically, where foods, and especially cereals, had to be imported due to crop failure or world prices for food items spiked drastically, developing countries had recourse to either the compensatory (export only) facility or the integrated (export and import) facility. Hooke, A.W. (1982) 46-47.

14. Quoted in Caufield, Catherine (1996) 99.

15. See McNamara's speech to the American Society of Newspaper Editors, May 18, 1966.

16. Kapur, Devesh, John P. Lewis and Richard Webb, editors (1998) 1:415-417.

17. Such land reform involves the transfer of rents from the landlord class to their tenant workers and not infrequently has been tied to revolts, revolution, conquest or independence from colonial rule. For more, see Binswanger, Hans P., Klaus Deininger and Gershon Feder (1995) 2683.

18. Ibid.:2666-2682.

19. Ayres, Robert L. (1983) 112-147.

20. Kapur, Devesh, John P. Lewis and Richard Webb, editors (1998) 1:253.

21. Ayres, Robert L. (1983) 176-208.

22. Caufield, Catherine (1996) 104.

23. He also organized and directed Argentina's central bank from 1935 to 1943. Love, Joseph L. (2001) 3. In 1949, Prebisch joined the staff of the UN's Economic Commission for Latin America and the Caribbean, where he stayed for 15 years, as a consultant for a year and executive secretary thereafter.

24. Emmerij, Louis; Richard Jolly; and Thomas G. Weiss (2000) 51-52.

25. Prebisch and Wladyslaw Malinowski, a Polish economist, were chiefly responsible in having UNCTAD made a permanent UN entity instead of a one-time conference. Malinowski was also instrumental in the establishment of the UN's regional economic commissions. See Love, Joseph L. November 2001) 5.

26. Emmerij, Louis; Richard Jolly; and Thomas G. Weiss (2000) 57.

27. Pearson, Lester B. (1969).

28. UN General Assembly resolution 3281, 29th Session, Supp. No. 31 (1974) 50.

29. Emmerij, Louis; Richard Jolly; and Thomas G. Weiss (2000) 186.

30. Chenery, Hollis B. (1974).

31. World Bank Operations Evaluation Department (2002) 77. The amounts are in current dollars, that is, not adjusted for inflation. Measured in constant dollars, annual commitment levels doubled in the 1970s.

32. This account draws on Harrison, Paul (1993) 93-94.

33. Quibria, M.G. (February 2002) 53

34. Food and Agriculture Organization (2000).

35. Food and Agriculture Organization (2004) vii-viii.

36. Ibid.

37. For more, see Persley, G.J. and Lantin, M.M. (2000).

5

Deeper Indebtedness (1971-80)

The Human Side of Development

During the 1970s, the issue of global poverty achieved prominence in the agenda of the United Nations. The previous two decades had seen unprecedented economic growth in the developing nations as a whole, averaging around five percent annually. Paradoxically, at least for trickle-down theorists, poverty, unemployment and income inequalities were also growing. Both trends persisted through the decade.

The concept of development itself underwent modifications as social issues came to the fore. Rural development as an end in itself gained support. The role of the largely undocumented but obviously significant informal sector of the economy of developing countries attracted increased attention.

Among agencies within the United Nations system, development was perceived more and more as a human, not simply an economic, issue. Employment and income distribution were placed on a par with overall economic growth.

The oil price shocks of the early 1970s led to increased borrowing by developing nations and the emergence of a full-blown debt crisis that had very human consequences for the world's poorest people.

Breakdown of Bretton Woods

In the first half of the decade, the gap between the developed and developing countries widened. Under the Bretton Woods Agreement of 1944, there was established a system of fixed exchange rates between currencies with support for countries that ran into problems with their balance of payments. For a quarter century after World War II, the Bretton Woods system maintained stable and adjustable international monetary exchange rates. To maintain equilibrium in the balance of payments there would be occasional devaluations of individual currencies.

The system was propped up by a United States commitment to redeem international dollar holdings at the rate of $35 per ounce of gold. On August 15, 1971, President Richard Nixon announced that the United States would no longer provide the gold backing for the dollar. With this unilateral U.S. action, the Bretton Woods system collapsed.

While unilateral, the U.S. action did not lack for a rationale. The amount of gold held by the United States in Fort Knox declined as a percentage of the volume of dollars circulating throughout an expanding international economy. Economic growth meant pressure for greater liquidity. Gold backing constituted a constraint if there was to be any meaningful relationship between gold and dollars.

With little or no relationship, the United States could at some point be flooded with dollars to be redeemed in gold, thereby exhausting its gold reserves. At the other extreme, if some fixed ratio were maintained between dollars and gold, it could constrict the growth of capital. The elimination of gold backing for the dollar was followed by the abolition of fixed currency relationships. It stimulated the expansion of international capital flows.

During and after 1973, prices for food, fuel, fertilizer, as well as capital goods, equipment and services rose sharply. During 1974, the prices of most commodities on which developing countries depended declined. The situation of these countries was worsened due to unfavorable climate conditions, which aggravated already existing agricultural imbalances, and led to recession in the developed countries.

Declining Flows of Official Development Assistance

Few of the developed market economies achieved the goal of providing 0.7 percent of their gross domestic product in the form of official development assistance. Arguments were put forward *against* any such predetermined level of assistance. Critics contended that aid should go to developing countries that would spend the funds effectively and demonstrate measurable improvements in areas like education and health.[1]

With declining flows of official development assistance, the developing countries turned to even more borrowing on progressively harder terms. Debt service payments grew from about 9.6 percent per year during the 1960s to 16.5 percent in the early 1970s. The burden of debt service payments in developing countries increased relative to export earnings.[2]

Some progress was made. Colombia, a showcase for the Alliance for Progress in Latin America, made strides with assistance primarily from the U.S. Agency for International Development, World Bank and Inter-American Development Bank. Initially, lending by these major donors supported infrastructure projects such as railways, roads, airports, power generating facilities, irrigation telecommunications, and industrial plants.[3]

Poverty Research at the World Bank

Officials interviewed by social scientist Robert L. Ayres for a 1983 book maintained that the World Bank was above all a bank, not a development agency.[4] It was concerned first and foremost with interest rates, amortization schedules and borrower creditworthiness. Over the next two decades that perception slowly changed 180 degrees.

Formal research began to play a role in the Bank's operations. Under Robert McNamara, the World Bank included research as a budget item for the first time in 1972. By fiscal year 1980 research expenditures reached $11.4 million in support of over 80 projects. The early studies covered a variety of poverty-oriented topics such as rural development, employment, migration and population trends.[5]

The Bank monitored the macroeconomic and microeconomic performance of individual countries. Sector analysis focused on familiar growth factors like investment, trade policy, exchange rates, interest rates and debt management. The newer poverty research and traditional economic analyses did not always mesh to guide sector allocation and country loan decisions.

From 1973 on, the Bank stressed rural poverty reduction through land reform, rural electrification and education. In 1975 the Bank established an internal Operations Evaluation Department to examine more rigorously its development projects. By 1983, the Bank could identify "significant gains in the standard of living of its people" in both rural and urban areas.[6]

World Employment Program

Under the impetus of research by the International Labour Organization, the UN system began to strategize more explicitly around the goals of economic *and* social development. Growth alone was insufficient; it needed parallel progress in employment creation, equitable income distribution and poverty reduction.

In 1976 the World Employment Conference at the initiative of the International Labour Organization emphasized productive employment creation as part of a "basic needs" strategy for eradicating poverty.

The International Labour Organization's World Employment Program broke new ground for this strategy. Its analysis of unemployment in developing economies differentiated among people willing to work at prevailing wages but unable to obtain jobs, younger people holding out for jobs more commensurate with their education and training, and the working poor—those whose earnings were insufficient to lift them out of poverty.

The notion of poverty as a function of unemployment shifted policy discussion from income redistribution schemes to job creation. Indeed it was argued that employment should supersede growth as a primary development objective.

The International Labour Organization highlighted the role of the informal sector, the network of small enterprise and *ad hoc* job creation that developed among rural migrants living at the urban margins. It emphasized the critical importance of education as an economic investment. It advocated "appropriate" technologies that accommodated the scarcity of capital but the abundance of labor in many developing countries.

As part of any development strategy, it underscored addressing basic needs in employment, income, education, health care, housing and, interestingly, access to culture. It called for greater consistency among macroeconomic, microeconomic, and sector policies.[7]

"The emphasis on distribution tended to benefit agriculture, since it was in rural areas that the majority of the poor were found and agriculture was often the lagging sector relative to industry."[8]

The World Employment Program was embraced by other elements of the UN system, such as the Food and Agriculture Organization; United Nations Educational, Scientific and Cultural Organization; United Nations Industrial Development Organization; United Nations Children's Fund; and the United Nations Population Fund.

An economic development strategy that took both employment creation and the alleviation of basic needs into account was valued as an idea whose time had come.[9]

Since the late 1970s the employment-intensive approach has fostered development assistance by international organizations that de-emphasizes large-scale industrial and infrastructure projects and supports small-scale job-creation projects. Such projects seek the application of appropriate technology, the promotion of rural development, enhancement of the informal sector, and small-scale industry.

Basic Needs First and Foremost

The United States and the World Bank both shifted away from supporting large infrastructure projects like roads, power and telecommunications. Instead they emphasized rural development and social services. Thus the newer aid projects highlighted food security, adult literacy, public health (for example, inoculations), credit for small farmers and technical assistance. They reflected a more explicit focus on meeting the immediate needs and longer-range aspirations of the poor.

In its strongest form, the basic needs element of development strategies advocated by the International Labour Organization faulted externally imposed policies. Instead it aimed at empowering populations to make their own development decisions through the redistribution of land, political power and other resources.

A weaker form of basic needs strategies emphasized growth over redistribution and contented itself with establishing scientifically-grounded and measurable objectives for health care, nutrition, education and the like.

The basic needs approach did not lack for critics. The G-77, which espoused the emergence of a new international economic order, wanted to see redistribution from developed to developing countries. Instead, as promoted by North-dominated international organizations, meeting basic needs meant redistribution *within* countries.

Until the mid-1960s, developing countries were treated as a homogeneous group except for their differing primary exports. The secretariat of the United Nations Conference on Trade and Development devised a typology of developing countries that highlighted their differences.

In 1971, drawing on this work and on recommendations from the Committee on Development Planning, the United Nations General Assembly approved the list of the Least Developed Countries. These were countries with structural handicaps that kept them in poverty and that were in greatest need of international assistance.

In 1974 governments attending the World Food Conference proclaimed that "every man, woman and child has the inalienable right to be free from hunger and malnutrition." The Conference set as its goal the eradication of hunger, food insecurity and malnutrition within a decade, a goal that was not met.[10]

At the sixth special session of the UN General Assembly in the spring of 1974, the nations of the South, as an outcome of an ongoing North-South dialogue, set forth a demand for a New International Economic Order.

In October 1974, a United Nations Conference on Resource Use, Environment and Development Strategies, held in Cocoyec, Mexico, issued "The Cocoyec Declaration." The Declaration contended that the primary goal of development should be the development of "man" not "things." Hence the most important concern for the international community was to satisfy the basic needs of the world's poorest people.

The international community, however, was turning its attention elsewhere.

Oil Prices and a Borrowing Binge

Until the early 1970s, large transnational corporations controlled the oil industry. With the creation of the Organization of Petroleum Exporting Countries in 1960, that slowly began to change. By the 1970s, OPEC had become a powerful player on the world stage.

At an October 1973 ministerial meeting, the Organization of Petroleum Exporting Countries voted to raise the price of crude oil. Prices rose fourfold and stayed high for the succeeding decade, triggering a worldwide oil crisis. The OPEC members racked up huge cash surpluses.

This was the first of several oil price shocks that occurred in the decades to follow. In countries dependent wholly or in part on oil imports, the cost of oil drove up other prices and triggered inflation. The 1973 oil crisis affected both developed and developing countries, the former requiring oil to sustain high energy consumption, the latter to foster industrialization.

The developed countries slowed their growth rates to combat inflationary pressures; this led to reduced demand for imports and lower prices in the types of commodities exported by the developing nations.

The effects were predictably adverse. Developing nations lacked the resources to pay for oil since the prices of the commodities they exported were dropping just as oil prices were rising. To meet their demand for oil and sustain capital investment, they borrowed.

What did they borrow? They borrowed the surplus cash that OPEC nations had stashed in commercial banks. Initially the developing nations were attracted by the low interest rates; the banks in turn sought new credit markets to take advantage of the excess liquidity in the international banking system.

The rise of OPEC diminished the reliance of the G-77 and other members of the United Nations Conference on Trade and Development on World Bank loans and on bilateral foreign aid.

Borrowing quickly turned into an addiction. It proved counterproductive (literally) as the developed nations fell into recession, bank liquidity began drying up and the cost of borrowing rose. Rapidly rising interest rates affected the ability of borrowers to repay their debts. One result was massive global payment imbalances.

Re-enter the IMF

By the early 1970s, the International Monetary fund had begun to respond to pressures that linked global monetary management with economic growth in its poorest members.

The International Monetary Fund helped developing nations cope with their balance of payments deficits through its "facilities". It had first introduced a compensatory financing facility in 1963 to address balance of payments deficits arising from temporary export shortfalls. It liberalized and extended the facility in 1966. In response to the oil price shock, it did so again in 1975.

The oil facility, conceived by the Fund's managing director, H. Johannes Witteveen, was established in 1974 to assist member countries to meet oil-related payments deficits. While open to all members, the facility was used most by developing countries.[11]

While small relative to the size of global payments deficits, the oil facility showed that developed and developing countries could cooperate in a monetary emergency.

In September 1974, the Fund introduced the "extended facility" as a form of medium-term assistance to its developing country members. A supplementary financing facility was approved in August 1977 and implemented in early 1979. The poorest developing countries could also obtain low interest loans through an IMF Trust Fund.[12]

Debt and the Trade Game

Debt servicing pushed poverty reduction off center stage and began to consume the energy of governments and international aid organizations.

The problem of debt was exacerbated by the commercial banks' resistance to more lending, reduced foreign capital investment, nascent protectionism in the developed nations that railed against so-called "cheap foreign imports", and declines in foreign aid.

For its part, the United Nations Conference on Trade and Development sought to change the rules of the trade game. It succeeded in getting developed countries to accept the notion of preferential tariffs for developing countries. At a 1976 trade conference in Nairobi the participants voiced their support for an Integrated Program for Commodities.

The goal was to maintain fair prices that would not fluctuate to the detriment of producers or consumers. The terms of trade for eighteen particular commodities would be subject to negotiation or renegotiation. However, a decade after the conference only one new commodity stabilization agreement had been completed; it was for natural rubber.[13]

Donors' Dilemmas

In the twenty years following World War II, the number of nations providing aid to the developing world grew substantially. While the United States remained a leading donor, its share of aid declined from about 60 percent in the 1960s to about 16 percent in 1981.[14] Donor nations provided aid both directly through bilateral programs and also indirectly with some aid channeled through multilateral organizations.

The United States and other members of the Organization for Economic Cooperation and Development regarded their aid as an instrument of foreign policy. Conceived in the context of the Cold War, aid was designed to foster the political, economic, cultural and developmental goals of both the donor and recipient countries. The OECD's Development Assistance Committee was created to stimulate the flow of donor aid and to establish guidelines for the provision of aid.

U.S. assistance is aimed at promoting U.S. security interests, economic and political stability, and self-sustaining growth in developing countries. Until the early 1970s, the U.S. Agency for International Development like other donors directed aid to economic sectors judged to have the highest potential for growth.

In practice this meant funding for dams, roads, buildings, industrial plants and similar large infrastructure projects.

The resulting economic benefits, it was widely assumed, would trickle down to the poor. Growing skepticism over the likelihood of this trickle down effect particularly in rural areas led to a shift in aid policy.

Private Non-governmental Aid

During the 1970s, there emerged greater collaboration between non-governmental organizations and official entities like the World Bank. Bank-financed projects increasingly began to incorporate a role for non-governmental organizations. "From 1970 to 1985, total development aid disbursed by international NGOs increased tenfold."[15]

Non-governmental organizations expanded the range of their antipoverty activities. Several macroeconomic and political factors accounted for this development.

During the decade, developing countries scaled back their own investments in infrastructure-building and social service delivery to cope with internal economic and fiscal problems, most notably their rising debt. The end of the Cold War brought in its wake political instability in many countries of the developing world. A global recession roiled the waters even more.

Non-governmental organizations were valued by international bodies like the United Nations and World Bank, as well as bilateral aid agencies, for their credibility with poor communities and their efforts to build community-based institutional capacity. They were called upon with greater frequency to provide emergency and humanitarian relief. As a result, funding from private foundations and bilateral government aid agencies increased.[16]

Oxfam became a more vocal advocate for the poor through its research and public affairs activities. In 1979 Oxfam received worldwide attention for aiding victims of the brutal Pol Pot regime in Cambodia. Oxfam led a group of agencies in a relief effort that included the importation of rice, seeds, tools, water pumps, and fertilizers for cities and rural areas.

In the 1970s, CARE responded to massive famines in Africa with emergency relief. It also supported long-term environmentally sound projects in agroforestry aimed at preventing drought and increasing food production.

Since the 1970s, the non-governmental world in both developing and developed countries has experienced exponential growth. Through their advocacy and research, both national and international non-governmental organizations played a significant role in focusing world attention on the debt crisis of the 1980s.

By the early 1990s, an estimated 15 percent of all overseas aid for development was being routed through non-governmental organizations like Oxfam, CARE and World Vision.[17]

New Directions in the United States

In the 1973 Foreign Assistance Act, the United States Congress reoriented the nation's aid programs under what became known as the New Directions Mandate. The Agency for International Development provided assistance through three main vehicles: Development Assistance to overcome barriers to growth, Economic Support Fund to promote economic and political stability, and Public Law 480 food aid.

The New Directions Mandate required that U.S. aid be targeted to the poor populations of the world to meet their basic human needs.

The loans and grants of the U.S. Agency for International Development were to be used to address problems faced by poor majorities, that is, for agriculture and rural development, nutrition, population planning, health, education, technical assistance and specialized development projects.

The agency was directed away from programming designed to promote macroeconomic reforms. Instead it adopted a rural-oriented development program "delivered primarily through a large number of discrete, small-scale projects."[18]

The U.S. New Directions approach demanded knowledge of the recipient country's needs and capabilities, as well as detailed social, economic and environmental analyses as part of any given project design.

Not infrequently project design work generated policy dialogues with the recipient country to determine the degree of compatibility between macroeconomic policy and local project objectives.[19] It entailed interaction with the ministries of the recipient country as well as the project's beneficiaries.

U.S. aid officials would advocate for changes in policy, particularly in cases of government subsidies, wage and price controls and other forms of market manipulation. They would press for macroeconomic reforms based more on private initiative, institutional development and technology transfer. The United States believed that its advice and technical assistance would be more acceptable politically under a project setting.[20]

The Scale of Antipoverty Projects

Under the New Directions Mandate, small-scale rural-oriented antipoverty projects increased from 1,550 in fiscal year 1975 to 1,970 in fiscal year 1980. Such project proliferation created management and monitoring problems for the field missions of the U.S. Agency for International Development.

In the early 1980, the agency's headquarters sought to streamline its project portfolio. It stressed a reduction in new project starts and concentration on fewer but larger projects.[21] The pros and cons of project versus non-project assistance were weighed.

A poverty reduction strategy based on a large number of small-scale projects geared to the basic needs of the rural poor is attractive in principle. In practice the strategy may bring about only limited and highly localized results without materially affecting the national poverty rate. Small localized projects increase administrative and other overhead expenses and diminish a donor's ability to exercise policy leverage with the recipient government.

Conversely large infrastructure projects like roads, bridges and power plants may be geared to a community or a region as a whole with the effect of increasing benefits to the nonpoor as much or more than to the poor and resurrecting the specter of trickle-down. More generalized nonproject assistance like commodity import programs and balance of payments support can help achieve overall development objectives but may fail to directly benefit the rural poor, at least in the short-term.

In contrast to the U.S. small-scale-many-projects approach, Canada, the United Kingdom, and West Germany emphasized capital development projects. France targeted education particularly in its former colonies. Sweden sought to integrate its aid with recipient country plans through sector aid and commodity imports.[22]

In 1975, Sweden became the first Development Assistance Committee member to achieve the official development assistance target of 0.7 percent of its gross national product. It was followed by the Netherlands in the following year and by Norway and Denmark in 1976 and 1978, respectively. At the other end of the scale, Portugal withdrew from the Development Assistance Committee in 1974, requesting that it be designated a developing country.[23]

In 1977, the members of OECD's Development Assistance Committee called for an aid policy that would help developing countries expand their capabilities to meet the basic needs of the poor.

In November 1977, the International Fund for Agricultural Development officially began life with a mandate to alleviate poverty, increase food production, and improve nutrition among the rural poor. Its establishment was an outcome of the 1974 World Food Conference. The Fund's target populations are the poorest of the world's people: small farmers, landless rural people, nomadic pastoralists, artisanal fisherfolk, indigenous people and rural poor women and children.

Global Perspectives on Development

In October 1974, the World Bank and the International Monetary Fund established The Joint Ministerial Committee of the Boards of Governors of the Bank and Fund on the Transfer of Real Resources to Developing Countries. Blessedly it is also known as the Development Committee. It advises the two groups on the financial assistance needed to foster growth in developing countries.

Over time since its establishment, the Development Committee has expanded its range to include global trade and environmental issues. The Committee has 25 members, mostly ministers of finance or development. Each is appointed for a two year period by one of the countries or groups of countries that designates a member to the Executive Board of the World Bank or the International Monetary Fund.

In August 1978, the World Bank released the first of its annual World Development Reports. Since then, each year's report has analyzed a specific aspect of development including over time such issues as the role of the state, transition economies, labor, infrastructure, health, the environment, and poverty.

The reports are the Bank's best-known contribution to its thinking about development. Critics like the Bretton Woods Project, which was established as an independent initiative by a group of British non-governmental organizations, complain that the World Bank presents the reports as embodiments of objective research and broadly held views.

For the critics, they are instead a means by which the World Bank justifies its actions and promotes its agenda.[24]

The collapse of the Bretton Woods system affected the functioning of the International Monetary Fund. Relying on pegged exchange rates, the Fund had provided short-term resources to help countries with balance of payments deficits.

After 1973, when President Nixon halted U.S. gold sales, the exchange rate system was no longer fixed. The International Monetary Fund shifted its focus more pointedly to the needs of developing countries. It did this through management of financial crises, lending, and technical assistance. It also expanded its economic data gathering for its 182 member countries.[25]

In some countries, reform measures had taken hold. Beginning in 1978, for example, China took steps to rectify unsatisfactory agricultural performance. The reforms at first were limited to giving farmers improved price and income incentives. These were quickly followed by more fundamental measures. There was a pronounced shift away from collective farming to a household-based farming system and reliance on prices and markets to determine production decisions.

The overhang of debt in the developing world posed an ominous obstacle to progress.

Fiscal Crises in the Developing World

While the World Bank had come to define itself as a development agency, it continued to function formally as a bank. In practice its assistance to developing countries came in the form of loans, whether "hard" or "soft", rather than grants.

The dependence of the developing world on loans had become self-defeating. Between 1978 and 1982, the foreign debt of Latin America doubled to $330 billion, of which four-fifths was owed to private banks.

By 1983, Brazil with a debt of $98 billion, and Mexico not far behind at $94 billion, headed a group of seventeen Latin American countries with debt repayment problems.[26] Warnings of possible default issued from these two countries and soon after from Argentina, Chile and Venezuela. Debt servicing had become a way of life.

During the 1980s, the debt problems of developing countries grew to crisis proportions. In 1970, the outstanding debt of developing countries was $70 billion; by 1980, it had ballooned to $438.7 billion. Private creditors held three-quarters of this latter total.[27]

International financial institutions, notably the World Bank and International Monetary Fund, added gasoline to the fire. They opted for improving the balance of payments and reinforcing the position of international commercial banks.

Governments needed outside assistance from the World Bank and other transnational financial institutions to service their debts. The needs of the poor receded as new loans were made to shore up governments on the edge of default.

By siding more with international lenders (in resisting calls for loan forgiveness, for example), the World Bank unwittingly insured that debt would burden the developing countries indefinitely.

Misalignment of Structural Adjustment

It was not in the interest of the World Bank, including in this case the International Monetary Fund, to allow financial management systems in the developing world to fall into total disarray. Each of these Bretton Woods institutions acted from different but complementary starting points.

The World Bank made capital available in the form of loans for long-term economic development projects. The International Monetary Fund typically provided balance of payments financing to countries with temporary or cyclical deficits in their current accounts.

Each needed structurally sound and sufficiently robust economies in which to ply their trade. The debt crisis undermined the potential for new investment and rendered the recipient country a bottomless pit for current account deficit financing.

Under its then operations chief Ernest Stern, the Bank crafted a structural adjustment loan scheme that linked new loans from the Bank to a program of macroeconomic reforms by the borrowers.

Under structural adjustment, developing nations were lent money on the condition that they adopt a panoply of Bank-imposed reforms. The recipient governments were expected to cut public spending, including social expenditures. Other reforms included curbing inflation, tightening monetary policy through higher interest rates, reorganizing state enterprises, liberalizing imports, and maintaining a flexible exchange rate.

Similarly the International Monetary Fund, beginning in 1976, provided loans on concessional terms to its eligible low-income member countries in support of their reform programs and their balance of payments deficiencies. The lending terms included an annual interest rate of one half of one percent, a five-and-a-half year grace period and ten-year maturity.

The funding for these loans came primarily from proceeds in the sale of the International Monetary Fund's gold holdings and from loans or grants to the Fund from member countries.

The approach in toto combined short-run stabilization under the aegis of the International Monetary Fund with the World Bank's focus on longer-run economic adjustment geared to open markets and freer trade. In order to be eligible for debt relief by the World Bank and International Monetary Fund, borrower nations had to agree to a range of reforms including an expanded role for the private sector.

The Ill Wind of Conditionality

Such conditionality arrangements were also part of aid packages from wealthy donor countries in the Organization for Economic Cooperation and Development. In the electricity and water sectors, privatization formed a key part of conditionality.[28]

Many loans were conditioned on the opening up of the recipients' economies and the increased export of commodities and raw materials. In order to pay off their debts recipients had to sell more abroad and earn foreign exchange. They competed with each other by lowering standards, reducing wages and providing their resources more cheaply to large foreign corporations and richer nations.

The richer nations and their corporations thereby obtained raw materials and commodities at bargain rates. Poor country governments spent less in an effort to stimulate their economies, but succeeded mainly in depriving their people of essential social services.

While fostering globalization of trade, this pattern led to greater poverty within developing nations. So-called "free" trade perpetuated and exacerbated inequalities between developing and industrialized nations.

Many developing nations racked up increased debt and experienced more widespread poverty. This was due in part to the policies of international lenders like the International Monetary Fund and the World Bank.

The goals of stabilization and structural adjustment relied heavily on market forces, austerity measures, and a diminished role for government. Reduced public spending was also expected to foster market-based reforms and private sector growth.

Structural adjustment policies have in some cases enabled recipient countries to shrink budget deficits, lower inflation and make more regular debt payments. They have fostered a movement toward more open and more accountable governments. Unfortunately, the same policies contributed to a rise in unemployment rates, reduced spending on health, education and safety net programs, and the persistence of extreme poverty.

The structural adjustment approach provoked resentment and protest in developing countries. It was derided as a "one size fits all" strategy that reinforced the hegemony of rich nations and transnational corporations while hobbling the economies of developing countries. The key components of structural   adjustment—trade   liberalization,   government   deregulation, privatization and fiscal austerity—had adverse effects on small entrepreneurs, working people, subsistence farmers, and women in poverty.[29]

Of Donors and Their Motives

By the end of the 1970s, the World Bank had helped make poverty alleviation a priority for both borrowing countries and other lending institutions. The tangible effects of its projects on overall poverty reduction are elusive. Many of its antipoverty initiatives in rural development, urban housing and water supply stood out as discrete showcases rather than the leading edges of global reform.

With the expansion of private capital markets, the Bank could contend plausibly that its role in financing poverty reduction on a global scale was small. Its overall lending mounted to less that two percent of the total investment in developing countries. Poverty lending amounted to only about a third of that two percent.[30]

The Bank's initiatives do foster global attention on poverty. In many cases, the projects serve as models for other countries. And they can help in building the capacity of governments to sustain their own wars on poverty.

Donor nations provided aid from a variety of motives.[31] Aid could strengthen ties with developing nations and ease the access of richer countries like the United States to strategic defense installations or raw materials. For some European donor countries it could preserve and expand cultural relationships with former colonies.

Donors could attach conditions requiring the recipient country to purchase the donor's exports or use the donor's goods and services. Aid could serve as a lever to promote ideological objectives like democracy, socialism, or private enterprise. Undeniably aid also often embodied genuine humanitarian values.

The Limits of Government Planning

In the 1970s, financing discrete development projects continued as a major part of World Bank and other donor operations. However, it was unduly optimistic to expect that such projects in the aggregate would release the recipient countries from the trap of poverty. Issues arose over the scale of antipoverty projects and whether to focus future aid on specific geographic areas or more general sectoral assistance.

In the first decades of post-World War II economic planning, government was viewed as the main agent of development. It controlled private investment and assumed a dominant role in key industries. Trade policy revolved around import substitution with high tariffs and limits on imports in order to foster domestic industries.

By the end of the 1970s it had become clear that such policies restricted competitiveness and efficiency and produced lower than expected growth rates. While governments were overly involved in industrialization, they were insufficiently attentive to social and human capital development.

This situation did not improve during the 1980s.

ENDNOTES

1. The argument was voiced more recently by former U.S. Treasury Secretary Paul O'Neill on a 2002 trip to Africa with popular music star Bono, lead signer for the U-2 rock group. While clearly appalled concerned by the poverty he saw and expressing support for increased aid, Secretary O'Neill stated: "I'll tell you what I don't like about [the 0.7 percent of GDP target]. I don't like working from the top down. I want to figure out what it is that we need to do. And then I want to cost it out, and then I'm ready to advocate it." See Washington Post (May 31, 2002) E1, E4.
2. See UN Resolution 3517 (XXX), "Mid-term review and appraisal of progress in implementation of the International Development Strategy for the Second United Nations Development Decade", December 15, 1975.
3. Cassen, Robert (1994) 252-56.
4. Ayres, Robert L. (1983) 10.
5. Op. cit. 27-28.
6. Ibid. This section of Cassen's book includes the World Bank quotes.
7. For more on this and the preceding paragraphs, see Emmerij, Louis; Richard Jolly; and Thomas G. Weiss (2000) 60-69.
8. Food and Agriculture Organization (2000) Part 2:15.
9. Emmerij, Louis; Richard Jolly; and Thomas G. Weiss (2000) 70-72.
10. See www.fao.org.
11. De Vries, Margaret Garritsen (1986) 140.
12. Ibid., 119.
13. In Anderson, Sarah, editor (2000) see Bello, Walden, "Building an Iron Cage: The Bretton Woods Institutions, the WTO and the South", p. 60-62.
14. U.S. General Accounting Office (1983) 2.
15. See http://www.gm-unccd.org/FIELD/Multi/WB/NGO.pdf
16. Lindenberg, Marc and Coralie Bryant (2001) 8-10.
17. Ibid.
18. Op. cit. 15-16.
19. Macroeconomic stability refers to the desired equilibrium in such key economic relationships as domestic demand and output, balance of payments, government revenues and expenditures, and savings and investment.
20. The French and British governments had a history of providing key advisers to particular developing countries, many of which were former colonies. Such an approach was considered less viable for the United States in dealing with developing nations. As a highly visible world power seeking to exert its influence, it needed to tread carefully in developing countries in sensitive political areas as wage and price controls and credit policies.
21. Op. cit. 38.
22. Op. cit. 3-4.

23. Portugal rejoined the DAC in 1991.

24. See, for example, www.brettonwoodsproject.org/topic/knowledgebank.

25. International Financial Institution Advisory Commission (Meltzer Commission) (2000) 2.

26. Reynolds, David (2000) 459, 462.

27. World Bank's *World Development Report* for 1981, as cited in Ayres, Robert L. (1983) 52.

28. Bayliss, Kate (January 2002) 3.

29. The World Bank eventually proved responsive to the protests. In 1997, an initiative called the Structural Adjustment Participatory Review Initiative (SAPRI) was launched as a joint endeavor of SAPRIN, a global civil society network, and James Wolfensohn, the new president of the World Bank. SAPRI brings together organizations of civil society, their governments and the World Bank to review structural adjustment programs and consider policy options that might alleviate their adverse effects. See www.saprin.org.

30. Kapur, Devesh, John P. Lewis and Richard Webb, editors (1998) 1:328-329.

31. This and the next several paragraphs draw on U.S. General Accounting Office (1983) 4-6.

6

Neoliberalism Unleashed (1981-90)

Reversal of Fortune

A global recession in the early part of the decade and swings in growth rates that adversely affected both developed and developing countries characterized the 1980s. The gap between rich and poor countries widened.

While the United States enjoyed an era of technological innovation and economic prosperity, elsewhere the decade witnessed falling growth rates, declining living standards and deepening poverty among developing nations and even some developed ones.

The debt crisis worsened in the early 1980s, leading to a reverse in the flow of resources, that is, from developing to developed countries. The response offered by a newly empowered neoliberal camp of economists was reliance on market forces, private capital flows and reduced government involvement.

The voices of poor people began to be heard more insistently through international organizations like ATD Fourth World.

There was a reaction to the dependence of the poor on higher growth rates and "safety net" welfare schemes. In Europe and subsequently in the United States, some analysts began advocating for a guaranteed basic income for their own citizens. Needless to say, such an approach lacked political viability. Still, in the presence of widening economic disparities within as well as among countries, it represented a noteworthy reaction to the prevailing neoliberal agenda.

The idea was not as far-fetched as one might think nor did it lack for precedents. In the United States, for example, Alaska established a Permanent

Fund through a constitutional amendment approved by the state's voters in 1976. The amendment set aside at least 25 percent of certain oil and mineral revenues paid to the state for deposit into a public savings account.

The funds are invested and dividends are paid each year to all permanent Alaska residents. By June 30, 2002, the Fund's value was $23.5 billion. The amount of the dividend varies from year to year, depending on market conditions and the investment decisions made by the Fund's trustees. It has become a dependable source of extra income for Alaskans.[1]

The Alaska model has more recently been proposed for oil-rich developing countries like Iraq and Nigeria. In Nigeria, for example, revenues from oil, which amounted to US$33 per capita in 1965, rose to US$325 per capita in 2000. However, per capita gross domestic product remained stuck at around US$245.

The country appeared victimized by the "natural resource curse", a condition in which abundant resources like oil or minerals generate not an improved standard of living, but instead productivity declines, institutional waste, public and private corruption, greater income inequality, and deepening poverty.[2]

This has led two economists to propose that oil revenues be distributed directly to Nigerian citizens rather than being appropriated by the government, which has misused them. From the government's perspective, this would convert an oil economy into a non-oil economy. That in turn would stimulate good governance and greater investment in other sectors besides oil. It would also raise per capita income and reduce the incidence of extreme poverty.[3]

A Third Development Decade

On December 5, 1980, the UN General Assembly proclaimed the Third United Nations Development Decade starting the following January 1.[4] The United Nations envisioned a new international economic order, under which the redistribution of resources would occur not only within countries but also among countries. This did not materialize

While hailing the adoption of an international development strategy under the Second Development Decade, the General Assembly acknowledged that the ambitious goals it had set for that period were largely unfulfilled.

The annex to the proclamation highlighted a number of familiar themes plus some new areas of emphasis: trade, industrialization, food and agriculture, financial resources for development, technical cooperation, science and technology, energy, transport, environment, human settlements, disaster relief and social development.

The international development strategy incorporated in the annex broke new ground by portraying not only the plight of poor countries but also of poor people. It observed that nearly 850 million people in developing countries had to contend with "hunger, sickness, homelessness and absence of meaningful employment."[5] Its vision for the decade involved the reduction of poverty along with accelerated development.

The policy measures proposed to reduce poverty included promotion of employment opportunities, increased access to education, adequate systems of primary health care, steps to control the rate of population growth and improvements in the status of women.

In the United States, conservative think tanks like the Heritage Foundation saw the new international economic order as an assault on private business capital flows and an effort to redistribute global economic power under the aegis of a South-dominated United Nations.

Such sentiments fed nicely into the agenda of Ronald Reagan, who was elected U.S. president in 1980. While combating communism was its highest foreign policy priority, the Reagan Administration also sought to curtail the influence of the Third World.

Under pressure from its largest shareholder, the United States, the World Bank and the International Monetary Fund began to add strong new conditions to their loans. Under adjustment lending, borrowers would have to commit themselves to programs of stabilization and structural adjustment.

Structural adjustment forced countries under severe fiscal constraints to jettison state-controlled enterprises and to open their doors to private investment. This had the effect of binding the economies of developing countries to the ebbs and flows in global capital markets, which developed countries dominated.

Under the Reagan Administration, the United States once again modified its aid strategy. The Agency for International Development underscored four main elements in its aid programming: policy reform, institution building, technology transfer, and increased private sector involvement.

Progress in these areas was made a condition of assistance to selected governments. Under balance of payments assistance provided through its Economic Support Funds program, the agency imposed conditions that were generally congruent with the International Monetary Fund's stabilization program and the World Bank's structural adjustment programs.

Changing Aid Patterns

By 1981 the patterns of aid from developed to developing nations had changed. Official development assistance in 1981 amounted to $35.9 billion. The share of this amount accounted for by the members of OECD's Development Assistance Committee twenty years after its establishment had declined to about 72 percent. Donors that were not members of the Development Assistance Committee provided a greater proportion of aggregate international aid.

These included members of the Organization of Petroleum Exporting Countries, notably Saudi Arabia, Kuwait and the United Arab Emirates, as well as another body titled the Council for Mutual Economic Assistance and consisting of the Union of Soviet Socialist Republics and eastern European countries.

The United States' share of global aid fell to about 16 percent. The United Kingdom, New Zealand, Austria, and Belgium also cut back on their aid levels. In the United States, the shifts in strategy and declines in aid levels in part reflected disenchantment with prior efforts to promote long-term economic growth, in part the unsustainable debt burdens accumulated by developing countries and in part the new administration's ideological predilections.

Most countries increased their aid considerably over the decade—Japan, France, Norway, Italy, Switzerland and Finland among others by more than 50 percent each. In 1988, Japan at $9.3 billion surpassed the United States as the largest donor.[6]

In 1977, on the heels of a proposal by the World Bank President, there was established the Independent Commission on International Development, known more popularly as the Brandt Commission after its chair, Willy Brandt, former Chancellor of the then-Federal Republic of Germany. The Commission was made up of eighteen members, including ten from developing countries.[7]

The Commission published two reports on international development, one in 1980 and another in 1983. It advocated a restructuring of the global economy, along with a comprehensive new approach to the problems of development, including an emergency program to eliminate poverty in developing nations.

In October 1981 an International Conference on Cooperation and Development was convened in Cancun, Mexico at the instigation of the Brandt Commission. It was organized by President Lopez Portillo of Mexico and Chancellor Bruno Kreisky of Austria.

Leaders from eight developed nations and fourteen developing nations, along with the Secretary General of the United Nations, attended the Cancun Conference. Discussions revolved around economic divisions between developed and developing nations. The leaders focused on improving international cooperation with respect to food security, trade, energy and development financing.

In Paris in 1981, the United Nations General Assembly held the First United Nations Conference on the Least Developed Countries. At the 1981 conference the international community unanimously adopted the Substantial New Program of Action for the 1980s for the Least Developed Countries.

Another Shift at the World Bank

At the World Bank, A. W. (Tom) Clausen, former head of the Bank of America, succeeded Robert McNamara as president. This signaled an abrupt shift away from poverty as a dominant theme in World Bank operations. Between 1982-1987, poverty sat on the back burner as the Bank focused on growth-oriented projects. Clausen's speeches highlighted macroeconomic policy, free markets and international cooperation, but included few references to poverty.[8]

A study on aid to Africa released by the World Bank in 1981 did more than recommend increased aid from the international community as a way to solve Africa's economic crisis. The report contended that African nations needed to help themselves through economic policy reforms in such areas as trade, exchange rates, agriculture and public sector expenditures.

International aid for development projects would produce few lasting benefits unless the recipient nation's policy and administrative deficiencies were corrected.

In short, the Berg report (so dubbed for its principal author, University of Michigan economics professor Eliot Berg) provided a rationale for lending conditioned on internal structural adjustments by the recipient countries.

The report in essence advocated that African governments diminish their overt role in development and instead foster expansion of the private sector. Macroeconomic policy and discrete economic development projects went hand in hand.

The report generated criticism in Africa and elsewhere on several grounds: inappropriate policy prescriptions (the state *did* have a role in development), intrusion into the sovereignty of African nations (colonialism revisited), or diversion of attention away from an unjust world economic order.[9]

Ironically the Berg report came out at a time when the Organization for African Unity, at a 1980 summit meeting in Lagos, Nigeria, produced its own plan of action. Contrary to the Berg perspective, it reinforced a state-led model of growth and promoted regional cooperation.

Whereas the Berg report focused on internal African reforms, the Lagos Plan of Action highlighted such international economic factors as declining terms of trade, falling commodity prices and rising energy costs.

The World Bank's Conservative Shareholders

In the early 1980s, conservative governments that had taken hold among some of the World Bank's largest shareholders, notably the United States, United Kingdom and Germany welcomed the Berg report. It was viewed as a charter for neoliberal orthodoxy. In the ensuing years, the Bank worked hard to build up its credibility in Africa and gain support for structural adjustment.[10]

Despite these efforts, a number of African leaders continued to oppose structural adjustment, armed in part by persistent criticisms from the United Nations Economic Commission for Africa. African leaders also resented the diplomatic style of some World Bank staff, who came across as a privileged foreign elite all too eager to dispense western wisdom to benighted Africa.

The hostility to structural adjustment and resentment at being preached to have diminished (but not disappeared) on the continent as the World Bank has sought to create a spirit of mutual respect and collaboration between it and its African borrowers.

In 1987, the World Bank, United Nations Development Programme and African Development Bank collaborated in the design of a Social Dimensions of Adjustment program. The program focused on the extent to which adjustment lending did or did not lead to a reduction in poverty and social inequalities. It highlighted the inequitable social welfare impacts of adjustment lending.

The Social Dimensions of Adjustment perspective emphasized the human basis of development. Development and adjustment strategies were seen as deficient unless they promoted education, acquisition of new skills, and economic opportunities for individuals and their communities.

In brief, transitional expenditures on behalf of the poor were needed to counter the adverse impact of macroeconomic and sectoral reforms. In light of persistent and growing inequalities, this meant giving priority to the community's neediest members, namely, women, children, seniors, persons with disabilities and particular racial and ethnic minorities.

Ascendancy of Neoliberal Dogma

In the 1980s the mantra for reducing poverty was economic growth through market friendly mechanisms. Governments, which hitherto were the solution, now were identified as the problem. They were advised not to be impediments to capital investment and private entrepreneurship.

Governments could underpin development through good governance, support for property rights, reduced spending, less regulation and greater reliance on private markets to achieve growth. Beyond that they should stay out of the way. This approach marked a return to trickle down.

World Bank president A.W. Clausen (1981-86) and his successor Barber Conable (1986-91), an amiable former congressman from upstate New York, reinforced these messages. However, Conable, without abandoning his advocacy for market reform, also began to reemphasize poverty reduction as a core mission of the World Bank. In Conable's view, growth was necessary but not sufficient. A more targeted antipoverty approach was required.

The Bank's *World Development Report 1990* on poverty broke new ground. The presidency of Lewis Preston, cut short by his death in 1995, reinforced the renewed emphasis on poverty reduction.

Near the end of McNamara's term and continuing through the presidencies of Clausen and Conable, China became a World Bank client. After thirty years of isolation, the world's largest nation was anxious to reintegrate itself into the world community. The Bank's lending to China appears to have been successful in reforming the country's urban grain price subsidies and promoting development within poorer inland provinces.[11]

During the 1980s China and India emerged from the list of the world's twenty poorest countries. Their success has contributed significantly to the reduction in global poverty. The standard of living for the 2.2 billion people living in just these two countries has risen remarkably over the past two decades.

In India, for example, the percentage of people in poverty declined from 44.5 percent in 1983 to 26.1 percent in 1999-2000. In absolute numbers for the two periods, the decline was from 323 million persons to 260 million persons.[12]

Without China and India, the picture looked much more bleak. With support from international donors, other developing countries addressed their mounting debt, investment needs, trade imbalances and failed growth strategies. Nevertheless, the economic situation as a whole for these countries worsened throughout the decade.

Subsidized Credit under Fire

Elsewhere in smaller countries, subsidized credit for the poor was judged disastrous. Lower interest rates were seen as distorting the true risks and costs of lending. The loaned money was often siphoned away from the poor in the form of transaction costs and rents.

Lending institutions felt political pressure to set interest rates very low (even to the point of being negative) and to forgive the debts of poor and non-poor alike. Subsidized credit for the poor was denigrated as overly draining of state resources and nonviable commercially.

Central banks were induced to expand credit to these clients to forestall their going bankrupt. This expansion of the money supply triggered inflation. The worst excesses occurred in Latin America. To offset these adverse consequences, the state therefore should stop providing direct credit support and instead foster competition among private financial institutions.

During this period the International Monetary Fund, whose influence had been declining as developing countries gained access to private capital markets, reasserted itself. It functioned as lead negotiator in the rescheduling of debt between Latin American governments and foreign banks.

The International Monetary Fund required debtor nations to adopt austerity measures to achieve balance-of-payments adjustments. Failure to comply meant that their foreign debt would not be rescheduled and new commercial loans and trade credits would not become available.

By now, the United States had concluded that the debt crisis posed an insupportable threat.

James Baker's Proposals

In October 1985, a series of proposals put forward by U.S. Treasury secretary James A. Baker III in essence conceded that, for highly indebted middle income countries such as Mexico, belt-tightening alone would not solve the debt crisis. Growth and creditworthiness were required as well.

Lending for a general capital increase under the so-called Baker Plan aimed at helping debtor countries to service their existing debts, support increases in exports, foster domestic investment, improve the balance of payments and trigger a new round of growth. Debtors could outgrow their lack of liquidity with the right combination of internal market reforms and new loans.

The Baker Plan sought to spur growth in fifteen highly indebted countries through some $29 billion in new loans. Of this amount, the Plan envisioned $20 billion in new loans from commercial sources and some $9 billion from the World Bank and other multilateral banks.

For the multilateral banks, the Baker Plan gave impetus to structural adjustment lending. As a condition of assistance, debtor countries would have to adopt macroeconomic and structural policies that would promote growth, reduce inflation and correct balance of payments distortions. The new loans they secured only added in the short run to already huge debt burdens.

Commercial banks resisted making new loans for fear that the debtor countries were facing long-term insolvency, not just temporary liquidity constraints. The Baker Plan fell far short of its objectives.

The world's poorest countries continue to owe billions to the World Bank, International Monetary Fund and to wealthy governments. Every year, they have to hand over huge sums in repayments. Precious little remains to invest in basic services such as primary education. In 1997 and 1998, Tanzania had to pay four times as much in debt repayments than the sum invested in primary education.[13]

These approaches reflected the continued dominance of neoliberal thinking. Essentially, as posited by analysts like Francis Fukuyama, with the collapse of the Soviet Union and the United States as the world's only superpower, humanity's future lay on the path of liberal democracy, free markets and industrial capitalism.[14]

If rigorously pursued with no modifications, such a scenario would eliminate any geopolitical incentive for focusing on the specific needs of the poor in the least developed countries. Foreign direct investment would flow to countries with stable political systems, market-friendly environments and promising growth prospects.

The Brady Plan

Since it was thought that the reduction or eradication of poverty could be left largely to private market dynamics, remedial rather than preventive measures were proposed. The possibility that market reforms could exacerbate poverty within countries' economic sectors and population subgroups received short shrift.

In 1989, Nicholas Brady, United States secretary of treasury, proposed a change in approach. His plan incorporated a degree of debt relief. Debt would be shifted from commercial lenders to international financial institutions like the World Bank and the multilateral regional banks.

Under the Brady Plan, debtor countries could exchange outstanding commercial debt for new securities, called Brady bonds, in which loans from multilateral banks and other official creditors would serve as guarantees.

Under a deal whereby the World Bank, International Monetary Fund and Japan guaranteed $7.1 billion in new bonds, Mexico was first to benefit from the Brady Plan, soon to be followed by a dozen other highly indebted countries.[15] To gain debt relief, a debtor country would have to agree to a package of macroeconomic reforms.

Adjustment lending provided balance of payments support to countries in deep financial trouble as a result of a second oil price shock in 1980, when the per-barrel price surged to $40.

The loans enabled countries to cope with fiscal and current account deficits. The attached conditions were intended to help stabilize the economies of developing nations and counter macroeconomic distortions.

Governments were urged to control inflation by reducing extremely high public sector deficits. Reduced spending entailed less government involvement in state-owned enterprises and greater autonomy for private sector development. Commodity prices, wages, interest rates and exchange rates, it was hoped, would find an appropriate balance.

Borrower governments committed themselves to programs of fiscal austerity in order to correct balance of payment problems. The conditions placed on the loans initially lacked a focus on poverty or sensitivity to the social consequences of reforms.[16] The distributive impacts of fiscal and monetary reforms were not fully examined. Macroeconomic stabilization offered few immediate benefits to the poor while cutting services and supports on which they depended.

To put it differently, what was considered good for the economy in general proved disastrous for people, especially poor people. Austerity measures unaccompanied by social safety nets provoked an angry reaction among adversely affected populaces.

The World Bank and the International Monetary Fund have acquired leverage over economic and social policy in the developing world. Not surprisingly, these institutions initially put the interests of international financial markets and wealthier nations ahead of borrower governments.

Loan conditions imposed by the World Bank and the International Monetary Fund forced developing nations to reduce the role of government, cut back on government expenditures, orient their economics toward international markets (rather than internal markets) and scale back social services.

In Latin America, countries experienced minimal to no growth, declining per capita income, rising poverty rates and greater income inequality. Gains made over the prior three decades were significantly eroded.

Africa: Deeper in Debt, Deeper in Poverty

The World Bank itself confessed that structural adjustment lending in the 1980s "was far less successful than hoped, due to an overreliance on lending conditionality and an underweighting of social concerns."[17] In the latter half of the 1980s, the World Bank began emphasizing the need for borrower countries to maintain social spending for the poor.[18]

In the 1980s, as economic conditions worsened, the forty-seven countries of Sub-Saharan Africa, comprising 85 percent of the continent's population, became more indebted than any other region of the world.

For example, thirteen African Countries had lower per capita incomes in 1989 than they did at the time of independence in the 1960s. The region's problems were caused by several factors, including drastically falling prices for exports, reductions in commercial loans and capital investment, and major debt problems arising from official bilateral and multilateral assistance.

From 1980 to 1988, twenty-five African countries had to reschedule their debts with creditors 105 times. Debt levels reached 100 percent of gross national product and 350 percent of export earnings.[19] Natural disasters like locust plagues and civil wars exacerbated these problems.

Hunger and malnutrition were prevalent. In 1985, Africa experienced the century's worst famine. More than one million people died. Private humanitarian organizations like Oxfam and CARE, as well as various governments, provided relief to millions of others.

African countries had the world's highest infant mortality rate, with a quarter of children dying before the age of five. Rapid population growth accompanied rising unemployment rates. Sub-Saharan Africa had over 70 percent of the world's victims of AIDS.

African governments contributed to the decline through policies that stifled growth. These included currency restrictions, price controls, trade barriers, budget deficits and state controls on the economy. In 1989, Africa's debt stood at 100 percent of its gross national product and more than 350 percent of its export earnings, making it the world's most indebted region.[20]

Women and Children in Poverty

In all regions of the world, women are disproportionately represented amongst the poor. One major cause is gender-based discrimination in many societies and particularly in their labor markets. Women find it more difficult to get jobs, especially well paying jobs with opportunities for advancement. Hence, once in poverty, they have a more difficult time escaping to self-sufficiency. The feminization of poverty is a global phenomenon.

Over thirty-two thousand children die each day from largely preventable malnutrition and disease. Compared to poor men, women in poverty generally work more and have less access to educational and economic opportunities. Directly aiding poor women in the developing world, it is argued, has immediate and positive benefits not only on family incomes, but also on child nutrition, health and education.

The poor in the developing world, particularly women, suffer from unstable employment and inadequate social safety nets. Many turn to self-employment; for example, in Africa, over 80 percent of employment is found in the informal sector of the self-employed poor.

Unfortunately, such poor entrepreneurs often remain trapped in poverty because they cannot obtain credit at reasonable rates. Many end up paying interest rates as high as 10 percent a day to lenders.[21]

The response of the United Nations to the problems of children evolved into a subset of the quest to eradicate poverty. The United Nations Children's Fund argued that children needed special attention because they suffered most from poverty. They could be seen as poverty's most sensitive barometer.

A Child Shall Lead Them

The United Nations Children's Fund published a report in 1987 that challenged the structural adjustment approach. As an organization that advocated for women and children, the United Nations Children's Fund insisted that meeting basic needs and investing in human potential should guide any development strategy.

Structural adjustment instead had worsened the human condition in poor countries by inducing cutbacks in health care, education, and nutrition. In short the goal of development was not just economic growth but more importantly human growth.[22]

Late in the decade, the World Bank's adjustment loans began to reflect a shift in thinking. They included provision for health, education and social safety net expenditures to protect the poor. The Bank's revised approach was influenced significantly by a rising chorus of criticism and was reflected in its seminal 1990 *World Development Report* on poverty.

The 1990 report defined poverty as "the inability to attain a minimal standard of living." It set forth an antipoverty strategy grounded in three complementary approaches.

First, labor-intensive growth was needed to generate income and employment for the poor. Second, the poor required special attention in such areas of human resource development as education, health care and nutrition.

Third, social safety nets were needed for those persons who could not benefit from growth and human resource development. These latter include persons with physical or cognitive disabilities, victims of civil conflict or natural disasters and persons living in isolation. While embracing targeted poverty projects and even welfare lending, the report paid due deference to growth including its alleged trickle-down benefits.

Yet Another Development Decade

While some developing countries recorded remarkable progress, most saw growth rates fall, living standards decline and poverty worsen. These conditions contributed to mounting political unrest. Early into the 1980s, developing countries were hurt by recession in developed countries, compounded by a debt crisis that brought commercial lending to a virtual standstill.

On December 21, 1990, under its resolution A/RES/45/199, the General Assemblyproclaimed the Fourth United Nations Development Decade. The resolution for the third development decade had noted that the goals for the second decade remained "largely unfulfilled." Similarly the resolution for the fourth decade noted that the goals for the third decade were "for the most part unattained." This ran the risk of sounding like a broken record.

The resolution took note of increasing interdependence among nations as reflected in the greater movement around the world of trade, finance, people and ideas.

With a more sober outlook than its predecessors, the resolution lamented the "debilitating deadlock" of the recent past. It underscored the danger that developing countries would become ever more marginalized and development itself would fade as an objective of international cooperation. Official development assistance had averaged only about half of the agreed-on target of 0.7 percent.

The resolution called for sustained growth rates of around seven percent annually in the developing world to achieve genuine economic transformation. At the same time it was recognized that the benefits of economic growth would not automatically be distributed equitably. While acknowledging the contributions of the private market, the resolution reiterated the essential role of the public sector in the development process.

The development strategy for the fourth development decade stressed the eradication of poverty and hunger. It portrayed the eradication of poverty as a "shared responsibility" of the entire world community. The strategy called for a style of development in which benefits were not concentrated within a few localities, economic sectors or population subgroups.

To insure more equitable distribution of economic benefits, special antipoverty programs were needed in several key areas. Employment could be fostered by activation of the informal sector of the economy and through expanded self-employment activities. The provision of cheap and subsidized food would alleviate hunger and malnutrition.

Measures to alleviate poor housing and homelessness were needed. Targeted maternal and child health care programs were needed, since women and children were disproportionately the victims of poverty.

The strategy adopted an approach that directly targeted the poor rather than subsuming them within welfare schemes for the general population. For example, food subsidies for the general population benefited people not in need, put strains on their governments, distorted prices and reduced production incentives.

While sustained economic growth is needed to raise living standards, developing countries do not need to wait for growth before assisting their citizens in poverty. Particularly in the areas of hunger, malnutrition and disease, developing countries can take steps to alleviate the extremes of poverty.

The four United Nations development decades indicate international concern over the development process. Each decade had its own theme, which when taken together show an evolutionary pattern.

The first decade emphasized financing for development, the second underscored equity through distribution, the third heightened awareness of global poverty and the fourth devoted attention to overcoming poverty mainly through employment creation and human resource development strategies.

Least Developed Countries Revisited

In Paris, September 3-14, 1990, the United Nations sought to highlight this disparity and expand international assistance to the least developed countries through a Second United Nations Conference on the Least Developed Countries. The Third United Nations Conference on the Least Developed Countries was held in Brussels, May 14-20, 2001.

These conferences sought to target special forms of assistance to these countries, such as grants and loans on highly concessionary terms, freer access to the markets of developed countries for their exports and expanded technical assistance.

The United Nations as a whole, as well as its component bodies, organs and organizations, has succeeded in making the international community more aware of and feeling responsible for worldwide economic development and poverty reduction. It has achieved this through research, conferences, negotiation of agreements and conventions, technical assistance and policy formulation.

Relative to other international forces, however, the United Nations system may be losing influence. The globalization of trade, finance and corporate activity has shifted the balance of power to the private sector. The United Nations continues to highlight the eradication of poverty as a global imperative.

The role and influence of non-governmental organizations like Oxfam and Caritas Internationalis were hampered by the faith of rich countries in market forces and other tenets of neoliberal orthodoxy. However, cooperation between non-governmental organizations and official aid agencies, both bilateral and multilateral, expanded.

And increasingly organizations of and for people in poverty began speaking out on their own behalf.

Voices from the Fourth World

The international ATD Fourth World Movement was founded in 1957 in a camp for homeless families outside Paris by Father Joseph Wresinski (1917-88), who himself had grown up poor. "Aide à Toute Détresse" (Aid in Total Distress) was the first name of the association.

The name Fourth World was added later. It hearkened back to the Fourth Estate of the French Revolution, which comprised the very poorest people struggling to be represented in the political changes of the time. ATD Fourth

World operates in eight Europeans countries, Northern and Central America, and several countries in Africa and Asia.

In addition to operating family-centered programs focusing on education and skill development, ATD Fourth World enjoys consultative status with the UN's Economic and Social Council, United Nations Children's Fund , International Labour Organization and the Council of Europe.

ATD Fourth World is also a member of the European Antipoverty Network, an independent coalition of national networks and trans-national organizations, that seeks the eradication of poverty and social exclusion in the member states of the European Union.

On October 17, 1987, one hundred thousand people gathered in Paris, following an appeal by Father Wresinski. Since then, each year on that date, very poor families have gathered with others to voice their rejection of extreme poverty and exclusion throughout the world and to emphasize the freedom and dignity of all persons.

On October 17, 1992, Javier Perez de Cuellar, former Secretary General of the United Nations, called for official UN recognition of October 17. In response, the United Nations General Assembly established October 17, effective in 1993, as the "International Day for the Eradication of Poverty." The day is set aside to spur efforts to eradicate poverty and destitution everywhere but particularly in developing countries.

BIEN

The Basic Income European Network (BIEN) advocates a basic income that is granted unconditionally to every individual without a means test or work requirement.

In the fall of 1983, Paul-Marie Boulanger, Philippe Defeyt and Philippe Van Parijs at the Catholic University of Louvain in Belgium jointly elaborated this idea, which one of them had proposed with the name "allocation universelle."

In April 1985, the group, then known as the *Collectif Charles Fourier*, spelled out the idea in a special issue of the Brussels monthly *La Revue Nouvelle.* They summarized their idea and its potential consequences in a prize-winning essay for a competition on the future of work sponsored by the King Baudouin Foundation.[23]

With the prize money gained from the competition, the *Collectif Charles Fourier* organized the first international conference on basic income, held in Louvain-la-Neuve, Belgium in September 1986, with sixty invited participants. This event brought together many hitherto isolated but kindred spirits.[24]

The conference led to the creation of a more permanent association, called the Basic Income European Network. Since 1986, BIEN has organized a major international congress every other year. From 1988 through 1999 BIEN published a newsletter, which more recently has been superseded by a regular

NewsFlash. The group maintains a website with among other items an extensive bibliography on the basic income concept.[25]

In the United States, the concept has gained footing through an informal network of advocates called the U.S. Basic Income Guarantee Network (USBIG). The group convened its first Congress March 8 and 9, 2002.[26] Organizations advocating a basic income exist in a number of other countries, including Australia, Austria, Brazil, Canada, France, Germany, Ireland, The Netherlands, New Zealand, South Africa, Spain, Sweden, Switzerland, and United Kingdom.

Better Data, Slowly But Surely

The quantity and quality of data on poverty in developing countries have improved in recent decades. In 1951, through its National Sample Survey, India started tracking household expenditures. The national statistics offices of various developing countries have undertaken national sample survey programs.

Examples from the late 1960s and early 1970s include the Additional Rural Incomes Survey in India, Malaysian Family Life Survey, and household surveys in Guatemala and the Philippines.[27]

The United Nations' National Household Survey Capability Programme "helped put household surveys on a sounder and more consistent basis."[28] Assistance from the United Nations and the World Bank has helped developing countries improve survey design, data collection, analysis and dissemination of results.

In 1980, the World Bank established the Living Standards Measurement Study. The Study explored ways of improving household data collection in developing countries in order to monitor their progress in raising living standards.

The first two living standards surveys were fielded in Côte d'Ivoire in 1985 and in Peru in 1985-86. These were followed by surveys in Ghana (1987-88), Mauritania, Bolivia and Jamaica (all three, 1988). Morocco, Pakistan and Vietnam conducted surveys in the mid-1980s. South Africa, Nicaragua, Guayanaand Ecuador did so in the early 1990s.

Surveys in Venezuela (1991, 1992, and 1993) monitored poverty conditions and government social programs. Living standards surveys have been carried out in some countries of Eastern Europe and the former Soviet Union.

Overall, some sixty Living Standards Measurement Study surveys have been conducted in forty countries. While not all countries follow the same format, they adhere to the same guiding principles. This has made the living standards surveys valuable resources for examining global poverty conditions.[29]

Other international agencies conduct their own surveys. For example, under contract with the U.S. Agency for International Development, ORC-Macro carries out Demographic and Health Surveys in developing countries.

These surveys grew out of two prior programs, the World Fertility Survey (1973-1984) and the Contraceptive Prevalence Surveys (1977-1985), both funded jointly by the U.S. Agency for International Development and the United Nations Population Fund with additional assistance from the United Kingdom, the Netherlands and Japan.[30]

The United Nations Children's Fund conducts Multiple Indicators Cluster Surveys. The wealth of new data from these sources has made it more feasible than ever to monitor progress in the world's war on poverty.

In the 1980s, the progress was disappointing.

A "Lost" Decade

The 1980s have been dubbed the "lost decade" insofar as it affected developing countries. In some countries, debt service payments exceeded what they could borrow. Both foreign investment and official development assistance declined. The prices of commodities on which many countries depended dropped.

The members of the Organization for Economic Cooperation and Development, rich countries all, reacted against "cheap foreign imports" of steel, auto parts, electronics, textiles, and agricultural products by imposing protectionist measures. Structural adjustment in poorer countries forced cuts in social spending.[31]

The neoliberal agenda was not completely discredited but its inadequacies were exposed. At the World Bank and elsewhere, there was renewed emphasis on meeting basic needs through education, health care and housing and working in more concerted fashion to reduce global poverty.

More radical notions began to get a hearing, for example, an unconditional basic income as a surety against extreme poverty.

ENDNOTES

1. A more detailed history of the Fund can be fund at www.apfc.org.
2. Sala-i-Martin, Xavier and Arvind Subramanian (2003) 4.
3. Sala-i-Martin, Xavier and Arvind Subramanian (2003) 17-26.
4. United Nations General Assembly Resolution 35/56 (December 5, 1980) Annex.
5. Ibid.
6. Cassen, Robert (1994) 5.
7. See Ayres, Robert L. (1983) 253-255.
8. Kapur, Devesh, John P. Lewis and Richard Webb, editors (1998) 1:333-336.
9. World Bank (1981).
10. Among other things, the Bank expanded the number and quality of its resident missions, established a Council of Economic Advisers in 1988 with which it met regularly for advice and support and launched an African Long-Term Perspective Study, the report of which was published in 1989.
11. Kapur, Devesh, John P. Lewis and Richard Webb, editors (1998) 1:24-25.
12. Planning Commission, Government of India (2002) 38.

13. See http://www.oxfam.org.uk/educationnow/debt.htm

14. Fukuyama, Francis (1989).

15. Kapur, Devesh, John P. Lewis and Richard Webb, editors (1998) 2:88-90.

16. World Bank (June 15, 2001) xii.

17. Goldin, Ian; Halsey Rogers; and Nicholas Stern (2002) 70.

18. World Bank (2000) 3-4.

19. U.S. General Accounting Office (1991) 8.

20. Ibid. 8, 10.

21. Committee on International Relations, U.S. House of Representatives, and Committee on Foreign Relations, U.S. Senate (June 2001).

22. Cornia, Giovanni A., Richard Jolly, and Frances Stewart, editors (1987).

23. The King Baudouin Foundation was established in 1974-1976 by the Belgian government as part of a celebration of the 25th anniversary of the King's coronation. The Foundation supports activities dealing with social exclusion, employment, sustainable development, local administration, citizen involvement, media, sports and culture, among others. After King Baudouin died in 1993, Queen Fabiola assumed the Foundation's Honorary Presidency. Since 1999, the Foundation's main emphases have been on poverty and justice. Among other activities, it manages a Poverty Fund that supports microcredit loans. The Foundation receives an annual grant from Belgium's National Lottery. For more information, see www.kbs-frb.be.

24. They included, among others, Gunnar Adler-Karlsson, Jan-Otto Andersson, Peter Ashby, Yoland Bresson, Paul de Beer, Alexander de Roo, Nic Douben, Ian Gough, Pierre Jonckheere, Bill Jordan, Greetje Lubbi, Edwin Morley-Fletcher, Claus Offe, Riccardo Petrella, David Purdy, Guy Standing, Robert van der Veen and Georg Vobruba.

25. See www.etes.ucl.ac.be/bien/Index.html. The website is the source of this brief overview of BIEN. Given its worldwide membership, there have been calls to change the name of the organization to Basic Income Earth Network.

26. www.widerquist.com/usbig/home.html. The group was founded in late 1999 by Fred Block, University of California-Davis; Charles M. A. Clark, St. John's University; Pamela Donovan, City University of New York; Michael Lewis, State University of New York-Stony Brook; and Karl Widerquist then of the Levy Institute, now of Oxford University. The most recent BIG conference as of this writing was held in Washington, DC, February 20-22, 2004.

27. The Indian survey was fielded by the National Council of Applied Economic Research, the Malaysian and Guatemalan surveys by RAND. See Strauss, John and Duncan Thomas (1995) 1891-92.

28. Lipton, Michael and Martin Ravallion (1995) 2565.

29. For more, see www.worldbank.org/lsms/guide/history.html.

30. United Nations Department of Economic and Social Affairs, Statistics Division (April 2003). This draft document is being restructured, reviewed and edited as of this writing. Hence a page reference could be misleading.

31. Hewitt, Tom, "Half a Century of Development", Chapter 13 in Tim Allen and Alan Thomas, editors (2000) 300-302.

Poverty Preeminent (1991-2000)

Poverty Reduction, Unevenly

Between 1990 and 2000, according to World Bank estimates, the proportion of people living on less than a dollar a day fell from roughly a quarter to a fifth of the world's population. See Table 3.

This progress was due largely to the experience of East Asia and the Pacific, where the drop-off was more dramatic. Over the period the proportion of the population in extreme poverty dropped from 32.9 percent to 16.1 percent in China and from 24.2 percent to 10.6 percent in the rest of East Asia and the Pacific. This region has reached the millennium development goal of halving its extreme poverty rate by 2015.

Elsewhere the picture was less cheering.

Of Miracles and False Prophecies

Over almost four decades starting in 1965 eight East Asian countries—Hong Kong, Indonesia, Japan, Malaysia, the Republic of Korea, Singapore, Taiwan (China), and Thailand—achieved such impressively high and sustained growth rates that they were dubbed the East Asia Miracle.

In Indonesia, for example, from 1970 to 1996, the percentage of people living in poverty (as measured by the government) fell dramatically from 50.6 percent to 11.3 percent and the absolute number of poor from 60.0 million to 22.5 million.[1]

To enthusiastic observers, this success was attributable to several factors, notably sound development policies, tailored government interventions, and rapid accumulation of physical and human capital.[2] Labor-intensive manufactured exports made a significant contribution to growth and poverty reduction.

Strong and effective national institutions were seen as the *sine qua non* of sustainable, equitable development. If these countries could do it, why could not others? Adopt their formula and enjoy equivalent success.

Table 3. People Living on Less Than $1 a Day: 1990, 2000

| Regions of Developing World | Millions and Percent of People in Each Region Living on Less Than $1 a Day | | | |
| | 1990 | | 2000 | |
	Millions	Percent	Millions	Percent
China	377	32.9	204	16.1
Rest of E. Asia/Pacific	110	24.2	57	10.6
South Asia	506	45.0	432	31.9
E. Europe & Central Asia	6	1.4	20	4.2
Latin America & Caribbean	48	11.0	56	10.8
Middle East & North Africa	5	2.1	8	2.8
Sub-Saharan Africa	241	47.4	323	49.0
Total-1	**1,293**	**29.6[a]**	**1,100**	**21.6[a]**
Total-2	**1,293**	**24.2[b]**	**1,100**	**18.1[b]**

[a]Percent of developing world population.
[b]Percent of total world population.
Source: World Bank (2003) 46; author's calculations.

Some cautionary voices were heard. East Asia's growth rates were said to be driven less by "inspiration," that is technology-grounded total factor productivity, than by "perspiration," or the mobilization of society's resources, and particularly its labor.

For example, Singapore enjoyed an average annual growth rate of 8.5 percent between 1966 and 1990. The proportion of the population in jobs rose from 27 percent to 51 percent. By 1990, two-thirds of the population had completed secondary school. Capital investment as a share of total output rose from 11 percent to 40 percent.[3]

Thus growth was based in part at least on input levels that could not be sustained. For Singapore, the proportion of the population employed is unlikely to nearly double again in a comparable period. The law of diminishing returns was bound to kick in.

Similar stories could be recounted for the other seven countries. The "miracle" may have been a one-time phenomenon, not readily replicable elsewhere. At the same time the countries do have a record of success that if not miraculous is at least enviable. Technologically they were not stagnant; mainly they played to their strengths, which was a large labor supply.

Over the period, the eight countries were relatively stable, reasonably well-governed and market-friendly. They promoted savings over rampant consumerism and encouraged investment. They were open to trade and technology and "responded quickly to the evolving skill needs of an outward-oriented economy."[4]

The relative contribution of these characteristics to high growth rates is uncertain. While the miracle economies have achieved growth and reduced poverty, they have had less success in overcoming income disparities. Thus growth contributes to the reduction of poverty, but may affect income disparities either not at all or negatively.

Aspects of the East Asian experience should have broader applicability. The lessons to be drawn continue to be debated. In any event lessons are not recipes and "policies and institutions cannot just be 'cherry-picked' from one empirical context to another."[5]

The World without China and India

China and India, whose combined population exceeds two billion people or one-third of the world total, have also achieved impressive economic growth rates. For the 1980-1995 period, the average annual growth rate for low-income countries excluding China and India was 1.8 percent. With those two countries included, the growth rate for the period rose to 5.9 percent.[6]

In other regions, there is cause for alarm. In Sub-Saharan Africa, the poverty rate in 1990 was 47.7 percent. It barely budged over the decade, "falling" by only a single percent. This situation is compounded by the scourge of HIV/AIDS.

"According to estimates from UNAIDS, an umbrella group for five U.N. agencies, the World Bank and the World Health Organization, 34.3 million people in the world have AIDS—24.5 million of them in sub-Saharan Africa."[7] In 1999, 2.5 million people died from AIDS; 85 percent of these were in Africa. Out of 13.2 million children orphaned by the disease, 12.1 million were in Sub-Saharan Africa.[8]

Worldwide, between 1990 and 2000, the number of people living in extreme poverty declined by 137 million, from 1.237 billion to 1.100 billion. In China the number of the extremely poor dropped by 157 million from 361 million in 1990 to 204 million in 2000.

In some other regions, most significantly in Sub-Saharan Africa, the number of extremely poor people went up, thereby offsetting the gains made by China. Thus, despite progress in some regions of the world, the number of extremely poor persons outside of China increased by 19 million over the 1990-2000 period.[9]

The world's population in the period rose from 5.3 billion to 6.1 billion persons. Despite a drop in the global poverty rate, such sheer population growth meant that the *number* of people in extreme poverty remained close to 1.1 billion.[10]

In order to cut the proportion of the world's population in extreme poverty in half by 2015, developing countries would have to attain an average 3.6 percent a year growth rate in their Gross Domestic Product. Not all regions will meet this target; for example, in Sub-Saharan Africa, average annualized growth rates of 1.5 percent are projected.[11]

From Structural Adjustment to Capacity Building

Developing countries with emerging markets have periodically suffered through financial crises related to levels of private investment, exchange rates, interest rates, balance of payments issues and overall capitalization. In the 1990s, economic woes in Latin America and East Asia shocked the international financial markets.

In December 1994, several months after its entrance into the North American Free Trade Agreement, Mexico experienced financial turmoil. The combination of greater privatization in Mexico and the country's prospects under NAFTA led to an infusion of foreign investment.

The country built up a large current account deficit that was financed largely by short-term portfolio capital. This type of capital was vulnerable to any loss of investor confidence. The government was forced to devalue a highly overvalued peso, precipitating just such a loss. Investors rushed to sell Mexican equity and debt securities.

To keep Mexico from defaulting on its obligations and to limit the spread of the crisis to other Latin American countries, a $48.8 billion multilateral assistance package was put together by the United States, Canada, International Monetary Fund and Bank for International Settlements.[12] Mexico underwent a period of economic hardship before being able to return to the international financial markets.

In late 1997, an Asian financial crisis roiled the economies of Thailand, Malaysia, Indonesia, Korea, and the Philippines. In Indonesia, for example, millions of people were plunged into poverty; Java, the country's most populous and developed island, suffered the most.[13]

As a result of overborrowing by private companies or, alternatively, overlending by international financial institutions, more capital investment funds had flowed into these economies than could be profitably used.

These conditions in turn generated high unemployment, food shortages in Indonesia and a region-wide recession. In the absence of stabilizing mechanisms, the reaction was massive outflows of capital from the region that led to depreciation of national currencies and high interest rates. The incidence of poverty rose sharply in Indonesia, Korea and Thailand.

Like Mexico, these countries faced large current account deficits. Unlike Mexico they did not receive a multilateral bailout package. Instead they were urged to make structural adjustments like devaluing currencies, cutting budgets, and raising interest rates.

While there is global governance of trade, no corresponding structure exists for international finance. Bailout arrangements are made on an *ad hoc* basis. Both Mexico and the East Asian "tigers" recovered from their financial crises and reembarked on the path to growth throughout the remainder of the 1990s. However, their experiences proved salutary.

Over the decade of the 1990s, donor countries and international bodies have been forced to reexamine the effects of macroeconomic policy on poverty. They can no longer assume that the market-friendly adjustment reforms they have advocated will *ipso facto* reduce poverty over the short- or even medium-term in developing countries.

The World Bank Group had shifted its emphasis from structural adjustment programs to more direct poverty reduction strategies. In the Bank's view, a successful attack on poverty required labor-intensive economic growth, human resource development (through better nutrition, health care, education, and related services) and social safety nets—welfare and social insurance.

The latter were intended for persons with severe mental or physical disabilities, victims of war and natural disasters, and others unable to benefit from growth and development opportunities.[14]

In 1987, the World Bank began supporting social fund projects. As distinguished from traditional lending for large capital investment initiatives, these projects have tended to be small, narrowly targeted, demand-driven, participatory, and multisectoral.

Social Funds allow poor people and communities to become actively involved in their own development. Local stakeholders largely determine the investment decisions. Social Funds support small projects ranging from infrastructure and social services to training and microenterprise development. Funding is often channeled though community-based, national and international non-governmental organizations.

Funds are used most frequently for school construction or rehabilitation, piped water supply systems, health care facilities and roads. During the 1990s, Bank lending for social fund projects grew. By May 2001, the World Bank had invested $3.5 billion in over ninety-eight social fund projects in fifty-eight countries.[15]

In 1991, Lewis Preston, Conable's successor at the World Bank, was fully committed to poverty alleviation. Even so, he was wary of seeing the priority given to poverty burgeon into a wholesale social agenda at the expense of the Bank's economic mission.

The pressure to expand social programs as part of the fight against poverty was strong, given obvious needs in the areas of education, health care, environment, gender equity, social exclusion, food security, housing and others. The Bank's mission began to appear larger and more diffuse. Greater weight was placed on aspects of development like governance, institutional reform, and social protection.

At the same time, the World Bank's own house needed to be put in order.

Portfolio Problems

On October 31, 1991, the World Bank announced that Vice President Willi Wapenhans would retire in twelve months, after thirty-two years of service. In the interim he headed the Task Force on Portfolio Management, also known as the Wapenhans Committee. Its report, delivered to the Bank's executive directors on November 3, 1992, triggered immense repercussions.

The Wapenhans Committee reviewed about eighteen hundred World Bank projects in 113 countries. For these projects the Bank had lent $138 billion and co-financiers an additional $222 billion. Its report stated that 37.5 percent of the projects completed in 1991 were deemed failures, more than twice the failure rate of 15.0 percent found ten years earlier.

The standard used to designate a failure was not clear. By the same token what constituted "success" for 62.5 percent of the eighteen hundred projects was no less ambiguous.

But the overall message was both inescapable and devastating. Even worse failure rates were found in certain sectors like water supply, sanitation and agriculture. Mexico and Brazil had failure rates exceeding 50 percent. Some African countries had failure rates as high as 82.8 percent. And the pattern of increased failure rates was spreading to other sectors like poverty, environment and infrastructure reform.

World Bank staff did little to determine the actual flow of benefits or assess the sustainability of projects beyond the expiration of the loan. Newly built roads need maintenance. Irrigation systems require ongoing water management. School buildings would remain empty unless curricula were developed and teachers trained.

These kinds of issues received insufficient attention. Loan approvals and the creditworthiness of the loan portfolio seemed to matter more than the purposes for which the money was lent.

The Wapenhans review raised alarm throughout the World Bank. The directors convened high level meetings with the Bank's management to try to stem the failures.[16] The Bank created an Inspection Panel to investigate claims against the Bank.

This did not mute criticism, which reached a peak at the 1994 annual meetings in Madrid. Since then all five components of the World Bank group have devoted themselves to improve internal efficiency and external effectiveness.

Nonetheless, specific projects have continued to come in for criticism.

The Qinghai Controversy

On July 7, 2000, the World Bank succumbed to pressure from several rich nations, most prominently the United States, and scrapped a controversial antipoverty project in China's Qinghai Province. The project included spending $40 million to resettle fifty-eight thousand Han Chinese from arid to irrigated areas in the province.

The Qinghai project was a component of China's $160 million Western Poverty Reduction Project, which targeted poverty in three arid western and northwestern provinces, namely Gansu, Inner Mongolia and Qinghai.

Tibetans made up about one-fifth of the province's population. However, protesters led by the International Campaign for Tibet contended that the Qinghai project had less to do with reducing poverty than with promoting further sinification of the province, where the Dalai Lama was born.

World Bank officials protested that China has reduced poverty through effective use of World Bank loans. China charged that rich nations were trying to dictate loan approval to the World Bank for political reasons.

A report by the Bank's independent Inspection Panel (the one created pursuant to the Wapenhans review) faulted the Bank for failing to comply with its own internal procedures in approving the loan. The combination of internal dissent, external protest and likelihood of final disapproval forced China to withdraw its loan request from World Bank consideration.[17]

A New Architecture of Development

The World Bank is supported by 181 member governments, the International Monetary Fund by 182. The World Bank is the largest official source of investment capital for developing countries. The International Monetary Fund promotes international monetary cooperation, exchange rate stability and short-term loans to member countries to address balance-of-payments problems.

The Board of Governors for each institution delegates policy decisions and loan approvals to a Board of Executive Directors consisting in each case of twenty-four executive directors appointed or elected by one or member countries. The Development Committee is composed of twenty-four members. It advises the Boards of Governors of the Bank and the Fund.

On October 6, 1998, in a speech to the World Bank's board of governors, Bank president James D. Wolfensohn asserted the priority of poverty reduction in the new "architecture" of development.

> "Development is about getting the macroeconomics right...but...also about building the roads, empowering the people, writing the laws, recognizing the women, eliminating the corruption, educating the girls, building the banking systems, protecting the environment, inoculating the children."[18]

In the Bank's new development framework, poverty reduction is not limited to raising the income of the poor above an official poverty line. It is part of a comprehensive strategy that also includes adequate infrastructure, access to basic services and opportunities for participation in the broader society. If previously economic development and poverty reduction stood side by side, now poverty reduction had pride of place.

The risk was that the World Bank would become ever more subject to pressures from outside interest groups portraying their goals as a form of poverty reduction. The more comprehensive and overarching the Bank's approach, the more "political" might become the decisions about the composition of its portfolio.

IMF's Poverty Reduction and Growth Facility

In 1999, the International Monetary Fund expanded its lending program to incorporate an explicit focus on poverty reduction. It signified this shift by changing the name of its concessional lending arm from the Enhanced Structural Adjustment Facility to the Poverty Reduction and Growth Facility through which it provides poor countries with long-term loans at below market interest rates.[19]

The new facility expanded the scope of its lending from balance of payments assistance to include support for growth that reduced poverty and improved living standards. Far from its original mandate to help remedy liquidity crises and stabilize the international balance of payments, the International Monetary Fund has evolved into yet another multilateral development bank.[20]

The lending process emphasized greater ownership of the macroeconomic framework by the recipient government, greater engagement by civil society in development planning, and evidence of improved prospects for the recipient's "graduation" from the concessional lending program.

By February 21, 2001, of seventy-seven countries eligible for assistance from the Poverty Reduction and Growth Facility, thirty-four had received approximately $4 billion in loan commitments; of these latter, twenty-two were in Sub-Saharan Africa.[21] From the evidence to date, it is unclear that these three conditions can be met.

For example, to graduate from concessional fund assistance, the thirty-two countries that borrowed from the Poverty Reduction and Growth Facility in 2000 will have to achieve average annual growth rates of 6 percent, a far cry from the average negative one percent annual growth rates of the preceding fifteen years.[22] A balance among macroeconomic stabilization, economic growth and poverty reduction such that all stakeholders concur remains to be found.

One thing the stakeholders could agree on was the need to alleviate the debt burden on developing countries. Poverty reduction would not occur without a comprehensive approach to debt relief.

Heavily Indebted Poor Countries Initiative

The Heavily Indebted Poor Countries initiative, begun in 1996 at the urging of the Group of Seven (G-7) highly industrialized nations, is supposed to lead to a write-off of external debt in the poorest nations by donors.[23] It is managed by the World Bank and the International Monetary Fund.

In 1999, at the Cologne G-8 meeting, world leaders agreed to cancel $100 billion of debts owed by the poorest countries. In September 1999, the World Bank and the International Monetary Fund enhanced the initiative by expanding the estimated amount of debt relief and adding the goal of reducing poverty in the poorest countries.

In 2000, the World Bank and the International Monetary Fund classified forty countries as heavily indebted and poor; of these, thirty-two were in Africa.[24] The total external debt of the forty countries was over $200 billion. To qualify for debt relief, developing countries had to agree to undertake economic and social reforms.

The World Bank's member governments contribute to the HIPC Trust Fund. The amounts they contribute are conditioned by domestic policy considerations. For example, the United States withholds funds for the benefit of countries engaged in patterns of gross violations of human rights or in civil or military conflict that impede their abilities to alleviate poverty.[25]

The HIPC initiative responded in part to political pressure from debt-relief advocates. In the United Kingdom, members of the coalition like the Catholic Fund for Overseas Development (CAFOD), Christian Aid, Tearfund and the World Development Movement lent their support to a new campaign launched by the New Economics Foundation, called Jubilee 2000.

On May 16, 1998, the Group of Eight (G-8), representing the globe's richest economies, held their annual meeting in Birmingham, England. The Jubilee 2000 campaign organized a human chain of some seventy thousand people who ringed the conference center and called for cancellation of the debts of poor countries by 2000.

In the months and years following, the activities of the Jubilee 2000 campaign have kept the issue of debt relief on the international agenda. Jubilee 2000's global petition collected over twenty-four million signatures.

Jubilee 2000 and its successor, Jubilee Research, have demonstrated the power of collective global action to remedy economic injustice. The campaign itself includes an extensive international coalition of faith-based and secular organizations. It operates with offices in sixty countries.[26]

HIPC's Critics

While well-intentioned, the HIPC initiative has run into criticism from a number of quarters. Based on an analysis of ten countries, the U.S. General Accounting Office concluded that the export growth rates assumed by the World Bank for these countries are overly optimistic.[27] This is particularly true for countries that rely on primary commodities for a majority of their export earnings.

A shift from loans to grants would lessen the debt burdens of the highly indebted countries and improve their ability to repay outstanding debts.[28] Absent such a shift by the World Bank (and, it can be inferred, other multilateral development banks), developing countries will remain mired in debt.

Under the proposed shift, the World Bank would operate more like an endowment, making its own investments and providing grants from the proceeds. It would not depend on loan repayments for capital. A name change may be in order since it would no longer operate like a traditional bank. Hand in hand with this shift could come a de-emphasis on compliance-oriented conditionality and a sharper focus on performance targets (the means being left to the recipient countries).

Absent adequate growth rates, many low-income countries will continue to depend on concessional (below-market terms) loans. As part of a concerted international effort to reduce poverty, the International Monetary Fund changed the name of its concessional lending window from the Enhanced Structural Adjustment Facility to the Poverty Reduction and Growth Facility.

In 2000, thirty-two countries borrowed on concessional terms from the International Monetary fund. Whereas they had an average negative one percent growth rate over the prior fifteen years, they would need average annual growth rates of six percent over the following fifteen years to "graduate" from the concessional lending window.

Under the General Accounting Office's analysis, they could remain eligible for assistance from the International Monetary Fund for an average of fifty-nine years or virtually an indefinite future.[29]

Finally the General Accounting Office found that governments face immense difficulty in developing poverty reduction strategies. Developing the strategies both taxes their limited resources and demands agreement on highly sensitive political and cultural issues.

No less significantly, the Heavily Indebted Poor Countries initiative has created tension between the goal of gaining rapid debt relief and the time and effort required to develop comprehensive and country-owned poverty reduction strategies. Coordinating a diverse set of factors like rapid economic growth, good governance, participation by civil society and targeted antipoverty measures can strain the capacity of any government.

Thus, the Heavily Indebted Poor Countries initiative will not provide a lasting exit from debt problems and the poorest nations will remain dependent on concessional loans and poverty reduction strategies. In part, this is because the developing countries will need to continue borrowing both to pay off remaining debt and to obtain new resources for poverty reduction.

Obviously, debt relief and poverty reduction are worthy goals. At issue is the extent to which they are achievable within reasonable time frames. A commitment to increased privatization is prominent among the conditions set for poor countries seeking relief under the Heavily Indebted Poor Countries initiative. The mechanisms by which privatization is expected to reduce poverty have not yet been spelled out in detail by the World Bank and donor countries.

Poverty, Debt and Commodity Dependence

Trade barriers and subsidies by rich nations continue to undermine the prospects for commodity-driven growth in the least developed countries. Competition from rich nations works against stabilization in commodity prices and growth prospects.

The United States and Europe erect high trade barriers against agricultural and processed food products while subsidizing the exports of their domestic producers. In the least developed countries, earnings from such commodities fluctuate considerably from year to year.

For instance, the European Union, the world's largest producer of tomato concentrate after the United States, guarantees tomato farmers a minimum price higher than the world market price. Tomato processors also receive a subsidy to cover the difference between domestic and world prices.

Such subsidies, which reached about $300 million in 1997, kept world market prices low and eventually forced the closure of tomato processing plants in several of the least developed countries in West Africa. In Senegal, for example, production of tomato concentrate dropped from seventy-three thousand tons in 1990-1991 to less than twenty thousand tons by the end of the decade. Burkina Faso and Mali have also increased enormously their imports of tomato concentrate from the European Union.[30]

In developing countries, inadequate infrastructure and inappropriate policies hamper diversification into more profitable economic sectors. Barriers to diversification include the failure to fully meet international labor and environmental standards; lack of access to the Internet and related information technologies; and inability to attract foreign direct investment. As global trade grows year to year, they risk falling further and further behind more industrialized and richer nations.

During the 2000-2010 period, prices for non-oil commodities like coffee, cocoa and cotton among others may recover from prior cyclical lows. However, over the long term their prices are more likely to decline in real terms. This is due in part to a slowdown in global population growth and in part to improved cost-saving technologies in agriculture and mining.[31]

Aid for Whom, Aid for What?

Total official development assistance from the members of OECD's Development Assistance Committee actually dropped from 0.33 percent in 1993 to 0.22 percent in 1997.[32] That all-time low was matched in 2000.

Presumably developing countries that adopt privatization policies will attract foreign capital, which in turn will stimulate growth, which in its turn will have spillover benefits for the poor. Even if this scenario were to occur, by no means a certainty, the timetable for many countries is unacceptably long. It is difficult to imagine a global war on poverty that excludes foreign aid.

Where should aid go? According to a model developed by researchers at the World Bank, a more efficient allocation of poverty reduction aid calls for targeting countries where, thanks to appropriate policies and a functional government infrastructure, the problem is at least potentially soluble. Aid that is used effectively and efficiently by a developing country can help improve its investment climate.

Conversely, aid should be diverted away from countries where the necessary conditions are lacking. Of course, efficiency need not be the only criterion. Putting aid into countries where policy and infrastructure are weak is often intended to induce reform. It may however only serve as a crutch for existing deficiencies and risks the leakage of aid resources into unproductive, possibly even corrupt, activities.[33]

In recent years the donor community has underscored good governance as a prerequisite for the receipt of aid by a poor country. In essence poor people in badly governed countries are made to wait until reforms acceptable to donors have been put in place.

This may make good economic sense, but whether it makes good sense geopolitically is another matter. Compared to an equally poor but better governed country, Afghanistan prior to September 11, 2001 would not have qualified for increased poverty reduction aid. An analysis grounded in better intelligence and geopolitical considerations might have come to a different conclusion.

From 1960 to 1995, almost $1.7 trillion in 1995 dollars were transferred from rich to poor countries as foreign aid.[34] This refers to aid provided under concessional terms and intended specifically for the social and economic development of developing countries.

In 1991, the European Bank for Reconstruction and Development was founded. Through its investments the Bank helps create market economies and establish democratic governments in 27 countries from central Europe to central Asia.

In 1991, Finland joined Sweden, Norway, Denmark and the Netherlands in exceeding the 0.7 percent official development assistance target.

Development Aid Guidelines

In 1992, OECD's Development Assistance Committee endorsed official development assistance insofar as it contributed to sustainable development, reduced poverty, and fostered participation in the global economy.

To qualify as official development assistance, aid must go to a country on the Organization for Economic Cooperation and Development's list of less developed countries or to a multilateral institution assisting such a country. It must promote economic development and welfare and be concessional in character with a "grant element" of at least 25 percent.[35]

The Organization for Economic Cooperation and Development publishes and periodically updates poverty reduction guidelines to assist its member countries in their provision of aid.

In general, the guidelines endorse a comprehensive approach that features the following elements: pro-poor economic growth, empowerment of the poor, basic social services such as adequate nutrition, safe water, education, affordable medical services, human security to withstand sudden man-made and natural shocks, gender equity and environmental sustainability.[36]

The main strategies for eradicating poverty fall into several categories: subsidized credit, public works employment, land reform, agricultural growth and technology (including biotechnology), and a range of social services to meet basic needs—education, health care, housing, social insurance and, in some circumstances, food distribution.

The Organization for Economic Cooperation and Development's guidelines support "country-owned, country-led" strategies for reducing poverty. They emphasize the need for closer coordination among donor countries to harmonize development initiatives and minimize administrative burdens on the recipient countries.

Eschewing externally-imposed agendas, they endorse instead partnerships between donor and recipient countries in pursuing poverty reduction objectives. The problem, of course, is that developing countries (like the donors) are not homogeneous entities.

They consist of individuals and groups pursuing different and often competing objectives. Central governments, regional and local governments, civil society organizations, unions, human rights groups, religious bodies, think tanks, the private business sector—all may endorse poverty reduction but differ on the means.

Donor countries cannot remain neutral if they intend for their assistance to have an impact on poverty. The people who enjoy wealth, power and privileges tend to resist any assault on poverty that threatens their status. Donors may be compelled to take sides in internal political and policy dialogues on poverty.

In structuring assistance to make it more "effective," they risk undermining country ownership of antipoverty strategies. Developing countries with limited administrative capacity often find themselves trying to comply with multiple planning requirements and reporting burdens from both bilateral and multilateral donors.

Developing countries are taking a more collaborative approach with one another and with donors in their development and antipoverty agendas.

A case in point is the New Partnership for Africa's Development. NEPAD is intended to enable African countries to confront collectively their major challenges, namely escalating poverty, underdevelopment and marginalization in world affairs.

On behalf of the Organization for African Unity, five member governments—Algeria, Egypt, Nigeria, Senegal and South Africa—generated a vision and strategic framework for continental development. The framework, which was formally adopted by the Organization for African Unity in July, 2001, aims at fostering sustainable development in Africa through conflict resolution, improved economic and political governance and greater regional integration.[37]

Prior efforts to foster continent-wide growth through cooperative action by African governments have yielded more promise than product.[38] Whether an initiative like NEPAD can reverse this trend remains to be seen.

Of Donor Fatigue and the Effectiveness of Aid

Official development assistance has fallen somewhat out of favor in light of persistent criticism over its effectiveness.

For example, the United States government in its 2002 national security policy statement acknowledges that a world where half the people live on less than $2 a day is "neither just nor stable." However, it goes on to charge that "[d]ecades of massive development assistance have failed to spur economic growth in the poorest countries."[39]

Critics charge that development aid has subsidized oppressive regimes, helped line the pockets of corrupt administrators, enabled governments to shift their own resources toward military expansion and had no discernible effect on growth or poverty reduction. In short, "[it] has often served to prop up failed policies, relieving the pressure for reform and perpetuating misery."[40]

Entities like the International Monetary Fund are concerned that large inflows of aid can cause exchange rate appreciation, trigger inflation and adversely affect the competitiveness of a developing country's exports. Unpredictable and erratic aid flows have additional harmful consequences. The lack of capacity and the prevalence of corruption prevent many countries from being able to use aid effectively.[41]

Despite the nearly two trillion dollars spent as aid to developing countries since the 1960s, growth in Sub-Saharan Africa, Asia, Latin America and the Middle East has remained erratic at best. Poverty rates in these regions are appalling. To critics, the nostrums of development economists have proven faddish and futile.

Recipient government reforms have availed little against their nations' landed and industrial elites. Bilateral and multilateral donors continued to provide aid because that is what they do. Grant and loan conditionalities were ignored by recipients and not enforced by donors.[42] Good governance and macroeconomic stability are seen as essential for effective poverty reduction.

Such criticisms cannot be ignored. That corruption occurs is undeniable but the scale of corruption in the development process and its impact on poverty reduction strategies are not well understood. While evidence for the effectiveness of official development assistance is wanting, so too is evidence of its alleged ineffectiveness. Clearly individual projects like road construction and potable water systems have benefited specific communities.

The "but for" question remains. How differently would conditions have turned out either locally or nationally but for such aid?

Assessments of the macroeconomic effectiveness of aid have not achieved overall consensus. A widely cited World Bank analysis concludes that to be most effective aid needs to be targeted toward countries where certain preconditions exist. These include low inflation, small deficits, open markets, and good governance.[43]

This assessment provided reinforcement to the Washington Consensus, which has been taken, not without demurral, as a summary expression of neoliberal dogma.[44] The problem is seen as lying more with recipients' behavior rather than donors' policies.

Development is complex, involving the interplay of economic and noneconomic factors. One extensive review of research over several decades on the impact of aid concludes that it has in fact contributed to improved economic performance. On balance, aid increases aggregate savings, investment and overall growth.

However, the marginal returns decrease, due to factors like limited absorption capacity and adverse effects on exchange rates. Indeed, aid can have a negative impact on growth once it reaches a quarter to a half of a recipient country's gross national product.[45]

Arguably, aid should not be provided to countries that cannot hope to make good use of it. Nor should it go to those that would make headway without it. Both waste scarce resources. At the same time, an *ad hoc* and uncoordinated approach to the provision of aid by multiple donors also undermines its intended impact.

Hence, the solution does not reduce to simple formulas. The aid allocation issue may be less about targeting a class of countries that meet certain preconditions and bypassing others less fortunate. Rather it seems to entail assessing each case individually and tailoring specific aid instruments to meet particular needs and circumstances.

Sectorwide Approaches

The 1990s also witnessed a shift away from the proliferation of assistance for unrelated projects toward a more systematic approach. This included identifying the country as the unit of accountability, promoting coordination of aid among donor countries, emphasizing sustainable development through good governance, and transparency.[46]

A sectorwide approach brings together all the major funding for a particular sector (say, health care) under a single policy and expenditure strategy devised by the recipient government. Sectorwide approaches were seen as a means of giving the recipient government ownership over the development process.

Concurrently they aimed at securing a more supportive policy environment within the recipient government. Specific policy and programmatic emphases were placed on high profile issues like gender equity, sustainable development and elimination of HIV/AIDS.

They represented a reaction to stand-alone donor-funded projects that distorted the development process. Piecemeal approaches led to multiple, even conflicting, donor expectations and redundant reporting systems that bogged down recipient governments.

At the same time, donors want to see evidence of effectiveness in the recipient's macroeconomic framework and financial management systems. Sectorwide approaches work better under conditions where donors and recipient governments see eye to eye on the role of government in development. Such consensus is more likely to exist in areas like health care and education, less likely in other areas like agriculture and the environment. Sectorwide programs are most prominent in Africa.[47]

In the United States and other G-7 donors the criterion of good governance is used in determining the level of their development aid. Under this approach, the main countries to benefit will be those that meet good governance standards as operationalized by multilateral lending institutions like the World Bank and bilateral donors like the United States, Germany and Japan.

This entails a risk that many low-income countries and the poor people in them may be abandoned. Such selectivity could stand in the way of countries where, despite flawed and even corrupt governance there is evidence of a commitment to poverty reduction.

Organizations like the World Bank and International Monetary Fund may function less as financial institutions and more as investment policy gatekeepers. They set the conditions under which capital flows to developing nations and the terms of development.

Major international bodies promoted the goals of human rights, democracy, market economies, reliance on the rule of law, transparency in governmental decisionmaking, reductions in military expenditures, and accountability.

With assistance tied to multiple related agendas, from sustainability to gender equity, the autonomy of developing countries risked being undermined in the name of global political correctness. [48] The least developed countries were particularly vulnerable to these pressures.

More UN Conferences on the Least Developed Countries

A Second United Nations Conference on the Least Developed Countries was convened in Paris from September 3-14, 1990. The conference generated the Paris Declaration and the Program of Action for the Least Developed Countries for the 1990s.

At the global level, the United Nations Conference on Trade and Development assumed responsibility for monitoring the implementation of the

Program of Action. Country-level reviews are conducted at meetings of the World Bank Consultative Group and the United Nations Development Programme Round Table. A mid-decade global review was carried out September 25-October 6, 1995 in New York at a high-level intergovernmental meeting.

In General Assembly resolution 52/187, passed December 18, 1997, the United Nations convened the Third United Nations Conference on Least Developed Countries. The goal was to foster sustainable development in these countries and their progressive integration into the global economy.

The General Assembly designated the United Nations Conference on Trade and Development as the organizational focal point and accepted the offer of the European Union to host the conference, which was held May 14-20, 2001 in Brussels. The challenge of eradicating world poverty was a predominant theme of the conference. The Brussels Declaration asserted that the eradication of poverty depended on economic growth and "sustainable development based on nationally owned and people-centred poverty reduction strategies."[49]

The United Nations' Approaches to Poverty

Compared to the Bretton Woods institutions, where orthodox economics dominates the intellectual framework, the United Nations has tended to be more multidisciplinary, and, to some observers, more creative in its approach to poverty reduction.

On macroeconomic policy, the World Bank and the International Monetary Fund control the agenda. Familiar themes like economic growth, inflation, debt, structural adjustment and governance predominate. The scale of World Bank lending for programs and projects is large compared to the United Nations agencies.

Lacking the deep pockets of those institutions, the United Nations agencies have sought to maximize the returns on smaller scale, lower cost projects through close coordination with host governments and more participatory approaches in local communities.

The United Nations has brought forth some of the key concepts that guide the world's war on poverty. Among others, these include human development, gender equity, and sustainable development. The United Nations Development Programme insists that human development should be the focus of economic growth, not just a byproduct.

Moreover, United Nations agencies have the benefit of more on the ground, country-level experience, and can bring to bear useful perspectives on the implementation of poverty reduction strategies.

It is therefore a welcome development that, in contrast to prior decades, during the 1990s the World Bank group moved toward closer cooperation with United Nations agencies. Both have sought to bring about greater harmonization of bilateral donor aid in conjunction with the Organization for Economic

Cooperation and Development. The notion of aid as a form of partnering with recipient countries has taken hold.

At times and in many developing countries, collaboration and cooperation among aid agencies appear to subsist more in rhetoric than in reality. However, all parties within the United Nations system have seen their share of failures. They have grown more sensitized to the counterproductive effects of a fragmented aid system.

The failure of past antipoverty efforts, disillusionment with national governments, and the search for innovative strategies and practices have caused all parties in the global war on poverty to collaborate more closely. The elements of a more coherent global war on poverty are at least recognizable if not yet fully in place. Among other things, they include a larger role for non-governmental organizations.

International non-governmental organizations have become more prominent in development and antipoverty efforts in part because they are seen as being in closer touch than other institutions, public or private, with the needs and aspirations of poor people. The Internet has made it possible for non-governmental organizations to share information and build alliances (or at least temporary coalitions) in pursuit of shared goals. The increase in open political systems domestically and internationally has made it easier for non-governmental organizations to join the debate over the direction of global policy.[50]

Oxfam International

In the 1980s Oxfam provided famine relief to Ethiopia and the Sudan. In 1992, to tackle worker exploitation in Third World countries, the Fairtrade Foundation was created by Oxfam, Catholic Agency for Overseas Development, Christian Aid, New Consumer, Traidcraft Exchange, and the World Development Movement.

In 1994, Oxfam UK and Ireland joined with relief and development agencies in Australia, New Zealand, America, Canada, Quebec, Hong Kong, Holland, and Belgium to form Oxfam International.[51]

In Africa that year, Rawanda experienced the genocide of an estimated 800,000 people and an exodus of some 1.7 million refugees. Oxfam installed clean water and sanitation for 700,000 refugees in refugee camps near Goma, Zaire (now Democratic Republic of Congo).

In the late 1990s, Oxfam International undertook a major strategic review of its aims, operating procedures and relationships with other organizations, public and private. Its twelve member organizations work in over one hundred countries to relieve poverty and suffering.[52]

While continuing to provide support for famine relief, disaster assistance and community-based antipoverty initiatives, Oxfam International has become more outspoken in lobbying for food security, fair global trade practices and the rights of workers.

Oxfam International and its twelve national affiliates have subscribed to a strategic plan for 2001-2004 called Towards Global Equity. The plan addresses the growing gap between rich and poor under globalization. It envisions alliances with other networks and organizations on behalf of a global movement to promote social justice.

Evidence of More CARE

During the 1990s, CARE continued to provide emergency relief assistance while addressing more fundamental causes of poverty. For example, in 1992, it delivered food to two million people during a famine in Somalia. It helped several hundred thousand Haitians cope with food shortages in 1993. It delivered food, water and sanitation in 1994 to refugees and survivors of the Rwandan genocide.[53]

In 1998, CARE responded to emergencies like Hurricane Mitch in Central America, war and civil strife in Kosovo, Serbia and cyclones in Orissa, India.

Over the decade CARE supported longer-range projects in family planning, small business development, agriculture, schooling and health care. In 1997, CARE's shift of emphasis toward poverty alleviation was reflected in its household livelihood security framework, an approach designed to cover all aspects of a poor family's life.

Like Oxfam, CARE has expanded beyond its original country's borders. CARE International is a confederation of eleven member organizations, including CARE USA. CARE International is coordinated by a secretariat based in Brussels.[54] CARE International is active in more than seventy countries in AfricaAsia , Latin America, the Middle East and Eastern Europe.

An Expanding World Vision

Throughout the 1980s World Vision developed programs to help people in poor communities build a better future. These programs included relief and rehabilitation in Ethiopia, support for destitute farmers in Mozambique, flood rehabilitation in Bangladesh, clearance of land mines in Afghanistan and food provision in drought-stricken Thailand and Laos.

New projects through the 1990s included water drilling in Senegal, environmental protection in Mali, rehabilitation of war victims in Cambodia, community health work in Kenya and agriculture in Tanzania. Emergency help was also extended to thousands in the aftermath of famine, floods and conflict in Sudan, Bangladesh, Philippines, India and Rwanda.

From its inception in 1950, World Vision has grown into one of the largest Christian relief and development organizations in the world. Independent national offices are located in Geneva, Bangkok, Nairobi, Vienna, Los Angeles, and San Jose, Costa Rica. A twenty-four member international board oversees the World Vision Partnership. In 2002, World Vision assisted an estimated eighty-five million people in ninety-six countries.[55]

Ubi Caritas . . .

Caritas Internationalis has grown into a confederation of 162 Catholic relief, development and social service organizations active in two hundred countries and territories. It has become one of the world's largest humanitarian networks.

Caritas works to empower people to participate fully in all matters affecting their lives and it advocates on their behalf at national and international forums. Acting on Christian, and specifically Catholic, principles, it emphasizes the dignity of the individual person.

In the United States, Catholic Relief Services, a member of Caritas Internationalis, operates in some eighty countries. Its programs fall under the general headings of emergency response, community health, education and peace-building. Sudan is a case in point.

Since obtaining its independence in 1956, the country has been embroiled in a series of civil wars. The Southern People's Liberation Movement has led the resistance to the Khartoum government, which has sought to impose Arabic culture, Islam and the *sharia* law on the non-Muslim, largely African, south. The SPLM has itself been plagued by internal dissension, creation of splinter groups and factional fighting. The wars have claimed millions of victims, mostly in the southern third of the country.

Catholic Relief Services has been operating in the country since 1972 and is the largest private relief organization in southern Sudan. The agency distributes tools and seeds to farmers who have lost what they owned in fleeing conflict. It also provides emergency relief, health, education and microfinance programs to Sudanese families and communities. It has worked for reconciliation between the south's two largest tribes, the Dinka and the Nuer, through a People-to-People peace process.[56]

Elsewhere, in response to the African tragedy of HIV/AIDS, Catholic Relief Services has set up home-care and education programs for people with the disease in Kenya, Uganda, Tanzania and Zimbabwe.

The Growth of Microcredit

Poor farmers and rural dwellers have suffered from lack of access to credit. Rural people need credit to invest in farms and small businesses and to better cope with adverse weather conditions and economic downturns. Lending to the poor was recognized as inherently expensive. However experience had revealed known pitfalls, criteria for long-term success and examples of replicable projects. One approach involves the use of microcredit.

Microcredit refers to small collateral-free loans to poor people at near-market interest rates. Financial institutions or non-governmental organizations make such loans through special community-based programs. The approach was pioneered in Asia by the Grameen ("Rural") Bank in Bangladesh, founded in 1977 by former economics professor Muhammad Yunus.

The Grameen Bank makes small loans directly to the rural poor and has experienced excellent repayment rates. In the early 1990s it had 1.4 million borrowers, lent $14 million a month and had a 97 percent repayment rate.[57] Its micro-lending approach has been adopted in Malaysia, the Philippines, and Sri Lanka among others.

In the 1980s, the Grameen Bank refused aid from the World Bank, persuaded that, in Yunus' words, its "experts and consultants take over the projects they finance."[58]

Dr. Yunus has been no friend of international development agencies in general. He was concerned about aid-funded projects spawning massive bureaucracies that "quickly become corrupt and inefficient, including huge losses."[59] He sees the elimination of poverty as a human rights issue, not the byproduct of an expanding gross national product.

The Grameen approach has been replicated in forty-five other countries and similar microfinance organizations have flourished as well. Direct lending to the poor has expanded to include groups like the Microenterprise Coalition among whose members are the Grameen Bank in Bangladesh and K-REP in Kenya, as well as networks like ACCION International, Foundation for International Community Assistance and the credit union movement.

Regulated microfinance institutions such as BRAC in Bangladesh, BancoSol in Bolivia, SEWA Bank in India, and ACEP in Senegal are able to raise funds directly from the local and international capital markets. Their lending alleviates poverty while reducing dependency on foreign assistance. In addition to providing credit, many accept deposits.

As of 1998, according to some estimates, there were some three thousand microfinance institutions. The industry as a whole reaches an estimated 12.5 million poor people worldwide. This is but a fraction of the roughly half a billion poor persons who potentially could benefit from microfinance assistance.[60]

Microenterprise is recognized by the U.S. Congress and others as a component of the emerging global financial architecture. It can broaden the reach of the financial sector to serve the very poor and women among others and thereby contribute to social stability and prosperity.[61]

Four Decades of ACCION

ACCION International has evolved into one of the premier microfinance organizations in the world, with a network of lending affiliates in Latin America, the United States and Africa. It stakes a claim to "first authorship" of microfinance.

ACCION International was founded in 1961 by Joseph Blatchford, an idealistic law student and amateur tennis player. Following a goodwill tennis tour of thirty Latin American cities, he returned to the United States haunted by images of Latin America's urban poor. He and law school friends raised $90,000 from private companies to start a community-based effort to help Latin America's poor help themselves.

In the summer of 1961, Blatchford and thirty volunteers flew to Venezuela. Initially greeted with skepticism, the fledgling "ACCIONistas" were soon working closely with local residents. Volunteers and residents installed electricity and sewer lines, started training and nutrition programs, and built schools and community centers.

Over the next decade, ACCION started programs in Brazil, Peru and Colombia. It placed over a thousand dedicated volunteers and contributed more than $9 million to development in very poor Latin American communities. The organization found that building schools and digging wells made better use of existing resources but did little to enhance the community's resource base. They saw the need for expanded economic opportunities.

Every year, drawn by the prospect of industrial employment, rural residents migrated to cities by the thousands. They discovered that jobs were scarce and available jobs did not pay a living wage. In desperation they started their own small businesses, weaving belts, banging out pots and selling potatoes. To buy supplies, they often borrowed from local loan sharks at rates as high as ten percent a day. Most of their profits went to interest payments, leaving them locked in a daily struggle for survival.

In 1973, ACCION staff in Recife, Brazil noticed the prevalence of these informal businesses. ACCION's Recife program began issuing small loans for what they termed "microenterprise." ACCION believes that these loans launched the field of microcredit. The experiment in Recife was a success. Within four years, the organization had provided 885 loans, helping to create or stabilize 1,386 new jobs.

ACCION had uncovered a way to generate wealth for the working poor. Over the following decade ACCION International helped start microlending programs in fourteen Latin American countries. With a loan repayment rate of 97 percent, ACCION's clients gave the lie to claims that the poor were bad credit risks. Microlending paid for itself. The interest each borrower paid helped cover the cost of lending to another.

ACCION's new loan guarantee fund, the Bridge Fund, enabled affiliates to connect with the local banking sector. As a result, between 1989 and 1995, the amount of money loaned by ACCION's Latin American network multiplied more than twentyfold. Still, the network was reaching less than two percent of potential borrowers.

In response, ACCION helped create BancoSol, the first commercial bank in the world dedicated solely to microenterprise. Founded in Bolivia in 1992, BancoSol's clients typically are market vendors, sandal makers and seamstresses.

BancoSol offers its more than sixty thousand clients a range of financial services including savings accounts, credit cards and housing loans. In 1994, ACCION helped BancoSol sell certificates of deposit in the U.S. financial market, a sure sign that investing in microenterprise was not charity but good business.

In 1991, concerned about growing income inequality and unemployment in the United States, ACCION brought its microlending model home, started a microlending program in Brooklyn, New York. In 2000, ACCION's U.S. initiative was renamed ACCION USA. By the end of 2001, ACCION USA had become the largest U.S. microlender with locations in California, Georgia, Illinois, Massachusetts, New Mexico, New York, Rhode Island and Texas, having lent more than $44 million to 6,600 low-income entrepreneurs.

In 2001, ACCION USA merged with Working Capital, a New England-based microlender, adding five new lending locations to the ACCION USA Network. In 2001 ACCION made loans, some as low as $100, totaling $562 million and serving over six hundred thousand borrowers in twenty countries.

In October 2000, as its first initiative outside the Americas, ACCION began working in partnership with microlending organizations in Sub-Saharan Africa. Currently, ACCION is providing technical assistance to microlenders in Benin, Mozambique, South Africa, Uganda and Zimbabwe.[62]

Consultative Group to Assist the Poorest

In 1995, Ismail Serageldin, vice president for special operations in the World Bank, and ten donor agencies collaborated to establish the Consultative Group to Assist the Poorest (CGAP). The Consultative Group to Assist the Poorest is a consortium of 28 bilateral and multilateral donor agencies and foundations that support microfinance. The consortium's secretariat is located at the World Bank in Washington.

Between 1995 and 1998, the consortium helped develop a common language for the microfinance industry, advocated for best practice performance standards, and worked to build consensus among industry stakeholders including donors, recipients, and analysts.

The Consultative Group to Assist the Poorest provides the microfinance network with technical assistance, training, research and strategic advice. It operates a small grants program to assist with local capacity building in microfinance.

It also seeks to build institutions that provide a variety of financial and non-financial services to poor individuals and their communities. It also works to establish supportive legal and regulatory frameworks for these institutions.

The Scourge of Chronic Hunger[63]

Globally, about 800 million people, a quarter of them children under age five, lack enough to eat on a continuing basis. Despite advances in agriculture, food production in many developing countries has not kept pace with the needs of rapidly growing and increasingly urban populations. Even where there is sufficient food to meet the needs of the population, people in extreme poverty often cannot afford to buy it.

Most poor and hungry people live in low-income, food-deficit countries. There are eighty-six such countries, half in Africa alone. For most agricultural production among poor farmers is critical. The agricultural sector is the main source of employment, food and income opportunities, as well as the spur for rural nonfarm development.

In 1994, the Food and Agriculture Organization initiated the Special Program for Food Security. By making available experts from many fields, the program helps these countries to increase agricultural productivity, reduce year-to-year variability in production on an environmentally sustainable basis and improve household access to food.

Consistent with national food security goals, the program can support a wide range of activities, such as peri-urban agriculture in Côte d'Ivoire, assistance for women seed farmers in Nepal, introduction of treadle pumps in Zambia, and support for farmer associations in the United Republic of Tanzania.

The FAO has responded to criticisms that the initial program design was rigid and inflexible by adopting a more participatory and multidisciplinary approach. Within developing countries the program is designed, planned and implemented by national governments and their rural communities, with technical assistance from the Food and Agriculture Organization as needed.[64]

The number of countries participating in the Special Program for Food Security has risen from fifteen in 1995 to over seventy in 2002. Funding has increased to over $500 million, of which developing countries have committed more than half.

At the headquarters of the Food and Agriculture Organization in Rome, a World Food Summit was convened November 13-17, 1996. The Summit brought together nearly ten thousand participants from 185 countries.

The Rome Declaration called for cutting in half the number of the world's chronically malnourished people by 2015. The Summit endorsed the Special Program for Food Security as a major step toward realizing this goal.[65]

Rural Poverty on the International Agenda

During the 1990s, poverty eradication assumed a prominent place on the international agenda. In 1992, a study by the International Fund for Agricultural Development highlighted the phenomenon of rural poverty, including its causes and the characteristics of the rural poor who make up 80 percent of the world's poor.[66]

The organization knew whereof it wrote. Since its establishment in 1977, the International Fund for Agricultural Development has financed over six hundred projects in 115 countries and independent territories with grants and loans amounting to $7.7 billion. External organizations have provided $6.4 billion in cofinancing.[67] The organization is a leader in supporting innovative, grassroots approaches to microeconomic development.

World Summit for Social Development

In March 1995, Denmark hosted the World Summit for Social Development. It was conceived by Ambassador Juan Somavia of Chile, whose energy and commitment helped make it a reality. Five years earlier a precedent had been set by the United Nations Children's Fund, whose executive director. Jim Grant, organized a conference on children, the first with a human development theme.

The 1995 Summit, attended by representatives from 185 countries including (remarkably) 117 heads of State or government, produced the Copenhagen Declaration and Program of Action. It committed the participants to eradicating poverty as an "ethical, social, political and economic imperative."[68] Each country would set a target date for meeting the goal.

Non-governmental organizations played a key role in preparations for the Copenhagen Summit, which led to a changed relationship between them and the United Nations. These organizations realized the importance of sustained and systematic follow-up to the goals and commitments reached at the Summit.

One product of the Summit was establishment of an international network called Social Watch, which monitors the follow-up at the national level by governments and international bodies on their commitments to eradicate poverty and inequality. Social Watch reflects the new way that non-governmental organizations like Oxfam and Caritas Internationalis build alliances with one another and exert influence on multilateral organizations like the United Nations and World Bank.[69]

The worldwide focus on poverty has triggered an outpouring of poverty-related research. In 1992, the International Social Science Council established the Comparative Research Program on Poverty (CROP). The original impetus was to keep track of the flood of poverty research in a global context.

The organization assists in the creation of a body of scientific knowledge that cuts across disciplines and can be used to reduce global poverty. The CROP Secretariat is located at the Centre for International Poverty Research in the University of Bergen, Norway

Critics see the current approach to development and poverty reduction as essentially unaccountable, corporate-led, and undemocratic. It is geared to integrating the world's economies through the diffusion of technology, large capital investments and expanded international trade.

Due to lack of training and low incomes, the poor may suffer rather than gain from this approach. Poor people are less able than others to take advantage of cheaper imports and an expanding job market's emphasis on technological skills.

One critic, the World Alliance of YMCAs, sees the emergence of a new global culture based on rampant consumerism in the "North" (economically advanced nations found mainly in the northern hemisphere) and impoverishment of the developing "South".

"The sinister aim of this monoculturalisation is the creation of a Global Factory, a Global Mall and a Global Financial Market with benefits unevenly accruing to the North. In the South, the advance of globalisation results in a fast and ruthless accumulation of wealth by a few at the cost of impoverishing large majorities of peoples."[70]

Structural adjustment only exacerbates the problem, since it reduces the government's role in developing human resources. Governments are forced to reduce overall expenditures in the name of fiscal austerity and to use an increasing share of available resources to service debt. One internal analysis of World Bank and IMF loans concluded that "economic expansions benefit the poor less under structural adjustment."[71]

First United Nations Decade for the Eradication of Poverty

In December 1995, under resolution 50/107, the General Assembly proclaimed the First United Nations Decade for the Eradication of Poverty (1997-2006). The year 1996 was designated the International Year for the Eradication of Poverty. In December 1996, resolution 51/178 stated the Decade's theme: "Eradicating poverty is an ethical, social, political and economic imperative of humankind."

The United Nations Development Programme, the UN's main development network, has made the eradication of poverty its highest priority. The UNDP assists less developed countries with the preparation and implementation of poverty reduction strategies in pursuit of sustainable human development. It supports some seven thousand development projects and programs in over 166 countries.[72]

World Trade Organization

The Agreement establishing the World Trade Organization was forged during the Uruguay Round of Multilateral Trade Negotiations and signed April 1, 1994. It includes recognition of the role of trade for "raising standards of living, ensuring full employment and a large and steadily growing volume of real income and effective demand...while allowing for the optimal use of the world's resources in accordance with the objective of sustainable development."

While poverty reduction is not a stated goal, it presumably can be inferred as part of raised living standards and sustainable development. Supporters contend that by establishing and enforcing uniform rules, the World Trade Organization protects developing nations from adverse actions by large transnational corporations, multilateral institutions and developed countries.

The World Trade Organization has cooperative arrangements with the United Nations but formally is a separate entity. The core notion of trade in agricultural and manufactured goods has expanded to include such "trade-related" issues as services (banking, insurance, media and the like), intellectual property rights and investment measures. This could be seen as the camel's nose under a country's sovereignty tent.

The World Trade Organization has built on this precedent. Other issues like the environment, labor standards, human rights, gender equity, tax systems and culture could make it onto the World Trade Organization's agenda as trade-related. The World Trade Organization serves as a potential policy development and enforcement vehicle for public interest groups advocating around these issues.

The developing countries of the South tend to perceive the World Trade Organization, whose decisionmaking processes are dominated in practice by richer North, as an instrument for "enforcing global economic governance."[73]

For example, a developing country may prefer to favor small domestic companies (with, for example, internal distribution rights) over large transnational firms, rather than risk having the latter dominate local markets. Developed countries within the World Trade Organization contend that such favorable treatment is a barrier to free and open competition. Developing countries come to the table around such issues in a weaker negotiating position.

Formally the World Trade Organization operates on a one country-one vote principle. In practice, formal votes are not taken; instead decisions are reached through "consensus." Often consensus is initially generated through backroom sessions where dominant actors like the United States, Japan, Canada and the European Union forge agreements favorable to their interests. Critics complain that the dominant nations then exert pressure on the entire membership to endorse these agreements.

The World Trade Organization's rules and agreements on balance favor large transnational corporations over domestic businesses in the developing world. The former easily overmatch the latter in a "free and open" competitive environment. The losers are small and medium business owners, small farmers and governments at all levels.

The countries of the South face a Hobson's choice. To participate meaningfully in the global trading system developing countries must join the World Trade Organization—an organization over whose decisionmaking processes they exert comparatively little influence. The perception that rich countries dominate international trade is a source of anger and resentment among those who are adversely affected by the WTO's policies and procedures.

Millennium Development Goals

At the United Nations Millennium Summit, held in New York from September 6-8, 2000, the member states of the United Nations committed themselves to poverty reduction through sustained development. The eight specific goals of the Summit were the product of agreements and resolutions of world conferences organized by the United Nations during the 1990s. The eight goals serve as a template for measuring global progress in development and poverty reduction.

The first seven goals aim at reducing poverty. The last goal, which is means-oriented, envisions a global partnership for development. The partnership entails increased foreign aid flows, debt relief, reduction of international trade barriers and national poverty reduction strategies. Even if the eight goals are met—a very large "if"—individual poor countries and regions or population subgroups within richer countries will lag behind. The eight goals are as follows:

- Between 1990 and 2015, cut in half (from 29.0 percent to 14.5 percent) the proportion of people whose income is less than $1 a day.[74]
- Ensure that by 2015 both boys and girls can complete primary schooling.
- Eliminate gender disparity in primary and secondary education preferably by 2005 and in all levels of education by 2015.
- Between 1990 and 2015, reduce by two-thirds the mortality rate for children under five years of age.
- Between 1990 and 2015, reduce by three-quarters the maternal mortality ratio.
- By 2015, begin to reverse the spread of HIV/AIDS, malaria and other major diseases.
- Integrate sustainable development principles into country policies and programs and reverse the loss of environmental resources.
- Develop a global partnership for development.

Reducing the proportion of people living in extreme poverty to half the 1990 level by 2015 would mean a drop in the proportion from 29 percent of all people in low and middle income economies to 14.5 percent. Extreme poverty is indicated by lack of sufficient income; the measure is living on less than $1 a day. If the goal were achieved, the number of people living in extreme poverty would drop to 890 million or even further to 750 million if plans for global economic growth stay on track. A modest goal indeed.

The World Bank and the Millennium Development Goals

Along with other bilateral and multilateral aid organizations, the World Bank has fully subscribed to the Millennium Development Goals. It has markedly increased its openness to outside scrutiny.[75]

As a share of total adjustment lending operations, those operations focused explicitly on poverty reduction went from 49 percent in 1992 to a high of 75 percent in 1999 before dropping back to 60 percent in 2001. In dollar terms, the trends are less impressive. Poverty-focused adjustment lending was $2.8 billion in 1992, rose to a peak of $10.7 billion in 1999, then was scaled back to $2.4 billion in 2001.[76]

In monitoring global poverty reduction, the World Bank relies principally on income measures, without ignoring the non-income aspects of poverty. Overcoming poverty means first and foremost putting more income into the hands of the poor. This can come about through paid work, conversion of assets, or societal transfers.

Among these options, paid work has pride of place. Higher employment rates and jobs paying a living wage occur best under conditions of overall economic development.

In its 2000/2001 World Development Report, the Bank proposes attacking poverty through the triad of opportunity, empowerment and security. This contrasts with the 1990 Report, where the watchwords were labor-intensive growth and expanded social services.

The new approach acknowledged that market reforms do not always segue smoothly into sustained growth and poverty reduction. Further, in the 1990s, while unskilled labor remained the chief asset of the poor, it was technology and high-end skills that fostered much of the growth.

For a variety of reasons, not least of which were internal and external pressures for structural adjustment (such as reduced public spending and greater attention to debt servicing), many developing nations scaled back their spending for health care, education and related social services during the 1980s and 1990s. The forces of global economic integration, technological progress and communications benefited some developing nations while skipping by others.

For the World Bank, such trends called for a broader antipoverty agenda. Opportunity strategies stressed making markets work better for the poor, increasing the assets of the poor through both market and non-market actions, and reducing wealth inequalities.

Empowerment referred to greater responsiveness by state institutions to the needs of poor people, elimination of barriers based on gender, race, ethnicity, and social status, and creation of appropriate social institutions. Security for the poor meant reducing the incidence of and managing the risks associated with ill health, violence, economic crises and natural disasters.

Despite its avowed commitment to poverty reduction as a necessary concomitant to economic growth, the World Bank has not quelled its critics. Few doubt its good intentions but instead focus on its structure, policies and decisionmaking processes.

In the United States, for example, the role and impact of international financial institutions has come under more severe scrutiny and led to calls for radical reform.

The Meltzer Commission

In November 1998, during the Asian financial crisis, the U.S. Congress created the International Financial Institution Advisory Commission (IFIAC). It was part of legislation that provided for an $18 billion capital contribution to the International Monetary Fund.

Better known as the Meltzer Commission, this eleven member group, chaired by Professor Allan Meltzer of Carnegie Mellon University, examined seven international institutions. These were: (1) International Monetary Fund (2) World Bank Group (3) Inter-American Development Bank (4) Asian Development Bank (5) African Development Bank (6) Bank for International Settlements and (7) World Trade Organization.

The resulting Meltzer Commission Report advocated substantial and, one might add, highly controversial changes at the multilateral development banks.

Since it had a short life of six months, the Commission relied heavily on experts on the seven institutions it examined. Its final report was approved by a majority eight to three vote and included vigorous dissents. The members did vote unanimously on two recommendations.

First, the International Monetary Fund, World Bank and regional multilateral development banks should write off all their claims against heavily indebted poor countries that implement effective economic and social development strategies. Second, the International Monetary Fund should restrict its lending to the provision of short-term liquidity; it should get out of the poverty reduction business.

There was less consensus around other recommendations for the World Bank and the regional development banks. The Commission would have the World Bank change its name to the World Development Agency.

Instead of functioning as a capital-intensive lender, it would offer technical assistance, provide regional and global public goods (literacy, access to health care, treatment of AIDS and tropical diseases, clean water, and infrastructure), and facilitate the flow of private sector resources to the least developed countries.

Dissatisfied by evidence that 70 percent of World Bank non-aid resources flowed to eleven countries that have easy access to the capital markets, the Commission recommended that official development assistance be phased out for countries with investment grade international bond ratings or with per capita incomes above $4,000 a year.

Grants would replace loans as the primary financing tool and services within countries would be performed by private sector entities—for-profit businesses, non-profit non-governmental organizations, and charitable organizations—under competitive contracts.

Essentially the Commission regarded the World Bank's performance in poverty reduction as having failed, in part for what we have come to call mission creep. It sought to refocus and circumscribe its mission for purposes of clarity and accountability.

The Commission perceived costly duplication and confusion over the roles of the World Bank and its regional counterparts. Over a five year transition period, all country and regional programs in Latin America and Asia should become the primary responsibility of the Asian and Inter-American Development Agencies.

The Asian Development Bank and the Inter-American Development Bank were judged sufficiently mature and professional to take full responsibility for poverty alleviation and structural reform in their respective regions.

Not so in Africa. Here the World Bank should become the principal source of aid until the African Development Bank was better prepared for that role. The World Bank would also be the development agency for the remaining poor countries in Europe and the Middle East.

While some of the Commission's dissenting members believed that the report did not go far enough—for example, one would abolish the International Monetary Fund altogether—others saw its recommendations as undermining the war on global poverty.

If the recommendations were carried out, the World Bank would eliminate its nonconcessional lending program and the International Monetary Fund would eliminate its Poverty Reduction and Growth Facility.

Evaluating the Evaluators

Dissenters from the Meltzer Commission's conclusions contended that these programs help hundreds of millions of the world's poorest people. Many of the world's poor are concentrated in very poor countries but others live in countries like Brazil and Mexico where average per capita income has exceeded the global poverty line.[77] The latter cannot be ignored by multilateral aid agencies.

The World Bank's Operations Evaluation Department took issue with the alleged 55-60 percent failure rate of World Bank-supported endeavors. The World Bank's own evaluations find a high rate of success—81 percent of dollars lent and 72 percent of projects assisted. Why the discrepancy? Different methods, different criteria.

The Operations Evaluation Department independently reviews and validates project completion reports and carries out field performance audits for 25 percent of all projects within seven years of project completion. A satisfactory outcome rating is given if the project has met its major relevant objectives and attained a real rate of return of at least 10 percent.

The Department also estimates the likely sustainability of the project beyond the loan period and its contribution to institutional capacity building in the recipient country.

The Meltzer Commission by contrast classified all projects with uncertain sustainability ratings as failures. This single standard approach appears overly rigorous. Capacity building merits attention as well. A high rate of return is not an insignificant consideration. Neither is the potential replicability of successful elements of the project design elsewhere.

Projects whose outcomes are assessed as unsatisfactory within the time frame examined may prove beneficial over a longer time frame. The World Bank points to its support for building community centers in slum areas under the First Urban Development Project in Colombia.

The centers would serve as a staging point for the coordination and delivery of services to the poor. Under Colombia's centralized government, the approach did not initially pan out. Staffing and funding lapsed after the loan period. The sustainability of the project was rated unsatisfactory. A decade later, however, when the government shifted to a more decentralized system of service delivery, the existence of the centers facilitated community-based service delivery.[78]

Obviously, just as projects considered failures can ultimately prove successful, the opposite can occur. Furthermore, success within individual communities does not necessarily translate into aggregate poverty reduction nationally.[79] The factors that produce local success, say, for example, charismatic and committed community leadership, are not routinely found everywhere.

Organization for Economic Cooperation and Development

Within the Organization for Economic Cooperation and Development, the Development Assistance Committee seeks to support the participation of developing countries in the global economy and the capacity of their people to overcome poverty. It does this by providing a forum where major bilateral donors can work together to increase their collective effectiveness.

In June 1998, the OECD's Development Assistance Committee established a subsidiary group called the Network on Poverty Reduction (POVNET). It grew out of the Committee's 1996 report *Shaping the 21st Century*, which included the benchmarks for monitoring progress against poverty.[80]

The World Bank and United Nations Development Programme participate in the work of POVNET, which helps bilateral aid agencies to sharpen the focus and effectiveness of their poverty reduction efforts.

The Development Cooperation Directorate, one of a dozen such OECD directorates, acts as a secretariat to the Development Assistance Committee. Members of the Committee generally subscribe to certain common objectives in their aid programs. The Development Assistance Committee issues guidelines for the benefit of its members.[81]

The guidelines emphasize country-led poverty reduction strategies based on local needs and priorities as determined by stakeholders. The guidelines provide information about poverty as well as successful antipoverty practices and policies. They set out parameters for building effective partnerships with governments, civil society, and other development actors.

With the decline of the state as the leading actor in development, the role of non-governmental and grass-roots organizations has expanded dramatically. However, over the decade of the 1990s, the volume of official development assistance declined markedly, in both absolute terms and as a proportion of total resource flows from developed to developing countries.

In 1991, total long-term resource flows to developing countries amounted to $123 billion, of which $60.9 billion (49.5 percent) was official development assistance, and the rest private flows from capital markets and foreign direct investment. By 2000, official development assistance had dropped to \$38.6 billion, while private flows had soared to \$257.2 billion or 87 percent of total resource flows.[82]

Notably, for the period 1991-2000, three-quarters of the foreign direct investment share of the private flows went to just ten of the world's developing countries.[83] This could be defended on grounds that these countries exhibited the right characteristics for investors: good governance, sound macroeconomic policies, commitment to open markets and an educated labor force.

There remained the question, however, of the level and type of support to channel to other developing countries. Official development assistance seems appropriate for these less-favored countries in their efforts to attract private investors. Otherwise a certain circularity prevails. Countries must show evidence of good governance (as defined and judged by donors) before receiving aid to reduce poverty—a contributor to "bad" or corrupt governance.

Antipoverty Strategies of Developing Countries

According to a 1990 report of the South Commission titled *The Challenge to the South*, a lack of organization impeded the ability of the South to fully exercise its leverage at the global level. The South Centre was initially established as a temporary follow up office of the South Commission. On July 31, 1995, the South Centre became a permanent intergovernmental body of developing countries.

The Centre, located in Geneva, seeks consensus or at least convergence of view and approach among the nations of the South on major policy issues. In 2002, its membership consisted of representatives from 46 developing countries.[84] It functions as a small-scale counterpart (and counterweight) to the Organization of Economic Development and Cooperation, which embodies the worldview of the industrialized and technologically advanced North.

Topics addressed by the South Centre include foreign direct investment, United Nations reform, financial flows, World Trade Organization agenda, science and technology and globalization.

The Centre works with and through South governments, institutions of South-South cooperation, intergovernmental organizations of the South, non-governmental organizations and the community at large. It provides a degree of support to related entities like the G-77 and the Non-Aligned Movement.

Since 1961, the Non-Aligned Movement's members have met in summit conferences roughly on a three-year schedule. With the breakup of the Soviet Union and the emergence of the United States as the world's sole superpower in the late 1980s, the terms "third world" and "nonaligned" are less apt.

The nations of the world tend to be grouped under the headings of "developing", "transitional", and "developed." However, these terms, which are used to classify sovereign nations, come with ideological freighting that makes them distasteful to some.

In 2001, the Non-Aligned Movement had 115 members. In recent years it has sought to expand dialogue with developed countries such as the G-8. The movement's members have tended to oppose protectionist measures in international trade and conditionalities as an element of bilateral and multilateral donor assistance. [85]

Emerging Donor Countries

In recent years, so-called "emerging donor" countries like Singapore and Thailand have been assisting other less developed countries. This South-South cooperation has contributed to bridging intra-regional gaps in technology, trade and investment.[86]

Partners in Population and Development is an alliance of 19 developing countries that share information and expertise on population planning and reproductive health. It was officially launched in 1994 during the International Conference on Population and Development (ICPD) in Cairo.[87]

Equally if not more interesting as a partnership model are the North-South arrangements embodied in the North American Free Trade Agreement. NAFTA incorporates ways for the United States and Canada to share technological expertise and organizational capacity-building with the developing and transitional economies of Latin America.

While trends in economic growth in many regions are positive, there are disturbing signs of gross inequality within and among countries and regions. The ratio in per capita gross domestic product between the more developed and less developed regions of the world stood at 3:1 in the early nineteenth century. The ratio had reached approximately 20:1 by the end of the twentieth century.[88]

For several decades, Latin America and the Caribbean have suffered from one of the most unequal income distributions in the world, particularly Haiti, Central America, the Andean region and Northeastern Brazil.[89] The demand for unskilled labor has not kept pace with growth and the wage gap between skilled and unskilled workers has increased. Lacking opportunities in the formal employment sector, unskilled workers must resort to an informal cash economy characterized by very low wages, lack of benefits and job transience.

Under annual per capita growth rates of three percent, it would take decades and, for some countries, literally a couple of centuries, to eliminate poverty in Latin America and the Caribbean.[90] It could take longer if national poverty lines were used (rather than the $1 a day standard), if growth rates declined or inequality accelerated.

The situation in some other regions, for example, Sub-Saharan Africa and parts of Asia, is if anything worse. Countries in these regions risk falling farther and farther behind the rest of the world economically and their people left not only in extreme poverty but also with an abiding sense of hopelessness. Because its benefits are spread so unevenly within and among countries, economic growth alone remains an insufficient condition for the eradication of poverty.

A Decade of Uneven Progress

During the 1990s, poverty declined as a share of the global population. Three factors dampened any budding optimism that the war on poverty would soon be won.

First, by subscribing to a dollar a day as the threshold of escape from poverty, the world community was making a statement more about global political conditions than a meaningful standard of living. Even if everyone on the planet cleared that bar, it would be ludicrous to claim anything other than that poverty, monetary as well as nonmonetary, persisted.

Second, while poverty rates declined impressively in some regions, notably East Asia, it remained stagnant elsewhere. Third, the absolute number of people in poverty remained unacceptably high due to rapid population growth.

While victory over poverty was conceivable, it remained doubtful that the war would be won by the end of the 21st century.

Unless some things changed…

_____

ENDNOTES

1. Nathan Associates, Inc. (2002a) 1.
2. World Bank (1993).
3. Krugman, Paul (1994).
4. Quibria, M.G. (2002) 5.
5. Ibid.: 79.
6. Soubbotina, Tatyana P. with Katherine A. Sheram (2000) 22.
7. Christensen, John (2000).
8. Ibid.
9. Because of overall population growth, the *proportion* of people outside of China living in extreme poverty dropped from 22.8 percent in 1990 to 18.6 percent in 2000. [My calculations, using World Bank data.]
10. World Bank (2002(a)) 11. Poverty is operationalized as living on less than one dollar a day as measured using the 1993 purchasing power parity index.
11. United Nations (July 2002) 4.
12. U.S. General Accounting Office (1996).
13. Narayan, Deepa and Patti Petesch, editors (January 2002) 182. This is Volume III in the World Bank's *Voices of the Poor* series.
14. World Bank (1990).
15. World Bank, Operations Evaluation Department (2002(a)) 1.
16. See www.globalpolicy.org/socecon/bwi-wto/wbank/2001/9410wap.htm.
17. New York Times, July 7, 2000. Also, see Bottelier, Pieter (Winter 2001).
18. See http://www.worldbank.org/html/extdr/am98/jdw-sp. The speech was titled "The Other Crisis."
19. This is a reorientation of what has been called the extended facility. The extended facility was created in September 1974 as a way to provide longer term financial support to members with endemic balance of payments problems. It gave their governments an

opportunity to address internal structural factors like production and terms of trade. Hooke, A.W. (1982) 44.

20. One critic, U.S. Representative Jim Saxton (Republican — New Jersey), Vice Chairman of the Joint Economic Committee in the U.S. Congress, contends that the broadened role of the IMF "could undermine its ability to act swiftly in a crisis." See "IMF Reform Push Is Welcomed," press release 108-120, April 27, 2004, Joint Economic Committee, Congress of the United States.

21. U.S. General Accounting Office (2001(b)) 3-4.

22. Op. cit. 6.

23. The members of the G-7 are Canada, France, Italy, Germany, Japan, United Kingdom and the United States. On the occasions when Russia participates, the group is referred to as the G-8.

24. In 1996, forty-one countries were classified as HIPCs. These included thirty-two with a per capita GNP of $695 or less and a debt-to-exports ratio of above 3.2 or debt-to-GNP ratio of 80 percent or more. Nigeria in 1998 and Equatorial Guinea in 1999 no longer met these criteria. Nigeria was replaced by Malawi, leaving a total of forty. See U.S. General Accounting Office (2000) 11.

25. Committee on International Relations, U.S. House of Representatives, and Committee on Foreign Relations, U.S. Senate. (June 2001).

26. The campaign has been succeeded by a permanent organization, Jubilee Research, which monitors the HIPC initiative and continues to press for complete debt cancellation in poor countries. Within the United Kingdom, the Jubilee Debt Campaign, a coalition of local and regional groups and national organizations, aims at changing its government's policy on debt to insure that the nation's influence is brought to bear on the World Bank and International Monetary Fund (IMF). See Greenhill, Romilly and Ann Pettifor (Jubilee Research); Henry Northover (CAFOD); and Ashok Sinha (Jubilee Debt Campaign) (2003).

27. U.S. General Accounting Office (2002) 17. The World Bank assumes that the ten countries will have export rates over the next twenty years that on average are more than double what they have achieved in the previous twenty.

28. U.S. General Accounting Office (2002) 6. According to the GAO's analysis, if grants replaced half of future multilateral loans, four of the ten countries would have favorable debt-to-export ratios for twenty years and two would be similarly debt sustainable for most of that period. The ten countries in the study were Benin, Bolivia, Burkina-Faso, Ethiopia, Mali, Mozambique, Nicaragua, Tanzania, Uganda and Zambia.

29. Bayliss, Kate (2002) 3. U.S. General Accounting Office (2000) and (2001(b)). The seven countries were Bolivia, Honduras, Mauritania, Mozambique, Nicaragua, Tanzania and Uganda.

30. United Nations Conference on Trade and Development (2002) 160.

31. World Bank (2001(a)) 23-24. Global population growth is slowing but the number of people added to the world's population each year remains large — approximately 90 million people. This means ever increasing demand for food, shelter, energy, and employment at a minimum. Population growth rates are highest in poor countries, that is, those that are least equipped to meet this rising demand. See Australian Agency for International Development (1997) 57.

32. U.S. General Accounting Office (2000) 81.

33. Collier, Paul and David Dollar (1999) 23.

34. Swaroop, Vinaya (1998) 1. The following treatment of fungibility benefited from the literature review and discussion contained in this draft paper.

35. U.S. General Accounting Office (1983) 76.

36. Organization for Economic Cooperation and Development (2001) 44-49.

37. For more, see www.nepad.org/en.html.

38. These prior efforts include the Lagos Plan for Action (1980-2000), African Priority Programme for Economic Recovery (1986-1990), Industrial Development Decade for Africa (IDDA), and United Nations Transport and Communications Decade for Africa (1978-1988).

39. United States Government (2002) 21.

40. Ibid.

41. Oxfam International (2003) 18.

42. All this is captured succinctly in an article in the Financial Times, July 3, 2001 by William Easterly headlined "the Failure of Development."

43. Burnside, Craig and David Dollar (1997).

44. As articulated in 1989 by John Williamson, the Washington Consensus was a set of ten policy prescriptions that revolved largely around macroeconomic discipline, a market economy, and openness to trade and foreign direct investment. The context involved preparation for a conference on the extent to which economic reforms had taken hold in Latin America. Williamson is senior economist at the Institute for International Economics. His view is that the Washington Consensus has wrongly been tagged as "neoliberal," since his list intentionally did not include such quintessential neoliberal ideas as capital account liberalization monetarism, supply-side economics, or a minimalist role for the state in social welfare. Rather it was geared to the situation in a specific region (Latin America) at a specific time (1989). See his remarks before the Center for Strategic and International Studies, November 6, 2002, which can be found at www.iie.com/papers/williamson1102.htm.

45. Hansen, Henrik and Finn Tarp (2000). Also, see United Nations Conference on Trade and Development (2002) 218.

46. Since 1987, "sustainable development" has become the mantra for international development policy. In 1987 the Norwegian Prime Minister Gro Harlan Brundtland chaired the World Commission on Environment and Development (the Brundtland Commission). The Commission's report, *Our Common Future*, defined sustainable development as that which "meets the needs of the present without compromising the ability of future generations to meet their own needs." See World Commission on Environment and Development (1987) 89.

47. See U.S. General Accounting Office (2001(c)) 45-46 and Centre for Aid and Public Expenditure (2000).

48. European Network on Debt and Development (2001 (a)).

49. United Nations General Assembly (July 2, 2001) A/CONF.191/12.

50. World Bank (2004) 120.

51. Oxfam Canada, the first of the international group of Oxfams, had started up in 1963.

52. The twelve members are found in Australia, Belgium, Canada, Germany, Hong Kong, Ireland, the Netherlands, New Zealand, Quebec, Spain, United Kingdom and United States.

53. Other international organizations played a significant role as well. The UN's World Food Program headed off starvation both during the flight to refugee camps in 1994 and during a mass movement back into Rwanda two years later.

54. The eleven member organizations are located in Australia, Austria, Canada, Denmark, Germany, France, Japan, Netherlands, Norway, United Kingdom, and United States.

55. www.wvi.org/wvi/about_us.

56. Catholic Relief Services (2003) 6.

57. World Bank (1994) 54.

58. Yunus, Muhammad (1999) 143. In 1993 Yunus did accept a $2 million World Bank grant for the Grameen Trust to support replications of the micro-lending program in other countries.

59. Ibid.:145.

60. Consultative Group to Assist the Poorest (2000) 10.

61. Committee on International Relations, U.S. House of Representatives, and Committee on Foreign Relations, U.S. Senate. (June 2001).

62. The history of ACCION relies largely on www.accion.org.

63. See www.fao.org.

64. Food and Agriculture Organization (2002).

65. The *World Food Summit: Five Years Later*, held in Rome, June 10-13, 2002, and attended by delegations from 179 countries and the European Commission, reaffirmed the commitments made at the 1996 gathering. Participants noted obstacles like insufficient water supplies, lack of access to technology, inadequate investment, depletion of natural resources, and lack of political will. One encouraging outcome was the addition of forty-five signatures on the International Treaty on Plant Genetic Resources for Food and Agriculture, bringing the total to fifty-six countries plus the European Community. The treaty aims at conservation of plant genetic resources.

66. International Fund for Agricultural Development (1993).

67. See www.ifad.org.

68. United Nations (1995) Commitment 2.

69. For more on the history of Social Watch, see www.socwatch.org.uy.

70. World Alliance of YMCAs. May 9-13, 2000. *Minutes of the 47th Meeting of the Executive Committee*. Geneva Park Conference Centre, Canada.

71. Easterly, William (2000) 2.

72. United Nations Development Programme (1999) 6.

73. See chapter by Martin Khor in Anderson, Sarah, editor (2000) 11.

74. More precisely, the standard adopted by the World Bank's standard is US$1 a day, first based on the 1985 purchasing power parity index, then later modified and updated using the 1993 index. The purchasing power parity index takes the value of a country's gross domestic product and converts it into U.S. dollars after making adjustments for price variations among countries in what they pay for equivalent goods and services.

75. Nobel prizewinning economist Joseph Stiglitz has stated that in government "openness is most essential in those realms where expertise seems to matter most. If the IMF and Treasury had invited greater scrutiny, their folly might have become much clearer, much earlier." *The New Republic*, April 17, 2000.

76. World Bank (2002(b)) 59. Annex E. Years are fiscal years.

77. Joint dissenting views of Commission members C. Fred Bergsten, Director, Institute for International Economics; Richard Huber, former Chairman, President and CEO, Aetna, Inc.; Jerome Levinson, former General Counsel, Inter-American Development Bank; and Esteban Edward Torres, U.S. House of Representatives, 1983-99.

78. This and the previous paragraphs in this section draw heavily on World Bank, Operations Development Department (Spring 2000).

79. In my opinion, projects funded by the World Bank and other donors, both bilateral and multilateral, should be treated (and funded) as demonstrations. They should be evaluated rigorously, using experimental or, if necessary, quasi-experimental research designs. In the allocation of aid resources, evaluation should have a higher priority than direct service delivery.

Why? Because ultimately poverty reduction depends not on the continuous infusion of external aid but on the recipient country's ownership of appropriate policies and programs. Developing countries can deliver services but lack the resources and often the political will to fund project evaluations on such a scale. Hence the actual project results and the factors accounting for them are endlessly and inconclusively debated.

Rigorous evaluation, which is expensive and time-consuming, can sort out the degree to which donor-supported projects account for reductions in poverty rates relative to other factors. It addresses the "but for" issue. Evaluation of a successful project shows the extent to which, but for the project, the outcomes would have been less satisfactory.

Insofar as a project's unique contributions can be demonstrated unambiguously, the recipient country will have an incentive to adapt the project design to conditions elsewhere. Getting to that point requires donors to concentrate their resources on fewer, better-designed and rigorously evaluated projects and programs.

80. Organization for Economic Co-operation and Development, Development Assistance Committee (May 1996).

81. The 23 members with date of membership in parentheses are Australia (1966), Austria (1965), Belgium (1961), Canada (1961), Denmark (1963), Finland (1975), France (1961), Germany (1961), Greece (1999), Ireland (1985), Italy (1961), Japan (1961), Luxembourg (1992), Netherlands (1961), New Zealand (1973), Norway (1962), Portugal (1961, withdrew1974, rejoined 1991), Spain (1991), Sweden (1965), Switzerland (1968), United Kingdom (1961), United States (1961), Commission of the European Communities (1961).

82. World Bank (2001(a)) 36 Table 2.2.

83. Ibid. 38. The ten favored countries were China, Brazil, Mexico, Argentina, Malaysia, Poland, Chile, Republic of Korea, Thailand and Venezuela.

84. The countries are Algeria, Angola, Benin, Bolivia, Brazil, Burundi, Cambodia, Cape Verde, China, Colombia, Côte d'Ivoire, Cuba, Egypt, Ghana, Guyana, Honduras, India, Indonesia, Iran, Iraq, Jamaica, Jordan, Korea D.P.R., Libya, Malawi, Malaysia, Mali, Micronesia, Morocco, Mozambique, Namibia, Nigeria, Pakistan, Panama, Philippines, Serbia and Montenegro, Seychelles, Sierra Leone, South Africa, Sri Lanka, Sudan, Suriname, Tanzania, Uganda, Vietnam, and Zimbabwe.

85. The summit conferences have occurred in 1961, 1964, 1970, 1973, 1976, 1979, 1983, 1986, 1989, 1992, 1995 and 1998. With the end of the Cold War and the breakup of the Soviet Union, "non-alignment" as a political construct has meant less. The movement has endeavored to reorient itself in a significantly altered global environment.

86. See Japan, Ministry of Foreign Affairs (2000).

87. At the end of 2002, the member countries were Bangladesh, China, Colombia, Egypt, The Gambia, India, Indonesia, Jordan, Kenya, Mali, Mexico, Morocco, Nigeria, Pakistan, Thailand, Tunisia, Uganda, Yemen and Zimbabwe.

88. Economic Commission for Latin America and the Caribbean (2002) 76.

89. Canadian Foundation for the Americas (FOCAL) (2001) 3.

90. Lustig, Nora and Ruthanne Deutsch (1998) i., 3-5.

8

Millennium Scorecard (2001-   )

Evaluation of Development Assistance

"Despite the billions of dollars spent on development assistance each year," states a World Bank publication, " there is still very little known about the actual impact of projects on the poor."[1]

This indictment, refreshing for its succinctness and honesty, speaks volumes. Forget the rhetoric on both sides of the aid question. We simply do not know the extent to which donor-subsidized interventions targeted to the poor in particular places at particular times have in fact reduced poverty.

Evaluation is expensive and time-consuming. It draws scarce resources away from direct service provision. Such factors are often cited as reasons for not evaluating projects.

Yet a case can be made that *every* project funded by external donors, whether bilateral or multilateral, should be seen as a demonstration and should therefore be evaluated rigorously. The reason is that sustaining and replicating projects most often falls to recipient country governments. They are more likely to do so when they have confidence in the project's potential for success.

The investment of time and resources going forward makes no sense unless there is a good chance of a social dividend. However, developing countries are less likely to have the evaluation research capabilities let alone sufficient resources for full-fledged impact evaluation.

The expansion of a program from demonstration status to ongoing can lead to a diminution in quality. Hence, even favorable evaluations of a demonstration program may not guarantee equivalent success when they are mounted on a large scale. More obviously, it makes little sense to expand a program in which controlled evaluation of a small-scale version shows little impact.

With increasing emphasis on independent, third-party evaluation, the World Bank is building a more scientifically-grounded knowledge base of successes, failures and lessons learned.[2]

For example, Argentina's TRABAJAR (To Work) Program, which began in 1996, is designed to create employment opportunities for the poor, who improve community infrastructures through their labor. Evaluation indicates that participants experience net income gains relative to comparison groups. However, performance has varied among Argentina's provinces.[3]

Take another example. After China and India, Bangladesh has the world's third largest population of people in poverty. For some individuals, microfinance programs offer an alternative to their dependence on private lenders, who often charge exorbitant interest rates and pursue defaulters ruthlessly. The microfinance programs of the Grameen Bank, Bangladesh Rural Advancement Committee, and Bangladesh Rural Development Board have served over four million clients in Bangladesh and been widely emulated by other countries and international institutions.

A World Bank 1991-1992 survey of eighty-seven villages and eighteen hundred households indicated that apparent gains in per capita consumption are due largely to mistargeting. Some 20-30 percent of loan recipients owned more land (and hence were less poor) than was permitted under the eligibility requirements.

It can be argued that even so the loans were made to groups that would not receive attention from the formal banking system. Whatever the merits of that argument, the evaluation findings underscore the need to verify how a program with claimed successes is actually functioning.[4]

Accurate targeting in economic and social development programs is often difficult to achieve. Bolivia's Social Investment Fund, established in 1991, provides sustainable investment in sectors like education, health care and sanitation. It has led to improvements in health care infrastructure and equipment, school achievement test scores, and access to water. There has been less success in improving school attendance and water quality.

The program is intended to benefit previously neglected poor communities but in fact is demand-driven. The communities that request assistance are not necessarily the poorest. Nonetheless, with a generally impressive track record, this innovative program has been a model for others in Latin America, Africa and Asia.[5]

Evaluation findings like these provide information on the net gains from particular programs and changes needed in program design and administration to improve performance. They also raise more basic questions over how much aid should go to particular types of programs and what might realistically be expected as a result of such aid.

Less successful has been Kenya's National Extension Project, begun in 1983. It relies on training and visits (T&V) in providing agricultural extension services. The World Bank evaluation determined that service provision was unsatisfactory with little impact on farm efficiency and productivity. The evaluation recommended a more diverse approach to the delivery of services, administrative decentralization and a focus on cost recovery.[6]

Despite widespread internal agreement on the importance of infrastructure in developing countries, the data on the impact of projects like roads, dams, power generation facilities and the like on poverty is surprisingly limited. An evaluation of the Vietnam Rural Roads Projects, which is still in progress, is aimed at remedying this problem, as the country shifts to a market economy.[7]

On a broader scale, economic and social development programs rely on the delivery of services to alleviate poverty. The services are intended to undergird the efforts of poor people and poor communities to help themselves. A hand up, not a handout.

Despite the good intentions, a dependency relationship between service providers and recipients can arise. There are endemic problems with program design, implementation and ongoing administration. Over time individuals in local communities can gain leadership and management skills.

Nonetheless, under a services approach, progress against global poverty will be incremental, not to say excruciatingly slow, at best.

The Goal of Aid Convergence

The United Nations, World Bank, International Monetary Fund, G-7/G-8, Organization for Economic Cooperation and Development, and regional development banks have signed on to the goal of global poverty reduction. They and individual donors are taking steps to harmonize their poverty reduction policies.

For example, the European Commission, which executes decisions of the European Union, has worked out co-financing guidelines with the World Bank and established regular high-level contacts with various United Nations agencies.[8] The European Union and its member states provide more than half of the international aid to developing countries.

The activities of donor governments and private humanitarian organizations have converged around the Millennium Development Goals. Increasingly international aid agencies are conducting crosscutting antipoverty policy analyses, sharing information and resources, and making their decisional processes more transparent.

At the same time, recipient countries are demanding a greater say in the selection and operation of aid projects and seeking to integrate them into broader economic development strategies. At the United Nations, there are proposals to establish a World Solidarity Fund.

Non-governmental, non-profit public and voluntary organizations have acquired official status at the United Nations. Based on Article 71 of the United

Nations Charter and ECOSOC Resolution 1996/31, adopted in 1996, such organizations may apply for consultative status with the UN's Economic and Social Council.

Representatives of qualifying organizations serve as technical experts, advisers and consultants to the UN Secretariat and individual member governments. They participate in international conferences, special sessions of the General Assembly and other gatherings. Many organizations use these opportunities to advocate for the interests of the world's poorest people.

As of 2004, there were 2,418 non-governmental organizations in consultative status with the Economic and Social Council (ECOSOC) and some 400 accredited to a subsidiary body, the Commission on Sustainable Development.

Acting singly or as members of coalitions, non-governmental organizations advocate on behalf of the poor at the World Bank, International Monetary Fund, World Trade Organization and European Union.

For example, in 2002, Oxfam International established an office in Geneva to advocate with the World Trade Organization (WTO) on trade policies and practices that benefit poor nations. More broadly, Oxfam works with like-minded organizations to strengthen the voice of civil society on such issues as trade, sustainable development, debt relief and monetary and fiscal policy.

The outlines of a new and more focused war on poverty appear more distinct. It does not come without constraints. The desired coordination among aid agencies, public and private, is difficult insofar as each pursues its own agenda and each wants a set of conditions reflecting that agenda included in any crosscutting program of assistance.

Non-governmental organizations that receive funding—and seek refunding—from budget-conscious aid agencies face new pressures to show quantifiable results sooner rather than later. This flies in the face of their traditional strength, namely investment in the building of long-term community-level capacity, an inevitably slow and not easily measured process.

With demands for accountability and operating efficiency, non-governmental organizations may be pushed toward greater professionalization, even bureaucratization, at the expense of a more charismatic commitment to their core missions.[9]

Developing countries are forced to give evidence of good governance and their capacity to use outside aid effectively. Evaluation of policy and program effectiveness is becoming embedded in the aid process.

At best, given all these circumstances, the progress in the war on global poverty will be modest and spotty at best.

Skeptics on the Right

The growing influence of non-governmental organizations has not gone unremarked in some conservative circles, particularly in the United States. In the conservative view, international non-governmental organizations, while doing valuable work in assaulting poverty and other global evils, have come to function like unelected quasi-governments.

Their policies are seen as reflecting a liberal international agenda that, at its core, is enamored of global governance. Conservatives groups perceive an NGO bias against free markets, transnational corporations and U.S. foreign policy.[10]

This tension is likely to persist. Whereas the governments of developed countries seek to promote trade and investment abroad, international non-governmental organizations—which often receive funding from their governments—tend to espouse humanitarian values. Depending on the degree and style of their activism in pursuit of these values, the latter may be portrayed by their critics as overtly political on issues like trade and human rights.

Fortunately, international non-governmental organizations retain a high level of public trust. So far this has enabled them (and, more importantly, their in-country personnel) to operate for the most part in poor, conflict-ridden countries without being identified as instruments for or against the interests of foreign governments or corporations.[11]

A Multiplicity of Mandates

Within most individual donor countries, aid to developing countries rarely achieves high priority status. Bilateral aid agencies often lack stature within the overall complex of government institutions. Aid agencies may be deluged with a wide range of legislatively imposed objectives rather than operating with a clear mandate to help reduce global poverty.

Aid is often tied to requirements that recipients purchase goods and services from the donor. This can distort the development process. Recipients may feel compelled to purchase lower priority goods and services from the donor rather than higher priority goods and services from other sources.

The question of fungibility clouds any assessment of aid effectiveness. In the absence of donor aid a government may have used its own resources for a particular public good. When aid is proffered, the government can free up those resources for another spending priority (for example, defense) or even tax reduction. This is not necessarily an adverse outcome; however, it means that donor aid is serving other government purposes rather than a designated good.

At one extreme, if the donor's aid completely substitutes for what the government would have spent on that good, the government can shift its resources to another good, which thereby indirectly (and unknowingly) is financed by the donor. Such scenarios make it hard to evaluate the net return on the donor's investment.

Furthermore, if donor aid diverts domestic resources away from a designated good, what happens when the donor's aid ceases? There is risk to the sustainability of the good.

In theory it is possible for donors to require as a condition of assistance that recipients maintain the level and allocation of expenditures that preceded the availability of aid. That maintenance of effort can then be monitored to make sure that donor aid represented a net addition for the designated good. In reality this is easier said than done.

Government budgeting anywhere in the world often seems like a mix of art, science and alchemy. The budgetary, financial management and banking systems of some developing countries are unsophisticated. Complete and accurate data are notoriously hard to come by. Fungibility in accounts can appear in the most unexpected ways. For developing countries with multiple donors, the opportunities for fungibility increase.

An alternative is for donors, both bilateral and multilateral, to become more deeply enmeshed in accounting, budgeting, and financial management system reforms. Donors support institutional and administrative reforms at the national level rather than discrete community-based projects. Donor assistance for community-based projects comes in the form of policy advice and technical assistance rather than hard cash.

The extent to which developing countries and poor communities within those countries endorse such a strategic shift in the provision of aid remains to be seen. The World Bank's public expenditure reform loans to countries like Ecuador, Guatemala, Jordan, Mauritius, and Turkey among others serve as test cases. Whether the poor will see benefits from these reforms in the near term or must wait (and hope) for them to trickle down eventually remains to be seen.

Rich Countries

Twenty-two highly developed nations comprise the membership of the Development Assistance Committee of the Organization for Economic Cooperation and Development.[12] The Committee provides a forum for bilateral donors to improve the effectiveness of their aid. Acting as a virtual secretariat, the OECD's Development Cooperation Directorate provides staff support for the Committee.

For its members, the Development Assistance Committee periodically issues revised guidelines to foster greater coherence and joint effectiveness in poverty reduction strategies. In 2001, the Committee recommended that official development assistance to the least developed countries be untied.

In other words, donors would provide aid without imposing conditions in such areas as the recipient's balance of payments, structural adjustment, debt forgiveness, sector targeting, investment project aid, import and commodity support, commercial services contracts and aid to non-governmental organizations for procurement related activities.

The recommendation was aimed at promoting a sense of partnership between donor and developing countries and giving the latter greater ownership over the development process.[13] The amount of development aid rose in 2002, reversing a prior downward trend. The 2002 amount was almost $57.0 billion, a 4.8 percent increase in real terms. The aid figure equates to 0.23 per cent of the donors' aggregate gross national product.[14]

Along with North America and Japan, the European Union has emerged as one of the three most prosperous areas of the world. According to the *Laeken Declaration—The Future of the European Union*, December 15, 2001, the members aspire to "benefit not just the rich countries but also the poorest" and to anchor globalization in a moral framework, one that promotes "solidarity and sustainable development."[15] Currently its member states in aggregate provide approximately half of the world's official development assistance.

In many rich countries, there are separate government departments for aid policy. Not infrequently the aid agency is a world unto itself, delinked from broader foreign policy concerns. As the government of the Netherlands has recognized, the distinction between foreign policy and development cooperation is less meaningful in a globalizing environment. Development policy can contribute to stability, peace building and security. And vice versa.[16]

Least Developed Countries

The least developed countries as recognized by the United Nations are characterized by extreme poverty that is persistent and pervasive. Life expectancy, per capita calorie consumption, school enrollment and adult literacy are all low.[17]

Increased awareness of the special needs of these countries has triggered changes among donor countries and multilateral institutions. Many target the least developed countries with a greater share of official development assistance.

Poverty in the least developed countries is related to their ability to accumulate capital, modernize governmental structures, improve productivity, diversify their economies and generate jobs. At the same time, because so many of these countries depend on single commodity exports, direct foreign investment and external donor assistance, they cannot be examined apart from global economic trends.

Over the past forty years the average per capita income in the least developed countries has diverged from that of the world's twenty richest countries. In 1960, per capita income in the richest countries was eleven times higher than per capita income in the least developed countries. By 1999, it was nineteen times higher. In relation to the subgroup of least developed countries that relied on exporting commodities other than oil, it reached *thirty-five* times higher.[18]

This is due in part to a long-term downward spiral in the prices of non-fuel commodities since 1960, most notably for items like cotton and coffee and grains.[19] Mergers and acquisitions have tended to concentrate control over prices in the hands of a smaller number of global enterprises. With information technologies, buyers and sellers can communicate more easily and quickly with each other, thereby crowding out middlemen.

As of December 2003, there were fifty least developed countries. Of these, 34 are in Africa, seven in Asia, seven are Pacific Island nations; finally, there is Yemen in the Middle East and Haiti in the Western Hemisphere. These countries have a combined population of 614 million people or 10.5 percent of the world's population.[20]

Table 4. Per Capita Gross Domestic Product for Selected LDCs, United States and World (2001)

Country*	Per Capita GDP**
Afghanistan***	$800
Burundi	600
Comoros	710
Democratic Republic of the Congo	590
Eritrea	740
Ethiopia	700
Guinea-Bissau	900
Kiribati	840
Madagascar	870
Malawi	660
Mali	840
Mozambique	900
Niger	820
Sierra Leone	500
Somalia	550
Tanzania	610
United States of America	36,300
World	7,600

*LDCS are selected based on estimated per capita GDP < $1000.
**Per capita GDP estimates are based on purchasing power parity (PPP) calculations.
***Estimate is for 2000.
Source: U.S. Central Intelligence Agency (2002)

The least developed countries make up thirty-two of the lowest thirty-five countries in the United Nations' Human Development Index. The average life expectancy in the least developed countries is fifty-one years, compared to seventy-eight years for members of the Organization for Economic Cooperation and Development.

Furthermore, 15 percent of children born in the least developed countries die before their fifth birthday. The group contains countries with the lowest literacy rates, lowest primary school enrollment rates and widest gender disparities in education.[21]

Of Income Inequality and Land Reform

Global income inequality is distressing. In 1970, the incomes of the richest 10 percent of the world's population were 19.4 times greater than the poorest 10 percent. By 1997, this ratio had risen to 26.9 to 1.[22]

In Brazil, in 1960 half the population received 18 percent of the country's income; by 1995, that had fallen to 11.6 percent. In 1997, at exchange rate conversions, the combined wealth of the world's 225 richest people exceeded one trillion dollars. This was about equal to the combined income of the poorest 47 percent of the world's population, about 2.5 billion people.[23]

The world's poverty population is predominantly rural and the risk of poverty is greatest for the landless. For several decades following the end of the Second World War, newly independent and other developing countries placed great stock in land reform. The goal was to provide ownership rights to small and marginal farmers and greater protection for tenants on large landholdings.

In the 1990s, there was a shift in favor of large-scale corporate farming. This diminished the impetus for traditional land reform and weakened enforcement of existing laws on land ceilings and tenant security. During the period of India's Ninth Five-Year Plan (1997-2002), little progress was made in detecting concealed surplus land for redistribution to the landless poor.

A ban on tenancy in some Indian States (Uttar Pradesh, Bihar and Orissa) has in fact hurt tenants, who are not recognized as such and therefore do not qualify for tenure or rent regulation. In a reversal of traditional practice, large commercial farms are leasing land from small and marginal farm families.[24]

Worldwide, patterns of semi-feudal agriculture persist in many areas while commercial and corporate farming expands elsewhere. These patterns exist within as well as among countries. Efforts to rectify inequities in land ownership are affected by the major changes in the agrarian economy over the past three decades. Non-farm wage employment, microcredit and rural enterprise development play a growing role in rural poverty reduction.

From the Richest to the Least Developed

In fiscal year 2002, the World Bank Group made $19.5 billion in loans to its client countries. It works in over one hundred economies, bringing a mix of finance and ideas to improve living standards and eliminate the worst forms of poverty. For each of its clients, the Bank collaborates with government agencies, non-governmental organizations, and the private sector.

Official development assistance from the world's twenty richest countries dropped from $53.7 billion in 2000 to $51.4 billion in 2001. The ratio of official development assistance to gross national product for the members of OECD's Development Assistance Committee stood at 0.22 percent, far below the internationally agreed-on target of 0.7 percent.

For the United States, the figure was 0.1 percent.[25] The United States government perceives a link between poverty and terrorism. It is not that poor people are more likely to become terrorists (they are not; terrorists tend to be well-educated members of the middle class). Rather it is that poor countries more easily function as safe havens for terrorist organizations.

In 2001, the United States provided $11 billion in official development assistance. However that figure understates its impact on the global development process. In the 1997-200 period, U.S. private capital investment in developing countries averaged $36 billion a year.

In 2000, U.S. private charitable donations to developing countries were $4 billion. In 2001, U.S. food and other humanitarian assistance totaled $2.5 billion. For the 2002-2003 period, the U.S. contribution to multilateral development banks is $1.4 billion.[26]

As a factor in the global war on poverty, U.S. aid has been weighed down by "larger" geopolitical concerns and multiple overlapping, even contradictory, objectives. Funds are targeted disproportionately to a small number of countries, notably Israel and Egypt. Aid administration is cumbersome. Many individual projects have registered success but the global antipoverty effectiveness of U.S. assistance remains at least debatable.

The terrorist assault on September 11, 2001 has influenced the attitude and the approach of the United States to global development and poverty reduction. President George W. Bush has proposed the creation of a Millennium Challenge Account. It would be administered by a government corporation and by 2006 would be funded annually at $5 billion. This would represent a 50 percent increase over current U.S. aid levels.

If implemented as advertised, the new Millennium Challenge Account would focus on meeting the development needs of a select number of countries. Those countries would become eligible for assistance if they showed evidence of acting in accordance with three main criteria: governing justly, investing in people, and encouraging economic freedom. Their performance would be measured by a set of sixteen indicators related to these criteria. See Appendix 1.

While the Millennium Challenge Account is a promising new initiative, it is dwarfed by larger geopolitical factors. As signified by the September 11, 2001 assault on the United States, terrorism represents a threat not only to global security but also to global prosperity and poverty reduction. Resources are increasingly reallocated toward anti-terrorism programs and away from investment. The wars waged by the United States and other partner countries in Afghanistan and Iraq have added new uncertainties to global economic prospects.

The World Bank's Boundaries

The World Bank's expressed goal is to reduce poverty by promoting sustainable economic development. The World Bank's 2000/2001 World Development Report, *Attacking Poverty* promotes a framework of opportunity, empowerment and security for alleviating poverty.[27]

As of June 30, 2002, of its 184 member country shareholders, the five largest were the United States, which has 16.4 percent of total voting power, followed by Japan with 7.9 percent, Germany with 4.5 percent, France with 4.3 percent and United Kingdom with 4.3 percent.[28]

Since its inception, the World Bank has financed some four thousand projects in one hundred thirty countries and lent over $300 billion. Debt issued by the World Bank has been rated AAA since 1959.[29]

Like other international development organizations, the World Bank suffers from a profusion of goals. It began as a bank to aid in post-war economic recovery. It evolved into more of a development agency with the trappings of a bank. It embraced poverty reduction as a test of true development.

More recently it has espoused the notion of a Comprehensive Development Framework. Along with traditional concerns for economic stability and growth, this incorporates a number of social goals, including gender equity, sustainable growth, good governance, population planning, education, and trade.

As a result the Bank has had "no clear demarcation around its appropriate zone of work."[30] As an illustration, take the thirteenth replenishment of resources for the International Development Association.[31] The policy priorities for poverty reduction read more like an inventory than a strategy.

Process in Lieu of Progress?

For poverty reduction strategies, the process associated with the Bank's concessional assistance emphasizes country ownership; government transparency and accountability in public expenditure management; anti-corruption initiatives; participation of the poor, civil society organizations and other affected parties in poverty reduction planning; donor coordination; and measurable outcomes.

In more substantive terms, reduction in poverty rates is seen as the result of actions along a large (and, it seems, ever growing) number of fronts. A simple list is therefore not exhaustive, only exhausting. Poverty reduction is assumed to depend on increased spending—or "investment"—in many if not all of the following:

(a) education, with priority given to primary schooling and schooling for girls;

(b) health care, with emphasis on fighting communicable diseases like HIV/AIDS;

(c) social protection funds for adversities like poor health, natural disasters and economic downturns;

(d) labor force reforms, such as (prominently) elimination of child labor;

(e) legal reforms, including women's property rights;

(f) gender equity as a mainstream element in society;

(g) private sector development, through entrepreneurship and market access;

(h) rural development, through enterprise expansion and productivity gains;

(i) protection against natural resource degradation (like deforestation); and

(j) reduced worker exposure to environmental hazards (e.g. in mining).

The International Development Association's thirteenth replenishment strategy also highlights trade, both regional and global, as an engine of poverty reduction, noting that "poor countries that are more integrated with international markets have grown faster than others less integrated."[32]

Poverty reduction and overall development aid in post-conflict situations require a stable political and security framework. This entails collaboration between donors and the United Nations with the latter's special conflict resolution and peacekeeping expertise.

Finally, in the wake of the September 11, 2001 terrorist attack on the United States, the thirteenth replenishment provides for steps to combat terrorist money laundering and related financial abuse. This last provision indicates how newly identified needs and threats can expand the number of elements included under the rubric of global poverty reduction. All this is supposed to take place in a "framework of broad-based and equitable growth."[33]

There is nothing to quarrel with and much to admire in the preceding list, seen as a list. The problem is that, as a part of a global assault on poverty, every item seems to carry the same weight. There is not a hierarchy of objectives upon which to base funding and operational decisions.

A Question of Ownership

In the most heavily indebted poor countries, debt relief under HIPC is tied to the development of national poverty reduction strategy papers.
These papers set forth a country's policies, programs and financing needs to promote broad-based growth and reduce poverty.

Member countries prepare the papers through a participatory process involving domestic civil society organizations and international donors. The process is designed to assure country ownership over its poverty reduction strategy. As of January 2003, twenty-six countries had completed poverty reduction strategy papers and twenty-five had presented interim or status PRSP reports.[34]

A country's poverty reduction strategy paper is intended as the vehicle for articulating its internal development and antipoverty priorities. However, these papers are subject to review by the World Bank and increasingly, in the name of coordination, by other multilateral and bilateral donors. These external donors must satisfy the expectations of their own governments and other constituencies.[35]

Reflecting the dominant concerns of these entities, the poverty reduction strategy papers tend to emphasize economic stabilization policies over employment generation.[36] Poverty reduction is viewed as a necessary by-product of economic growth and macroeconomic stability.

A donor like the U.S. Agency for International Development, for example, may use its influence to foster economic policy reform and sustainable development strategies as the key to poverty reduction in contrast to more direct social service, job creation and income redistribution approaches that a developing country may prefer.

Developing country ownership over their poverty reduction strategies is therefore constrained by the ability of the World Bank and other donors to impose conditions on loans and grants that are geared more to donor demands than the recipient's priorities.

Within developing country governments, the ministries of finance or economy typically have the lead role in developing poverty reduction strategy papers, often without active involvement by other ministries like planning, industry, labor and agriculture. The influence of civil society organizations over the process and especially the content of the papers tends to be limited.[37]

Despite the very different economic and cultural contexts in which they are prepared, the papers as a group display more homogeneity than diversity or creativity in their approaches to poverty reduction.

The more that Bank funds are devoted to program or adjustment lending for macroeconomic reforms, the fewer the resources there are for more targeted antipoverty projects. During the 1990s, the Bank sought to ameliorate the adverse effects of this approach by steering its borrowers toward labor-intensive growth strategies and the maintenance of social services and safety nets.

The World Bank has in fact made adjustment loans that are explicitly poverty-focused. In 1999, three-quarters of the Bank's 48 adjustment lending projects were poverty-focused.[38]

Such loans assist borrower countries that redirect public expenditures more toward the poor, eliminate policies and regulations that impede the income-generating opportunities of the poor, and/or support social safety nets. However, the loans in effect co-opt recipient country ownership of the process.

Pure country ownership can be purchased only at the risk of being turned down for assistance from the Bank and other donors. To the extent that donor priorities hold sway, there is a risk of diverting poverty reduction programs away from the poor and in favor of other population subgroups.

The more multidimensional and multilateral the aid process becomes, the less possibility there is for recipient country ownership over its antipoverty strategy and the greater the risk that macroeconomic poverty will persist.

Donors tend to assume that poverty reduction in developing countries depends on several key elements. Among these are good governance reforms, human capacity building, HIPC-related debt relief, private capital investment and entrepreneurship, open markets, deregulation, and integration of social policies with overall development objectives. While donor coordination is desirable, it is secondary to a recipient country's focus on these elements.

In short, donors tend to place the responsibility for global poverty, including failed policies and bad management, within individual countries. Missing is sufficient emphasis on international economic relationships that themselves help perpetuate poverty conditions.

The fragmented aid system disrupts the ability of a developing country to efficiently deploy its available resources, whether domestic or foreign-born. The impact of a fragmented aid system and policy conditionality has eroded the governmental autonomy and capacity of developing countries and may have undermined prospects for economic growth and poverty reduction.

Despite efforts like the World Bank's Heavily Indebted Poor Countries initiative, the debt burden appears unlikely to go away any time soon. This has contributed to donor fatigue, as new aid goes to service old debt rather than poverty reduction initiatives. International capital lenders remain skittish about their prospects in poor, debt-ridden countries and therefore invest elsewhere.[39]

The IMF as an Antipoverty Organization

Many developed countries persist in subsidizing their own producers of certain commodities in competition with developing countries that rely disproportionately, in many cases exclusively, on precisely those commodities as exports and means of earning foreign exchange. Price fluctuations in these commodities over time have had an adverse impact on the economies of developing countries and their ability to earn foreign exchange.

The International Monetary Fund is responsible for ensuring the stability of the international financial system. It makes its financial resources available to its members through a variety of financial "facilities" or loan programs. The International Monetary Fund's regular facilities include Stand-By Arrangements; Extended Fund Facility; Supplemental Reserve Facility; Contingent Credit Lines; and Compensatory Financing Facility).

Beyond them it provides concessional assistance under the Poverty Reduction and Growth Facility and debt relief under the Heavily Indebted Poor Countries initiative. The International Monetary Fund also offers training and technical assistance to countries in the areas of institutional capacity-building, fiscal and monetary policy, statistics and macroeconomic and structural policy. As of June 30, 2002, it had some $88 billion credits and loans outstanding to 88 countries.

Private Sector Development Strategies

According to the Universal Declaration of Human Rights and many United Nations Conventions, people have a right to education, health and water services. To deliver such services, the World Bank has developed a Private Sector Development Strategy.

This reflects disenchantment with the performance of public sector agencies in developing countries and increased prominence of privatization as the preferred pathway to development. Private enterprise is promoted as the engine of jobs, investment and tax revenue, as well as a source of openness and innovation.

The strategy expands the role of the International Finance Corporation and Multilateral Investment Guarantee Agency, two bodies that deal directly with the private sector. The International Finance Corporation traditionally has made loans to and taken equity positions in large-scale private ventures like power plants.

The Multilateral Investment Guarantee Agency seeks to attract foreign investment to developing countries by insuring against non-commercial risks.

The Private Sector Development Strategy argues that governments with weak capacity should welcome the privatization of services, even if that approach entails higher costs.

However, such governments may lack capacity in regulation and oversight as well as service delivery. Privatization could foster unregulated monopolies for essential services. It could adversely affect labor rights, environmental protection and democratic consultative processes in favor of higher profit margins.

Poor people can benefit from privatization if it results in the availability of more goods and services at prices they can afford. Increased private investment can expand employment opportunities. However, the transitional costs can be significant. In the case of utilities like water and electricity, governments have tolerated access to service by non-payers and illegal connections. Privately run utilities may be less forgiving.[40]

At a World Trade Organization conference in Doha, Qatar in November 2001, trade ministers from 142 countries committed themselves to building an open and nondiscriminatory trading system with sensitivity to environmental effects. They agreed to launch a new World Trade Organization round—the Doha Development Agenda—covering further trade liberalization and new rule-making to support economic growth through trade in developing countries.[41]

This provided impetus for constructive forward movement. At the United Nations-sponsored International Conference on Financing for Development in Monterrey, Mexico, March 2002, several major donors agreed to increase their official development assistance. Lack of aid should not be a deterrent to achieving the Millennium Development Goals. The United States and the European Union committed themselves to aid that would total $12 billion annually by 2006.[42]

A subsequent round of global trade negotiations began in January 2002. For this new Doha Development Round, members of the World Trade Organization have set a deadline of January 2006 for completion of negotiations. High on the agenda is a comprehensive agreement on agriculture that lowers tariffs dramatically, expands quotas, eliminates export subsidies and reduces trade-distorting domestic support.

Other issues for Doha participants include the reduction of tariffs on industrial goods, liberalization of trade in the services sector, rules governing Trade-Related Intellectual Property Rights (TRIPS), standards for investment, and environmentally accurate product labeling.

In conjunction with the increased emphasis on the role of the private sector, concerns were voiced that the poor would continue to be marginalized unless growth strategies were adapted to their needs.

Pro-Poor Growth Strategies

Global growth has depended on large international capital flows and widespread adoption by businesses of advanced technologies including robotics, biotechnology and telecommunications. These in turn have fostered improvements in productivity, inventory management and quality control. Pro-poor growth instead favors "appropriate" (usually, the minimally required) technology and maximum use of available labor.

The notion of poverty as a function of unemployment may no longer fit the circumstances of a 21st century world. At a minimum there is uncertainty as to the long-term effects of employment-intensive programs on aggregate poverty alleviation.[43]

A country whose entire growth strategy is "pro-poor" risks falling behind one whose strategy is more capital- and technology-intensive. The notion of pro-poor growth, for example, usually implies a greater allocation of a country's resources to health care and education. A healthier and better-educated populace, it can be plausibly argued, will yield a more highly skilled and productive labor force. A key term is "will". The strategy is future-oriented.

As observed by Sir Arthur Lewis half a century ago, the process can be accelerated. Traditionally, skill development has entailed stages of education, training, and apprenticeship. The process has tended to lengthen as a given occupation comes under the control of a union, guild or professional society.

During World War II, when skill shortages had to be met rapidly, belligerent nations developed new training techniques. Compared to traditional training, people acquired essential skills "in as little as a quarter of the time."[44] Overcoming skill deficits in a developing economy may require less time and expense than often assumed.

Even so, increased spending on education and health care diverts resources from economic investment in public and private enterprise that could generate growth in the near term. Furthermore, such spending could be inflationary if the government has to borrow money to finance it. The country's annual deficit and overall debt level could increase unless there are additional revenues.

Expenditures on health care and education will reduce poverty only if these services are delivered effectively and in fact reach the poor. If they are spent on private schools and universities rather than public sector primary schools, or on urban-based tertiary hospitals rather than rural primary care clinics, the middle and upper income groups may benefit disproportionately and greater inequities may result.

It may happen that as a result of such pro-poor spending the poor do receive more schooling and better health care. This in turn would contribute to a more skilled and productive work force. However, this by itself is no guarantor of growth. In addition to labor, growth depends on other factors like land, capital, technology and markets. Without these factors, jobs for a more productive labor force will remain scarce.

Most countries that are eligible for concessional loans from the International Monetary Fund's Poverty Reduction Growth Facility have experienced low to negative growth rates over the past decade. Without commensurate job opportunities, a better-educated and more skilled but still unemployed labor force could be a source of social instability.[45]

Thus, a pro-poor growth strategy could have the opposite of the intended result. Does this possibility suggest that a more effective strategy is to *reduce* spending on education and health care? Of course not. Rather, it suggests that pro-poor strategies need to be crafted carefully to be sure that growth actually occurs and the poor actually benefit.

Social Safety Nets

Over half the absolute poor in the developing world live in South Asia. The area experienced strong economic growth in the latter half of the 1980s. While the percentage of the population in absolute poverty dropped by 2.8 percent in this period, the number of poor people rose by 30 million. "At this rate it would take South Asia almost a century to eradicate absolute poverty."[46]

Due to more uneven income distribution, poverty in China actually worsened in the latter half of the 1980s. In other regions either weaker economic growth, population increases or both led to increases in the number and percentages of people in poverty.[47]

To forestall such trends requires public spending on social safety nets that protect the most vulnerable members of society, whether the economy is expanding or contracting. This of course implies that maximum economic growth unfettered by other considerations is not the overriding goal.

In developing countries poverty is concentrated heavily in rural areas where many people lack skills, literacy and access to productive assets. Several decades of land reform initiatives have foundered in large part because of resistance by large landholders who wield the bulk of political and economic influence.

This suggests that fundamental land reform may not be politically feasible in many developing countries. Under one alternative approach land is redistributed in small but economically viable units without threatening those with large landholdings. Another alternative, for tenant and sharecroppers, involves assurance of fair land rents and security of tenure.

Beyond agriculture there are additional means for absorbing excess rural labor capacity while improving skill levels and raising incomes. These include the development of private agro-industries (e.g. fish farming, food processing plants) and expansion of public sector jobs programs in areas like road-building, water and waste water treatment systems, school construction and health center staffing.

With advances in mechanization, information and communications technologies, and biotechnology, agriculture in the future will make productivity gains possible in both developing and developed countries. In the former, the declining demand for farm labor accompanied by high population growth rates means that long-term solutions are required to avert a worsening poverty situation.

This has implications for both rural and urban areas. By 2025, it is anticipated that close to half (47 percent) of the population in developing countries will live in urban areas compared to 29 percent in 1995.[48] Clearly employment opportunities can come about only by expanding alternatives to agriculture, such as industrialization, service sector development, tourism and the building of infrastructure.

Combinations of private sector enterprise, both large and small-scale, with public sector employment to build infrastructures can be used to expand job opportunities for the urban poor as well.

If stable jobs paying a living wage are the key to self-sufficiency, then training in the skill sets required for those jobs is a critical mediating factor. Income of course matters only if needed goods and services can be purchased.

In the private sector this requires the availability of consumer goods and services at reasonable prices. For public services like safe drinking water, liquid and solid waste treatment facilities, and environmental protection, the form of "payment" can be taxes and user fees. Adequate food, housing, and health care in poor communities may require a mix of public and private interventions.

World Solidarity Fund

In December 2002, as one outcome of the World Summit on Sustainable Development, the United Nations General Assembly endorsed establishment of a World Solidarity Fund to combat poverty and finance development in the least developed countries. It is modeled on a National Solidarity Fund established in Tunisia.

Tunisia's National Solidarity Fund was created, December 8, 1992, by a presidential decision after visits by President Zine El Abidine Ben Ali to rural areas that lacked basic amenities like potable water, electricity, housing, health care, education, and roads.

Commonly called "26-26" after its postal account number, the Fund is financed by public and private sector organizations and Tunisian citizens. The Fund invested more than 546.7 million dinars (about $400 million) in various projects between 1993 and 2000. It focuses largely on employment, housing, health, education, culture and social integration. It is credited with having reduced poverty in Tunisia to about four percent within a few years.

The Tunisian experience was cited as a model human development program by the 1995 Copenhagen Summit and by the United Nations Development Programme. The new World Solidarity Fund for Poverty Eradication was created at the initiative of President Ben Ali. The administrator of the United Nations Development Programme, Mark Malloch Brown, voiced pleasure at the willingness of the United Nations "to try out this innovative mechanism worldwide."[49]

The World Solidarity Fund was established formally in February 2003 as a trust fund managed by the United Nations Development Programme. Projects supported by the Fund will emphasize access to drinking water; education and health services; access to national electrical grids; improvements in housing; road and track construction; and support for microfinance and microenterprise.

The Fund will be supervised by a "Committee of Wise Persons" composed of internationally renowned personalities, and entrusted with the task of elaborating the Fund's strategy and helping with the mobilization of its resources.

Performance, Not Just Promises

With the adoption of the Millennium Development Goals, the world had a way to measure progress in its war on poverty. The goals provided a framework within which antipoverty organizations of all types could seek to coordinate their efforts. However, even if all the goals were met, an unlikely prospect, poverty would persist well into and even beyond the century. The pace of progress under the most optimistic scenarios would be slow at best.

Goodwill was not lacking, nor were moves toward closer coordination between developing countries and international donors and investors. No, what was lacking was a new paradigm.

ENDNOTES

1. Baker, Judy L. (2000) vi.
2. In recent years the World Bank has been pressured by the U.S. Congress and other observers to improve its internal evaluation capacity and accept external audits of its overall performance. These critics contend that evaluation at the Bank is not disinterested and "hard-nosed". Bank employees from other units serve in the Operations Evaluation Department on a rotating basis. For advancement purposes, they have an incentive to make the Bank look as good as possible. Evaluation measures of impact are often based on subjective judgment calls rather than hard data.
3. Baker, Judy (2000): 94-100. TRABAJAR began in 1996, followed by an expanded TRABAJAR II in 1997 and TRABAJAR III in 1998. These findings refer to TRABAJAR II.
4. Ibid: 101-104. Technically any positive findings about the impact of the loans could be attributed to selection bias.
5. Ibid.: 109-113.
6. Ibid.: 77-78. The program has been controversial, as mirrored in disagreements over its impact between The World Bank's Operations Evaluation Department and the Bank's Africa Region Department.
7. Ibid.: 165-68.
8. European Commission (2002) 205.
9. Lindenberg, Marc and Coralie Bryant (2001) 18-22.

10. In 2003, the American Enterprise Institute and the Federalist Society for Law and Public Policy Studies created a website to monitor the funding and operations of non-governmental organizations. It aims "to bring clarity and accountability to the burgeoning world of NGSs..." See www.ngowatch.gov. Australia's Institute of Public Affairs is another prominent critic of the NGO world.

11. This situation may be changing. On October 27, 2003, an ambulance packed with explosives slammed into the Baghdad headquarters of the International Committee of the Red Cross, leaving twelve casualties and much physical devastation. This was one of four well-coordinated car bomb attacks that day on dispersed targets in Baghdad in which thirty-five people were killed and 230 wounded. Medecin Sans Frontieres (Doctors without Borders) charged that, in attacking Iraq, the United States-led coalition had tried to link the work of humanitarian relief organizations to its "war on terrorism." According to Medecins Sans Frontieres, such politicizing of independent international non-governmental organizations put the lives of their personnel at risk. See www.msf.org. Click on press releases for October 31, 2003.

12. The original (1961) members of the OECD are *Austria, Belgium, Canada, Denmark, France, Germany, Greece,* Iceland, *Ireland, Italy, Luxembourg, the Netherlands, Norway, Portugal, Spain, Sweden, Switzerland,* Turkey, *United Kingdom,* and *United States.* Countries that joined later are: *Japan* (1964), *Finland* (1969), *Australia* (1971), *New Zealand* (1973), Mexico (1994), Czech Republic (1995), Hungary (1996), Poland (1996), Korea (1996) and the Slovak Republic (2000). Note: Countries whose names are in italics are members of the Development Assistance Committee.

13. Development Assistance Committee (2001) 2.

14. Figures released in Paris, April 22, 2003 at the OECD Development Assistance Committee's annual meeting.

15. See europa.eu.int/futurum/documents/offtext/doc151201_en.htm

16. The Netherlands, whose foreign policy has global poverty reduction as one of its highest priorities, has come to grips with this issue. Under a reorganization that took effect in early 2002, the Minister of Foreign Affairs is assisted by two junior ministers (or "state secretaries"). One is the Minister for European Affairs. The other is the Minister for Development Cooperation. By this means, development cooperation policy has been integrated into the Ministry's overall agenda. The reorganization has meant that the Netherlands Development Corporation (SNV), which had been attached to the Ministry for 36 years, now operates as an independent organization, though it continues (for a time) to receive an annual core subsidy. See speech in Tokyo by Agnes van Ardenne, Dutch Minister for Development Cooperation March 24, 2003. For more information go to www.minbuza.nl and www.snv.nl. The Dutch arrangement is the exception, not the rule.

17. For inclusion on the United Nations list of least developed countries, a country must meet the following criteria: gross domestic product per capita of less than $900 a year; inadequate performance on quality of life indicators, namely, nutrition, education and adult literacy; instability of agricultural production; instability of export of goods and services; low share of manufacturing and modern services in the gross domestic product; a handicap from economic smallness; and population of less than 75 million. See www.un.org/special-rep/ohrlls/ldc/default.htm.

18. United Nations Conference on Trade and Development (2002) 122.

19. United Nations Conference on Trade and Development (2002) 137-38.

20. United Nations Conference on Trade and Development (2000) Overview: 2.

21. United Nations Conference on Trade and Development (2000) Part 1:8.

22. United Nations Development Programme (2001) 20. Note that this comparison is based on the Purchasing Power Parity (PPP) measure, not the exchange rate conversions that the UNDP had relied on until 1999. The latter shows much higher measures of income inequality between the richest decile and the poorest (51.5:1 in 1970, 127.7:1 in 1997). However, PPP approaches, while not lacking in theoretical and practical issues, are a better way to capture and compare living standards. In comparing the richest 20 percent to the poorest, the PPP approach yields a decline in income inequality between 1970 and 1997, from 14.9:1 to 13.1:1.

23. United Nations Development Programme (1998) 29-30.

24. Planning Commission, Government of India (2002(b)) 301.

25. United Nations (2002(a)) 13.

26. Ibid.

27. The World Bank has produced a World Development Report every year beginning in 1978. Poverty has been the major theme in 1980, 1990 and 2000/2001. In June 2000, a few weeks before its release, the report team's director, Ravi Kanbur, resigned in protest over the emphasis of the main messages in the final approved version.

28. A 2002 information statement is found at www.worldbank.org/debtsecurities.

29. See www.worldbank.org/debtsecurities/html/about.html.

30. Kapur, Devesh, John P. Lewis and Richard Webb, editors (1998) 1:1216.

31. International Development Association (2002).

32. Ibid.:18.

33. Ibid.: 12.

34. See www.un.org/special-rep/ohrlls/ohrlls/cca_undaf_prsp.htm

35. For example, in the United States, the "earmarking" of appropriated funds by Congress for specific purposes limits the programming flexibility of the U.S. Agency for International Development. A case in point. In Mali, congressional earmarking of funds for child survival and development prevented the agency from funding badly needed education programs. See U.S. Agency for International Development (2003(b)) 20.

36. United Nations Development Programme (2004)

37. Ibid.

38. World Bank (2000) 5-6.

39. The preceding discussion draws considerably on United Nations Conference on Trade and Development (2000) Overview.

40. Bayliss, Kate (2002) 12-13.

41. Officially, Doha was the fourth ministerial conference since the World Trade Organization came into being January 1, 1995. The prior three conferences were held in Singapore, December 9-13, 1996; Geneva, May 18-20, 1998; and Seattle, November 30-December 3, 1999. The fifth conference was held in Cancun, Mexico, September 10-14, 2003.

42. U.S. Agency for International Development (2002) 6.

43. For example, see Keddeman, Willem (1998) Section IV.3.

44. Lewis, W. Arthur (1955) 186.

45. See U.S. General Accounting Office (2001(c)) 55-58.

46. United Nations Economic and Social Council (1995).

47. Ibid.

48. Ibid.

49. Islamic Republic News Agency, "Antipoverty Fund" (December 24, 2002). Tehran, Iran.

9

Facing Forward

Poverty's Future

For the moment, we have run out of history, so it is time to face the future. Since this chapter is more of an assessment than actual history, my bias, which has leaked through in the previous pages, will be made more explicit.

As the war on global poverty proceeds, there will be grand new strategies, occasional project and program successes, dispiriting failures, solemn international pronouncements, endless conferences, heavily footnoted research studies, stimulating new lines of inquiry, and more books like this one.

Oh yes, and major reductions in poverty rates in this or that community and this or that country.

For the world as a whole, the results will be less than dramatic. There will be progress in the war on global poverty, but the pace will be glacial. Throughout the 21st century, billions of people will live in appalling conditions before dying prematurely. Unless something radically different is done.

The World Bank has developed three poverty reduction scenarios to assess the likelihood of reaching the Millennium Development Goals by 2015.[1]

Even under the most optimistic growth scenarios, the number of people living on less than $2 a day in 2015 would be 2.3 billion out of a total world population of 6.1 billion. "Thus, the global war on poverty is likely to be with us well into the twenty-first century."[2] Likely, but it does not have to be that way.

Consider some stylized facts.[3] In 2000, the gross world product was about $32 trillion and the global population was about six billion people. That comes out to roughly $5,300 per person and over $21,000 per four-person household.

By 2015 the gross world product would, under the World Bank's baseline scenario, rise to about $50 trillion, while the global population would go to 7.1 billion persons. This works out to slightly more than $7,000 per person.[4]

In theory, if the world's growing income were distributed equally or at least less unequally among its inhabitants, poverty could be made to disappear. Obviously the world has chosen a more circuitous route.

Many Antipoverty Agendas

The war on global poverty has engaged a great number of entities in all regions of the world. The *Directory of Development Organizations* (2003 edition) lists 29,500 agencies and organizations whose work in some degree bears on poverty reduction.[5]

These include international bodies such as the United Nations, individual governments or government ministries, financial institutions, universities and related training organizations, non-governmental organizations, consulting firms, information providers (newsletters, journals, etc.) and funding resources like philanthropic foundations.

The war on global poverty is merged with (and often submerged in) a number of allied causes, like overall economic development, protection of the environment, elimination of AIDS, gender equity, universal primary education, private market expansion and good governance.

Each of these issues is worthy of the world's attention. Poverty provides a foothold for issue advocacy groups. Once its issue linked to the war on global poverty, each group can claim a share of antipoverty resources. The risk is that, to the degree progress is made on an issue (say, environmental protection or gender equity), correspondingly less attention will be paid to the plight of the poor. In the world's war on poverty, the poor may stand last in line for benefits.

The cumulative political pressure of many groups with an interest in poverty reduction, or at least an interest in their own issues under the banner of poverty reduction, can lead to short-term expansion of antipoverty resources. However, the political base consists of an unwieldy mix of governments, donors and advocacy groups lacking overall coherence.

Progress in achieving the associated goal, say, minority rights or gender equity, may lead to upward mobility for some persons in the affected groups and leave countless others in poverty The same scenario can be imagined for women, children, seniors, persons with disabilities, and others.

Once the poor are delinked from particular social groups, they become a formless mass, differentiated only by their inhuman living conditions but devoid of political allies. Concern for their welfare is relegated to rhetoric instead of action.

Take an example. Women constitute a disproportionately high share of the world's poverty population. The feminization of poverty requires antipoverty strategies addressed to the needs of women. But consider the extreme case, in which one hundred percent of the world's antipoverty resources are devoted to poverty reduction among women.

Advocates of other low-income constituencies would resist. What about men in poverty? Or children? Or the elderly, regardless of gender? What about the special problems of rural communities? Indeed, what about overall growth patterns? Poverty reduction strategies are mediated through a host of competing as well as complementary interests.

At the same time, resources for the war are limited. Large economic interests can play one group against another. Fostering a scramble for limited resources serves the agenda of those whose priority is not the elimination of global poverty (except perhaps as a byproduct) but political predictability, capital-intensive growth and quiescent citizenries.

A Clear Objective?

In 1997, the Australian Agency for International Development or AusAID published a report titled *One Clear Objective* with the subtitle *Poverty Reduction Through Sustainable Development.*

The report thoroughly examines Australia's overseas aid program in an international context. It recommends changes aimed at making the program more effective in reducing poverty, with emphasis on the countries of East Asia and the Pacific.

Clearly the report's title conveys an objective—one shared by many other donor countries—but whether the objective itself is clear is debatable.[6] First, the objective is to reduce rather than eliminate poverty. Reduction is a slippery term, crying out for an operational measure. It boils down to what one considers satisfactory poverty reduction.

Second, the objective of reducing poverty is immediately circumscribed by the means, namely development. Arguably, as a means rather than an end, development does not belong in the subtitle. Aid might be used to help reduce poverty in other ways but these are ruled out from the start.

Furthermore, the approach to development itself is circumscribed. It must be sustainable. In the report itself, the notion is amplified as "sustainable economic and social development."[7]

In purely administrative terms, progress toward an objective like reducing (or, preferably, eliminating) global poverty would be measured against a single unambiguous standard. That standard would guide the development, execution and evaluation of global antipoverty strategies.

Instead, the objective as laid out in the report's title summons up potentially conflicting issues around the definition of poverty, its measurement, the degree of its reduction, overall social development, economic growth and sustainability. In the general scheme of things, poverty reduction is treated as a byproduct rather than a driver of development. The approach to poverty reduction is indirect, not direct.

In short the global war on poverty, as neatly reflected in the Australian report's title, embodies a political, not an administrative, objective. The allocation of antipoverty resources does not result from an overarching global strategy. Instead it arises from a welter of discrete political and policy decisions made at the subnational, national and international levels. It depends on the continuing cooperation of many diverse constituencies.

For poverty reduction, the extent, depth, nature and duration of such cooperation cannot be taken for granted.

Priorities of Developing Countries

Within developing countries, a war on poverty may conflict with other strategic priorities like overall growth, national security or structural reform.

Even for a clearly defined poverty problem, the solution may involve significant tradeoffs. Take, for example, a rural community that has embarked on logging as an economic activity. Its type of logging, say, clearcutting, degrades the environment and threatens sustainability.

To stop or cut back the activity would safeguard the environment and the area's economic prospects for the area's future inhabitants. However, this comes at the expense of the existing inhabitants for whom clearcutting provides a more immediate escape from poverty.

A solution is possible as a function of careful analysis, short and long term considerations and compromise among various stakeholders. But the solution is not the most direct route to poverty alleviation. One community or, for that matter, one country's government, might come up with a solution that differs from another's.

Deciding which of several options to highlight as the measure of true progress involves tradeoffs. Furthermore the tradeoffs will tend to be local, that is, country-specific and community-specific, rather than global. For a comparable set of circumstances, the actual tradeoffs may well vary from one locality to another.

This problem is compounded to the extent that poverty reduction strategies entail decentralization to a country's regions, provinces and municipalities where adequate planning and administrative mechanisms are even less developed.

A goal may be to develop such capacities at the subnational level. This takes time, money and commitment. Unavoidably, however, it diverts resources away from a more direct assault on poverty. Even with technical assistance and financial support from external donors, developing countries find it hard to mount an all-out assault on poverty conditions.

Prodded by international donors and their own people, many developing countries set exceedingly ambitious goals for the eradication of poverty, while at the same time they lack the administrative capacity to take action and monitor progress for even a small subset.

Poverty Reduction—A Passing Fashion?

The World Bank Group currently advertises poverty reduction as its highest priority. Indeed for most of the past three decades, the World Bank's lending has been geared to growth strategies that benefit the poor. However, fundamentally the Bank and the Fund are financial institutions and as such are beholden to their shareholders and the international financial community, not the world's poor.

In the early to mid-1980s, preoccupation with structural adjustment and debt trumped poverty reduction. With a larger resource base than other multilateral development organizations, the World Bank will remain a leader in the field of development economics. What remains in play is the long-term direction of that leadership.

At the microeconomic level the Bank has amassed an impressive portfolio of lending for antipoverty purposes. However, the macroeconomic and sectoral effects are more difficult to assess.

For example, in rural South Asia, the Bank tends to support individual projects such as irrigation systems, credit schemes, and dairy cooperatives, while avoiding major structural issues like land reform. In such cases, the Bank's war on poverty reduces to a series of skirmishes.

In recent years the Bank has sought to link individual project lending to adjustment lending for macroeconomic reforms in areas like currency valuation, improved balance of payments and privatization. The jury is still out on the impact of this approach.

As countries progress from the developing to the transitional economy stage, the pressures will be to divert official development assistance to needier areas of the world. Thus rather than reaching the "takeoff" stage, progress may slow as outside resources diminish.

How far they are willing or even able to go to foster sustainable development and long-term poverty reduction as distinct from short-term palliatives remains a concern. By targeting the poor in less developed countries, the Bank risks an adverse reaction from more prosperous groups in those countries.

Pro-poor growth will be portrayed as retarding the overall economic growth of a developing country, thereby perpetuating global inequality. The neoliberal line will reassert itself. Countries in transition from developing to developed status may seek the Bank's assistance through loans or loan guarantees with infrastructure projects like roads, bridges, dams and power plants to maintain their momentum.

They may feel shortchanged if their projects are given lower priority and come to regard the Bank's pro-poor stance as unbalanced. Over time the Bank may experience political pressure to modulate its poverty reduction focus. How well it will deal with such pressures remains to be seen.

No one has found a policy mix that neatly balances the goals of macroeconomic stability (lowering of deficits, debt and inflation rates), growth (availability of labor, land, capital, technology, markets) and poverty reduction (access of the poor to employment, social services, and safety nets). When push comes to shove, growth will trump poverty as the highest priority.

Some Good News

There is good news. Multilateral and bilateral donors have embraced the goal of poverty reduction as a key element of development cooperation. They value partnerships with each other and with aid recipients. All the parties assault poverty on a number of fronts.

Some promote good governance and stable macroeconomic environments while others direct development resources to rural areas, where most of the world's poor live. They support adult literacy programs and increased access of girls and women to educational and economic opportunities.

They seek to integrate poor people into a country's economic life through labor-intensive production, microcredit, and development of small and medium enterprises. They seek the civic and political empowerment of persons and groups historically subject to social exclusion. With respect to aid effectiveness, donors and recipients are more inclined than ever to endorse transparency, accountability and evaluation.

The Bad News

Despite good intentions and exemplary models of cooperation, the overall picture is not encouraging. Donors do not always engage in meaningful dialogue with either a recipient country's government institutions (national, regional or local) or its civil society. Aid projects are not well integrated into a developing country's domestic and foreign policy agenda.

Operationally, many aid projects do not reach the intended target group, namely a country's poorest people. Projects designed to support entire communities tend to benefit disproportionately the wealthier residents of those communities.[8]

The key asset of the poor, namely their labor, argues for a development strategy geared to universal primary education, small business enterprises and labor-intensive production. The approach entails a relatively large role for the public sector reinforced with foreign assistance.

Unfortunately, such a strategy runs exactly counter to the forces of globalization, which are driven by extraordinarily large private capital flows, technology-based growth strategies and the investment decisions of transnational corporations. The governments of developing countries may understandably feel that their future lies in that direction.

Once barriers to upward mobility are removed for particular groups, those who advance up the economic and social ladders are tempted to settle into middle class comfort. The drive to advocate for and act on behalf of their compatriots diminishes. Indeed there may even be a sense of shame at being identified with one's poor relations and an effort to distance oneself from them.

Maximum economic growth does not translate automatically into maximum poverty reduction. In every country, but particularly in developing countries with land scarcity and expanding populations, the trickle-down of benefits to the poor occurs too slowly to make a significant dent in poverty rates.

In a sign that, as World Bank President James Wolfensohn put it, the world is "out of balance", one billion people own 80 percent of the gross world product while another billion survive on less than a dollar a day. The world's population stands at about six billion persons. By 2030, the population of rich countries will increase by 50 million people while that of poor countries will increase by 1.5 *billion*. This dims the prospects for a safer, more stable planet.[9]

Some of the assumptions underlying the war on global poverty deserve reexamination.

Revisiting the Work Ethic

At present social policy in both developed and developing countries dictates that the poor must at all costs be kept busy. The task for a developing country is to absorb as much of its unskilled labor force as possible without unduly sacrificing points in the overall growth rate.

For people in poverty, income is disproportionately dependent on their labor compared to the non-poor who are more likely to receive some income from sources like investments, savings and inheritances.

Individuals can have either an overdeveloped or underdeveloped work ethic. Since there is more to life than paid work, a balance is needed. So too for society. The question is not simply whether human work effort is reduced due to a guaranteed income but whether it is reduced to the point of being detrimental to society.

As the 21st century unfolds, productivity gains will depend less on human labor and more on technological innovation and diffusion. There will be advances in renewable energy, information and communications, transportation, biotechnology, and medicine.

Furthermore, labor-intensive growth strategies do not necessarily make the most sense over the long term for developing countries. That approach could leave them forever unable to catch up with more developed countries whose productivity gains are due more to advances in technology and the migration of capital than reliance on human labor.

Robotics, For Instance

"We are standing right now on the threshold of the robotic era. Once robots start arriving in the job market in significant numbers—something that we will see happening within a decade or so—they have the potential to dramatically change the world economy."[10]

Advances in technologies like robotics will offset to some degree the potential decline in work effort among the poor (or others) resulting from a guaranteed income. Indeed, the poor without skills will find work harder to find, as robots and other advanced technologies substitute for more and more of the world's unskilled labor.

This is hardly news. In the 1960s, economist Robert Theobald, an early proponent of a guaranteed income, predicted that employment in a technologically advanced economy will depend largely on "the level and skill of the job applicant...[T]he decline in job opportunities will be most severe for those who perform repetitive tasks and whose work can most easily be done by machines."[11]

Rapid advances in robotics already have led to the replacement of humans by robots on many industrial assembly lines. During the 1990s, robotics improved due to advances in computing, telecommunications, software, electronic devices and lightweight materials. Robots have become ever smarter, smaller and less power hungry. To no one's surprise they are found overwhelmingly in developed economies.

In 2002, Japan accounted for over half the world's 740,000 industrial robots, followed by the United States and Germany. Other countries making more and more use of industrial robots include Italy, Republic of Korea, France, United Kingdom, Russian Federation, and Spain.

The United Nations Economic Commission for Europe has estimated that in the year 2003 the number of operating industrial robots worldwide will approach 900,000. The most common application is in vehicle manufacturing. Robots are also appearing in service sectors, like lawn care, housecleaning, firefighting, courier delivery, and security.[12]

Over the next decade or two, robots will continue to replace human beings in certain types of employment, especially those involving repetitive tasks, heavy lifting and hazardous conditions involving smoke, chemicals, intense heat and the like. Robots can also be used for surgery, undersea exploration, surveillance and demolition.

In this context, of course, robotics is used as synecdoche for all forms of technology-based, capital intensive growth that relies less and less on the prime asset of the poor, their labor. Advances in artificial intelligence, biotechnology, nanotechnology and a range of information and communications technologies will exert powerful influences on the world's economy.

The long-cherished goal of full employment through free market mechanisms will fall by the wayside. Two possibilities will remain. There will not be full employment. Or, there will be full employment but it will not result from free market mechanisms.

In the latter case, unskilled workers will become increasingly dependent on their governments, which will be endlessly pressured to institute retraining schemes, create labor-intensive public service jobs and expand welfare and related social protection benefits.

Guaranteeing Income

Impatience with the pace of progress in the world's war on poverty has led to calls for more targeted approaches. In a recent book, Peter Townsend and David Gordon include an antipoverty Manifesto. Among its 18 items for international action, the second calls for legally enforcing the right to an adequate standard of living. This right would be recognized through "state-defined minimum earnings [plus] state-defined minimum cash benefits for those not in paid work."[13]

One can extrapolate from this to a global guaranteed income based on transfers from the more well-off to the extremely poor. Under one possible scheme, the amount of the transfer would be sufficient to lift every extremely poor person above the $1 a day threshold.

Put another way, the scheme would guarantee each person on the globe an income of at least $365 a year. This level of income would not eliminate poverty but it would accelerate progress toward that goal.

A global guaranteed income scheme must confront two fundamental objections. First, it flies in the face of those whose *summum bonum* is the creation of wealth with little or no regard for those excluded from its benefits. Second, it also runs up against those who want to expand the welfare state through services rather than risk letting people make the "wrong" choices with their additional income.[14] With respect to the poor, the former attitude reflects conservative dismissiveness, the latter liberal paternalism.

A guaranteed income does away with employment status as a condition of eligibility and with the application of marginal tax rates. For example, in the United States, the Earned Income Tax Credit requires that at least one member of the household be an earner; the value of the tax credit drops as earned income increases until at some point it is phased out. A guaranteed income, by contrast is jobless income.

As a route to increasing self-sufficiency for individuals and overall economic growth for developing countries, a work requirement approach is questionable at best. The mandatory search for work as a condition for receiving benefits all too often leads to former welfare recipients being trapped in low-wage jobs and encumbered by heavy transportation and childcare expenses.

A guaranteed income as a form of poverty alleviation would do away with the stigma of means-tested welfare programs with mandatory employment elements. The additional income would expand the range of choices for recipients.

Arguably, the potential for reduced work effort occasioned by a guaranteed income could be positive. Reduced work effort may spur more cost-effective alternatives. In addition, the labor pool could make up in quality what it lacks in quantity. To borrow a military analogy, an all-volunteer work force could prove more productive than one that relies on draftees.

It would free individuals from the trap of dead-end jobs and give them some flexibility to upgrade their skills and pursue more remunerative work. Or it could enable one or both parents to spend more time with their children. Or it could enable young people to study rather than be forced to seek work.

Based on the evidence from a series of negative income tax experiments in the United States and Canada during the 1970s, complete withdrawal from the labor force is unlikely. The pattern observed in the earlier experiments was longer periods of unemployment between jobs and fewer hours worked per week.[15]

Under a guaranteed income scheme, any foregone labor will be disproportionately unskilled, precisely where demand is diminishing proportionate to total labor demand. Unskilled guaranteed income recipients will have the option to reduce their participation in the labor force or use part of their income to acquire skills demanded by a globalizing economy.[16]

Some modest beginnings are on record. On April 11, 2001, Brazil created a Guaranteed Minimum Income Program. Under the guarantee, each child aged six to fifteen receives 15 reales a month up to a maximum of 45 reales per eligible family. To be eligible a family must earn less than half the minimum wage of 180 reales a month. Payment of the benefit is conditional on school attendance by the recipient child.[17]

The evolution of income support strategies in Brazil has gone still further. Due in large measure to the long-term dedication of Senator Eduardo Suplicy, the Brazilian Congress committed the nation to pursuit of an unconditional basic income for all citizens. On January 4, 2004, Brazil's President Luiz Inacio Lula da Silva signed a law stipulating that basic citizenship income "will be realized in steps, at the discretion of the Executive, giving priority to the neediest layers of the population."[18]

A guaranteed income would hardly satisfy everyone's needs and wants. The incentive to work, accomplish something useful in life and upgrade one's living standard would persist to a large extent. In any event, leaving people in extreme poverty when there are means to eliminate it runs counter to elemental notions of social justice.[19]

On a global scale, a guaranteed income is preferable to the expansion of welfare-to-work programs in developing countries. Such programs tend to spawn complex eligibility criteria and benefit determination rules. They are subject to relentless politicking by self-interested groups. They engender administrative inefficiencies, periodic fraud, ever more complex regulations, mistargeting of benefits and maldistribution of services.

Along with other factors (such as migration pressures), "disillusionment with both conventional aid and neoliberal development policies" will lead those who are really concerned about winning the war on global poverty to consider more "radical" approaches like a global guaranteed income.[20]

A guaranteed income by contrast will provide workers with a degree of economic security plus the freedom to pursue a wider range of career options. As an underpinning of society, it will enable the private sector to invest more readily in advanced technologies as a source of economic growth.

The diffusion of advanced technology plus a guaranteed income for all could lead to overall improvement in the global quality of life. With a guaranteed income system in place, governments could direct their attention to supporting high tech, capital-intensive production. Emphasis would shift from creating jobs for the unskilled to building a skilled labor force capable of incorporating new technologies.

These processes are already underway in developed countries. By contrast, developing countries are encouraged to engage in labor-intensive growth strategies. While touted as "pro-poor", these strategies may undermine the long-term growth prospects of the developing world. There is an alternative. A global guaranteed income system could serve as a vital precondition for technologically driven growth in the developing as well as the developed world.

Administrative Mechanisms[21]

There remains the question of what form a global guaranteed income program should take. A number of arrangements can be envisioned. Most straightforwardly, on a regularly scheduled basis, say, monthly, a check could be mailed to individuals or the funds deposited electronically in an individual's account. We may call this the grants approach.

Under a grants approach, an individual would continue to file a tax return. The administration is more complex, since the individual must factor in the basic income amount to determine his or her tax liability. The same funds could be sent back and forth, first from the government to the individual as a check or electronic transfer and then from the individual to the government as part of the taxes due.

An administratively simpler and far less costly option is a negative income tax. The negative income tax could take the form of a reimbursable tax credit. To receive the credit, households of one or more persons would need to file a tax return. For those whose annual income fell below $365 per household member, the government would transfer an amount that made up the difference. Thus, an individual's minimum income guarantee would be set at $1 a day.

In most poor countries, this amount in the aggregate would strain national budgets. Hence, the international community, as represented by the United Nations, would take up the slack, according to an agreed-on cost-sharing formula. The United Nations would establish a global guaranteed income fund, which would rely on periodic replenishments from its members.[22]

Under a negative income tax, only one step is involved for each party. This lowers transaction costs and reduces the chance for error. The approach has intuitive appeal but obviously depends on an honest and efficient tax system. Fraud, abuse and error are inevitable, most especially in the start-up phases. The system would be vulnerable to dishonest reporting and corrupt administration, though decreasingly over time. Simple mistakes could be made in eligibility determination, benefit calculations and payment transfers.

Poor people would have an incentive to hide income in order to qualify for the benefit. This would appeal to some persons with intermittent or unstable employment histories.

Others would resist converting non-liquid assets into cash in order to remain eligible for the guaranteed income. Taxpayers would work harder to avoid or evade taxes. Administrators might set up sham accounts and pay themselves.

Such possibilities underscore the need for advanced information and communications technologies, adequate recordkeeping systems and the imposition of severe penalties for cases of fraud and abuse. Some developing countries, for example, are turning issue smart cards to tax filers as a way to store, encrypt and update data. With international support and adoption of new technologies, equitable and efficient administration of a negative income tax system in developing countries is within reach.

A guaranteed income approach would not necessarily lead to elimination of social services but some reduction and consolidation could be anticipated. This would lower the total effective costs of a guaranteed income.

The United Nations could serve as the administrative agency for a global guaranteed income program in collaboration with participating national governments. Such an arrangement would permit participation by the poorest countries that lacked the financial and administrative capability to implement the program on their own. Some of the financing could come from new sources of revenue like the proposed Tobin Taxes.[23]

What would it cost? Assume that on average, each of the world's 1.1 billion poorest had incomes averaging $.50 a day. They need an equal amount to reach $1 a day. The poverty gap to be financed is thus $.50 a day times 365 days times 1.1 billion people or about $200 billion a year. To simplify the calculations, arbitrarily add $25 billion for administrative and transaction costs. If we assume (unrealistically) one hundred percent participation by the world's extremely poor people, there would be a total annual program cost of $225 billion.

In 2002, based on purchasing power parity, the gross world product stood at an estimated $49 trillion or $7,900 per capita.[24] Hence a global guaranteed minimum income of $1 a day provided through a negative income tax would absorb less than one-half of one percent of the gross world product ($225 billion divided by $49 trillion).

If the average poverty gap per person (the amount needed for that person's income to reach $1 a day) were, say, $.25 rather than $.50, the total cost would be cut in half. And the share of the gross world product would drop to less than a quarter of one percent.

In either case, the cost would be far less, particularly in the early years of implementation, due to low take-up rates by developing countries and by their poorest citizens. An incremental approach has advantages. It will permit countries to modernize their tax systems and establish the integrity and credibility of the approach. It will give the United Nations and participating governments an opportunity to counter corruption and improve administrative efficiency.

An actual plan as opposed to this hypothetical one would look different. However, the essential point is that eliminating extreme global poverty is not only desirable but also affordable. The plan will gain global acceptance once the people of all countries are convinced that a guaranteed minimum income is required to defeat extreme global poverty and, furthermore, that they can have confidence in its administration and financing.

Summing Up, For Now

The war on global poverty will go on, but books about it must end. I conclude with a brief retrospective and a glance ahead.

Over half a century ago, the United Nations launched the war on global poverty by identifying adequate health and well-being as a human right. In these early years of the 21st century, billions of people remain deprived of that right.

The term "poverty" has come to subsume many meanings, ranging from insufficient income to the lack of "freedom." Without denying its nonmonetary aspects, the global community has adopted an income standard for purposes of measuring progress in alleviating poverty.

For the first couple of decades in the war, overall economic growth through rapid industrialization was the world's preferred strategy for (and usually by) developing countries. Even if it took a while, and even if, a la Kuznets, the poor actually suffered in the process, the benefits of growth would eventually bring about significant poverty reduction.

Economists in the emerging field of development economics concocted a variety of growth formulas. Falling into or out of favor at various times were public management of the economy, private investment, expanded foreign aid, a key role for technology, population control, labor-intensive growth strategies, liberalized trade policies, stability in financial markets, debt reduction, pro-poor planning and government reform.

And, indeed, during the 1960s and 1970s, global growth occurred everywhere, including in the developing countries. However, its pattern showed an uneven distribution regionally and its benefits were not shared by all, either within or among countries. Sub-Saharan Africa lagged and the Middle East stagnated while parts of East Asia leaped forward. Poverty persisted, inequality grew and global tensions mounted.

Overshadowing all was the Cold War between the industrialized western democracies led by the United States and the communist nations of Eastern Europe and China. Ostensibly aimed at growth and poverty reduction, the foreign aid programs of the United States and other countries served a political agenda.

For their part, the developing nations of the third world sought with varying degrees of success to work the conflict to their advantage. Western aid went to nations whose leaders opposed communism, often regardless of government corruption and repression.

Disenchantment with state-led strategies, signs of increasing inequality and growing pessimism over the prospects for trickle-down led development in new directions.

At the United Nations and within the Bretton Woods Institutions, poverty reduction emerged as a more explicit objective. Their aid and loan programs began to emphasize not only discrete (and disconnected) self-help projects, but also broader institutional reforms, community-based planning and empowerment of the poor.

Resources were targeted toward specific groups most vulnerable to poverty, like women, children, rural residents and ethnic minorities. Issues like environmental protection, gender equity and the elimination of HIV/AIDS gained salience internationally.

In the private sector, international humanitarian organizations like Oxfam, Caritas Internationalis, and CARE shifted their emphasis from emergency relief to poverty reduction and long-range community self-sufficiency. Microfinance programs like those of the Grameen Bank and ACCION gained stature as antipoverty strategies.

During the 1970s and early 1980s, a slowdown in the global economy, falling prices for their primary exports and unprecedented increases in oil prices forced developing nations deeper into debt. They grew ever more reliant on borrowing to stave off imminent fiscal catastrophes.

International financial institutions, including the World Bank and its regional counterparts, often abetted these borrowing binges, which created unsustainable debt burdens in the developing world.

To remedy the situation, the World Bank's new loans came with conditions that required recipient countries to undertake structural reforms, promote private investment and cut public spending on safety net and social service programs.

Thus, debt reduction came with a price, which was largely paid by the poor. This continues, despite efforts like the Heavily Indebted Poor Countries initiative.

Following the collapse of the Union of Soviet Socialist Republics and the demise of communism, the United States has emerged as the globe's sole superpower. With its neoliberal leanings, the country has used its disproportionate influence in international institutions and with developing countries to promote private investment, liberalized trade and market economies.

The world's adoption of the Millennium Development Goals, particularly with respect to poverty reduction, gave a degree of cohesion to international aid efforts.

International development assistance continued to evolve from a project-by-project mentality to preference for sector-wide approaches, broader policy development and an expanded role for civil society. Multilateral and bilateral donors sought to minimize duplication and overlap in their aid programs.

Nevertheless, despite tens of thousands of antipoverty projects and programs around the world, the aggregate effectiveness of aid in alleviating global poverty remains in question. Donor fatigue has taken hold, as private capital flows have come to far outstrip official development assistance. At the same time, the world's antipoverty agenda is at risk of being overwhelmed by multiple and sometimes conflicting priorities.

While global poverty rates fell during the 1990s, it is axiomatic that the hardest cases are saved for last. It is likely that there will be declining progress in poverty reduction at the margins. People and nations that remain in poverty are those least equipped to take advantage of technology, trade and globalization. In that context, labor-intensive growth strategies appear almost oxymoronic.

The world must continue to wage war on poverty, if only to salve the global conscience. How the world community wages this war in the future will determine the prospects for success. If the past is prologue, success will remain far off. A new paradigm such as represented by the global guaranteed income approach would considerably brighten the prospects of the world's poorest people.

ENDNOTES

1. The scenarios differ only in terms of the assumed growth rate for the global economy as a whole. They are derived from country-specific assumptions about overall economic growth; population growth; growth rates in per capita consumption; and changes in the distribution of per capita consumption. They are affected by changes in endogenous factors like inflation, savings and school enrollment rates as well as by changes in exogenous factors like world trade growth rates.

Scenario A reflects solid "base case" growth rates that average 3.6 percent a year for 2005-2015. This assumes that countries in all regions achieve reforms and improve economic performance in line with World Bank expectations. Scenario B reflects lower case growth rates under which reform and performance fall below World Bank expectations in one or more regions (say, Sub-Saharan Africa and/or East Asia). Scenario C, the lowest case, assumes that average growth for developing countries as a whole fails to exceed what they experienced in the 1990s (1.7 percent in per capita terms). See World Bank (2001(a)) 25-41.

2. World Bank (2001(a)) 42-43.

3. That is, facts that are accurate, if not particularly precise.

4. World Bank (2001) 29.

5. This extremely valuable resource, produced by development economist Bert Wesselink, can be found at www.devdir.org

6. In what follows I do not quarrel with the content of the report, which is a valuable resource for anyone interested in global and regional development issues. I hang my hat on the title solely to make a point.

7. Page 2.

8. Halvorson-Quevedo, Raundi and Hartmut Schneider, editors (2000) 9-22.

9. "Urgent Action Needed to Fix Global Imbalance", World Bank news release, April 19, 2004. See www.worldbank.org.

10. See http://marshallbrain.com/robotic-freedom.htm. Marshall Brain is a writer and consultant who has written extensively on the impact of robotics on the U.S. and world economy. He advocates giving every U.S. citizen a stipend of $25,000 to distribute the benefits of the robotic revolution equitably and guarantee economic freedom for all.

11. Theobald, Robert (1965) 8.

12. United Nations Economic Commission for Europe (2002).

13. Townsend, Peter and David Gordon, editors (2002) 433 (Appendix A).

14. Bergmann, Barbara R. (2002).

15. Widerquist, Karl (2002) 10.

16. For more, see Murray, Michael L. (1997)

17. See www.etes.ucl.ac.be/bien/Archive.

18. Basic Income European Network (2004).

19. For a more extensive discussion of these issues, see Van Parijs, Philippe (October 2000).

20. Van Parijs, Philippe (1995) 228.

21. This section provides a sketch of a plan that I elaborate more fully in a forthcoming book, provisionally titled *Giving Credit Where Due: A Path to Global Poverty Reduction*.

22. The idea is not so farfetched as one might suppose. The International Labour Organization estimates that only 20 percent of the world's population has any form of social protection. It is investigating the feasibility of establishing a Global Social Trust, a body funded through voluntary international contributions. The Global Social Trust would help poor countries establish their own national Trusts and would assist them in financing essential health care, basic education and income security benefits. See International Labour Organization (2002).

23. Tobin Taxes, first proposed by Nobel laureate economist James Tobin, is a sales tax on international currency transactions. Currency speculators trade over $1.0 *trillion* a day across borders. These transactions would be taxed at a rate in the 0.10 to 0.25 percent range. The tax could dampen currency speculation and help head off financial crises. Of equal or greater importance, it could generate an estimated $100-300 billion a year for urgent international priorities like environmental protection, disease prevention and poverty eradication. Global citizen action is needed since national legislatures would have to pass Tobin Taxes and international cooperation would be required for enforcement. For more information, see www.ceedweb.org/iirp.

24. U.S. Central Intelligence Agency (2003).

Appendices

Appendix 1. Illustration of the Poverty Gap[*]

Take a population of twelve persons and an annualized poverty income threshold of $4,000, the level at which one exits poverty. (Table A-1.) Three of the twelve have annual incomes of $1,000, $2000 and $3,000 respectively. Everyone else has incomes at or above the $4,000 poverty threshold, leaving a poverty gap of zero.

The aggregate poverty gap is ($4,000 minus $1,000) plus ($4,000 minus $2,000) plus ($4,000 minus $3,000) for a total of $6,000. Dividing this $6,000 gap by the $4,000 poverty threshold yields a multiplier of 1.5.

Dividing 1.5 by the total population of 12 persons in effect "spreads" the multiplier among the total population. In this case, the result is .125. This is the mean proportionate poverty gap across the population. In dollar terms it comes out to $4,000 times .125 or $500 per person.

Table A-1. Poverty Gap (Illustration)

Person(s)	Annual Income	Poverty Gap
1	$1,000	$3,000
2	2,000	2,000
3	3,000	1,000
4-12	$667+ over poverty line	0
Total	N/A	$6,000

A redistributionist scheme would take from the nonpoor and give to the poor. In this case the 1.5 multiplier would be divided only by the nine nonpoor persons to yield a poverty gap ratio of .167. That figure times $4,000 comes out to $667 per person, the amount to be transferred so that the three poor persons can reach the poverty threshold. This of course implies that the transferors have incomes above $4,667 so that they are not themselves impoverished by the transfer.

A more feasible redisributionist scheme would not involve equal shares from each transferor. Instead, under the formulas of either a proportional or a progressive income tax system, the higher the transferor's income, the higher would be the share transferred from that transferor.

Under a proportional system, a fixed percentage of each transferor's income would be taxed for transfer to the poor. At ten percent, the share for a person with a $10,000 income would be $1,000; for a $20,000 income, $2,000; and so forth. Under a progressive system, linked to one's "ability to pay", the proportion taxed would rise as income rises. For example, a person with a $10,000 income might be taxed at ten percent, a $20,000 income at fifteen percent, and so forth. The total amount to be transferred would average out to $667 per transferor in order to completely overcome the poverty gap.

---

[*]The endnotes for these appendices are found following Appendix 8.

Appendix 2. Rates of Return

Success for an individual project is often measured by its economic internal rate of return. To oversimplify, "rate of return" is the ratio of forecasted values of benefits to costs minus one. "Internal" refers to the costs and benefits within the project itself. Thus if costs are 100 units and benefits are 125 units, the rate of return is (125/100)-1 or 25 percent. The question is what to count as costs and what to count as benefits.

For private investors, a *financial* internal rate of return may suffice. They will focus on the market value in prices of the project's output compared to the financial cost (that is, capital and labor) of producing it.

Public investment economists use a wider lens. They typically employ shadow prices, that is, the costs of goods and services as affected by market imperfections like monopolies or high marginal tax rates. For traded items, the world price can serve as the shadow price. For some nontraded items a standard conversion factor like exchange rates may suffice, for others more complicated calculations may be required.

Public sector economists also take into account externalities like labor supply, environmental impacts, taxes, trade, transportation, and exchange rates. Employing various conversion factors, economists estimate the total economic costs and benefits of the project. Since a project will usually run for a number of years, the economic rate of return will fluctuate. [1]

In part this may be due to real changes in the benefit-cost ratio, in part to artificial factors like inflation. To adjust for the latter, a discount rate is applied that yields the estimated net present value of costs and benefits over time. All this is rolled up into the economic internal rate of return.

To test the extent to which the economic rate of return is affected by changes in one or more variables, alternative assumptions may be made. Techniques like sensitivity analysis or risk analysis can indicate the variables on which the success of the project most depends, such as pricing, operating costs, taxes, scheduling delays and exchange rates.

The success or failure of a project can have implications for macroeconomic planning and sectoral development. An irrigation scheme designed to increase rice production may have a satisfactory economic internal rate of return.

It may in turn stimulate public irrigation investments elsewhere and over time affect the balance of public and private investment into rural development on the one hand and urban industrialization on the other. [2] Thus, in assessing the impact of a project (or series of projects), economists incorporate an external economic rate of return to society as a whole including estimates of national poverty reduction rates.

Appendix 3. United States as a Bilateral Aid Donor

The foreign economic assistance program of the United States grew out of the Second World War and the Marshall Plan. The $12 billion Marshall plan, created by the Economic Cooperation Act of 1948, was designed as an emergency assistance tool to stabilize a Europe devastated by war. It ended June 30, 1951.

By this time the government had shifted its emphasis from post-war reconstruction to long-range foreign development through economic and technical assistance.

During the 1950s, several different federal agencies provided aid, which at times became entwined in political and military functions. These agencies included the International Cooperation Agency, Development Loan Fund, Export-Import Bank and the Food for Peace Program of the U.S. Department of Agriculture.

By the end of the decade, there was little evidence that the recipients of aid had moved toward greater economic stability. And there was dissatisfaction with the awkward, slow and fragmented bureaucratic aid structure.

The Foreign Assistance Act of 1961 consolidated bilateral development assistance within a newly created Agency for International Development. Through a reorganized aid effort, the Kennedy Administration sought to foster stability and growth in the poorer nations of the world.

President John F. Kennedy linked "widespread poverty and chaos" to the collapse of political structures and the advance of totalitarianism. He asserted a moral and political obligation for the people of the United States "as the wealthiest people in a world of largely poor people" to counter the adversaries of freedom.[3]

The Foreign Assistance Act of 1961 included several programs: a development *loan* fund, and development *grant* fund, a guaranty program (to protect U.S. businesses operating overseas), a "supporting assistance" program and an appropriated contingency fund.

During the 1960s, assistance from the U.S. Agency for International Development was directed to economic sectors in developing countries with the greatest growth potential. It largely supported new capital-intensive infrastructure projects like dams, roads, and industrial plants.

The Alliance for Progress, set up under the 1960 Act of Bogota and confirmed in 1961 by the Charter of Punta del Este in Uruguay, became the framework for the Agency for International Development's strategy in Latin America. In Asia, AID's development efforts aimed at offsetting the export of communism, especially from China. To carry out its projects, the Agency for International Development typically contracted with outside organizations, including universities, private voluntary organizations, consulting firms and host government agencies. The benefits of growth were assumed to trickle down to the poorest elements of society.

By the early 1970s disenchantment with this approach had settled in. In the U.S. Congress, aid was seen as a "giveaway" program with few tangible benefits to the United States. In the House of Representatives, the Committee on Foreign Affairs redirected the thrust of aid away from financing of large-scale infrastructure projects in developing countries.

The 1973 amendments to the Foreign Assistance Act expressed what became known as the "New Directions" mandate. They required the U.S. Agency for International Development to target its assistance to the poor in countries trying to meet basic human needs. The New Directions policies focused on areas like nutrition, education, jobs, family planning, and rural development. The Agency for International Development pursued its objectives through a large number of small-scale projects with a rural development orientation.

During the 1980s, the agency began stressing aid for policy reform and institutional development needed to sustain broad-based economic growth over the long term. This approach persisted throughout the 1990s.

Several attempts have been made in Congress to update the Foreign Assistance Act.

In 1978, Senator Hubert H. Humphrey (Minnesota Democrat) introduced legislation to revamp the foreign assistance management structure. The bill became bogged down in legislative and bureaucratic wrangling. In 1979, as a way out of the impasse, the Carter Administration established by Executive Order the International Development Cooperation Agency and reorganized the interagency Development Coordination Committee. Neither proved effectual.

In 1988, the House Foreign Affairs Committee again reexamined the foreign assistance program. The Committee's report (or Hamilton-Gilman report) highlighted such impediments to effective foreign assistance as excessive congressional earmarking of funds, one-year instead of multi-year appropriations, costly and time-consuming reporting requirements and overemphasis on process rather than results.[4]

Few would argue that agencies with a single clear mission work best. Tellingly, as a reflection of the congressional tendency to micromanage federal agencies, the report identified 75 different, sometimes conflicting, mission priorities.[5] However, efforts to rewrite the Foreign Assistance Act based on such findings failed in 1988 and in succeeding years.

The architecture of the American foreign aid program remains the 1961 Foreign Assistance Act, as amended. At the same time, the foreign assistance program has been "buffeted" by groups with a stake in its activities, including other federal agencies, Congress, and lobbyists for special interests.[6]

The United States Congress has declared that the nation's foreign policy should support the people of developing countries in building economic, political, and social institutions that will improve the quality of their lives. Development cooperation policy should pursue five main goals:

(1) the alleviation of the worst physical manifestations of poverty among the world's poor majority;

(2) the promotion of conditions enabling developing countries to achieve self-sustaining economic growth with equitable distribution of benefits;

(3) the encouragement of development processes in which individual civil and economic rights are respected and enhanced;

(4) the integration of the developing countries into an open and equitable international economic system; and

(5) the promotion of good governance through combating corruption and improving transparency and accountability.[7]

Organizationally and managerially, the Agency for International Development cannot stay abreast of an ever more diffuse set of goals and the increasing number of countries in which it operates.

In the Foreign Assistance Act of 1961, as amended (P.L. 87-195), the U.S. General Accounting Office identified over thirty different objectives, namely:

(1) alleviating poverty;

(2) promoting equitable economic growth;

(3) integrating countries into the international economic system;

(4) assisting the poor to participate in the development process;

(5) reducing infant mortality;

(6) controlling population growth;

(7) fostering small-farm, labor-intensive agriculture;

(8) making improvements in the health of the poor;

(9) reducing illiteracy and increasing training for job skills;

(10) developing and effectively using energy resources;

(11) promoting the role of the private sector in development;

(12) integrating women into national economies;

(13) supporting human rights;

(14) reducing environmental degradation;

(15) encouraging conservation of tropical forests;

(16) preserving biological diversity;

(17) using voluntary organizations for development activities;

(18) strengthening cooperatives;

(19) eliminating production of illicit narcotics;

(20) upgrading developing countries' institutional capacities;

(21) demonstrating American ideas in education and medicine;

(22) marshaling resources for low-cost shelter;

(23) providing encouragement to democratic institutions;

(24) fostering development capacity in U.S. educational institutions;

(25) educating the American public about foreign aid;

(26) providing disaster assistance;

(27) promoting smaller, cost-saving, labor-using technologies;

(28) encouraging U.S. private investment in development;

(29) encouraging regional cooperation among developing countries;

(30) promoting policy reforms for economic growth with equity;

(31) increasing national food security; and—last but not least—

(32) meeting needs in public finance, safe water; and infrastructure.[8]

The United States Agency for International Development pursues objectives in six areas: economic growth and agricultural development, democracy, human capacity development, family planning, environment, and humanitarian assistance.

While poverty reduction may be a byproduct of work in these areas, it does not have status as a stand-alone objective. The agency has no official definition of poverty. In fact, neither poverty nor the poor are mentioned in the agency's mission statement. In an era of results-oriented management, what is not highlighted is not measured and is more easily ignored.[9]

Under its budget the United States' Agency for International Development manages four program accounts: (a) development assistance; (b) child survivor and diseases program fund; (c) international disaster assistance; and (d) transition initiatives.

It also administers the food aid program, which comes under the budget of the U.S. Department of Agriculture. The program, which was established in 1954 under the Agricultural Trade Development and Assistance Act (Title II, P.L. 480) seeks to foster recipient countries' development while expanding commercial markets for U.S. agricultural products.

The program assists victims of natural disasters such as 1999's Hurricane Mitch in Central America, and other victims in countries like Sudan and Sierra Leone affected by droughts, floods and ongoing civil conflict. It supports initiatives like farm-to-market roads, irrigation systems, food storage facilities and technical assistance to farmers aimed at improving agricultural productivity.

The Agency for International Development and the State Department jointly administer the Economic Support Fund; assistance for Eastern Europe and the Baltic States; and assistance for the independent states of the former Soviet Union. Development Assistance is provided under loans and grants to overcome the recipient country's constraints in meeting basic needs and to support sustainable growth.

The Economic Support Fund, which grew out of the supporting assistance program, is a flexible instrument whose allocations are made in line with political and security considerations but whose purpose is to foster growth and stability. Since the late 1970s, the principal beneficiaries have been Israel and Egypt, which together absorb over half the annual appropriation. Smaller amounts go to other recipients, most notably in Africa.

Another entity, the Overseas Private Investment Corporation, which grew out of the guaranty program, was created as a public corporation in 1969. It stimulates U.S. private sector investment in developing countries through loans, loan guarantees, political risk insurance and pre-investment assistance to U.S. firms.

Of all these foreign aid mechanisms, Development Assistance was most closely aligned with the goal of meeting basic needs in developing countries.

Other countries pursued a similar basic needs strategy but in different ways. Canada, United Kingdom and Germany supported capital development projects to provide the infrastructure for economic development. France emphasized education as the key to development while Sweden focused on non-project assistance like commodity imports linked to a country's own internal development plans.

The United States relies heavily on non-governmental organizations to deliver goods and services under its foreign aid programs. During fiscal year 2000 the Agency for International Development's obligations totaled $7.2 billion. Of this amount, about $4 billion went to non-governmental organizations.

These organizations included private voluntary organizations such as Catholic Relief Services, CARE, Save the Children and Johns Hopkins University. For-profit recipient of Agency for International Development funding included Development Alternatives, Inc., Barents Group, LLC, and Chemonics, International, Inc.

The United States provides significantly less official development assistance as a share of gross domestic product than other developed countries. In 1998, the share was 0.10 percent, which was less than half the 0.24 percent figure for the other 21 members of the OECD Development Assistance Committee.

This approach to foreign aid is changing, in part as a response to heightened international terrorism.

On March 14, 2002, in an address to the Inter-American Development Bank, President George W. Bush stated: "Poverty doesn't cause terrorism. Yet persistent poverty and oppression can lead to hopelessness and despair. And when governments fail to meet the most basic needs of their people, these failed states can become havens for terror."

The President proposed the creation of a $5 billion Millennium Challenge Account. It is designed to counter the "growing divide between wealth and poverty, between opportunity and misery," with priority given to countries that "root out corruption, respect human rights and adhere to the rule of law, as well as encourage open markets and sustainable budget policies."[10]

As proposed, the Millennium Challenge Account will be administered by a new government corporation designed to support innovative strategies and to ensure accountability for measurable results. The Corporation will be supervised by a Board of Directors composed of Cabinet level officials, chaired by the Secretary of State. Assistance provided through the MCA will be based on evidence of sound policies in developing nations.

A limited number of countries will be selected as targets of aid based on their performance under three broad criteria: governing justly, investing in people, and encouraging economic freedom. Performance will be measured using a set of sixteen indicators to determine country eligibility. The indicators with their sources in parentheses follow.

Criterion 1: Governing Justly
- Civil Liberties (Freedom House)
- Political Rights (Freedom House)
- Voice and Accountability (World Bank Institute)
- Government Effectiveness (World Bank Institute)
- Rule of Law (World Bank Institute)
- Control of Corruption (World Bank Institute)

Criterion 2: Investing in People
- Public Primary Education Spending as Percent of GDP (World Bank/national sources)
- Primary Education Completion Rate (World Bank/national sources)
- Public Expenditures on Health as Percent of GDP (World Bank/national sources)
- Immunization Rates: DPT and Measles (World Bank/UN/national sources)

Criterion 3: Promoting Economic Freedom
- Country Credit Rating (Institutional Investor Magazine)
- Inflation (IMF)
- 3-Year Budget Deficit (IMF/national sources)
- Trade Policy (Heritage Foundation)
- Regulatory Quality (World Bank Institute)
- Days to Start a Business (World Bank)

Appendix 4. Other Selected Bilateral Aid Agencies

Canada

Canada's bilateral assistance program began in 1950 at the Colombo Plan Conference of Commonwealth nations. There, Canada and other participants agreed to assist the newly independent nations of India, Pakistan and Ceylon (subsequently, Sri Lanka). In the early 1960s Canada began providing assistance to French-speaking or Francophone nations of Africa. In 1968, the External Aid Office of the Department of External Affairs became the Canadian International Development Agency (CIDA).

The agency is responsible for about 78 percent of Canada's aid. The remainder is administered by the Department of Finance and the Department of Foreign Affairs and International Trade. CIDA supports some three thousand projects in more than 120 countries.

Other bilateral aid channels include the International Development Research Centre, a public corporation created in 1970 as an alternative to traditional aid mechanisms. It fosters the creation and dissemination of scientific, technical and other knowledge as the engine of development.

The Centre's mission was strongly influenced by a 1969 report of the Commission on International Development, chaired by Lester B. Pearson. The report, *Partners in Development*, emphasized global interdependence and promoted multilateral cooperation. The Commission also stressed the central importance of building the capacity of developing countries.[11]

Petro-Canada International is another public corporation that was created in 1980 to help oil importing countries reduce their reliance on such imports. Since 1995, CIDA has administered a special budget allocated for cooperation with the countries of Central and Eastern Europe and the former Soviet Union. Overall, CIDA supports sustainable development projects in over one hundred countries that include four-fifths of the world's population.

France

The Agence française de Développement traces its origins to World War II London, December 2, 1941, when Charles de Gaulle in exile there ordered the creation of the Caisse Centrale de la France Libre (Central Bank of Free France). This was changed on February 2, 1944 to Caisse Centrale d'Outremer and later by the French General Assembly on December 30, 1958 to the Caisse Centrale de Cooperation Économique. In October 1992, decree number 92-1176 defined its terms of reference. It took its current name under decree number 98-294, dated April 17, 1998.

The agency consists of eight credit institutions, three regional development corporations and three property development companies. It provides loans and subsidies for economic development by financing public or private investment.

Its structural adjustment funding—loans to middle-income countries and subsidies to low-income countries—supports national economic and financial recovery programs.

PROPARCO (Société de Promotion and Participation pour la Coopération Économique), a subsidiary established in 1977, specializes in financing and developing the private sector, through loans or equity investments.

The Agence française de Développement has a presence in over sixty countries, especially in Sub-Saharan Africa, the Mahgreb, Lebanon and Palestine, the Indian Ocean, the Pacific, the Caribbean and Asia. It contributes to the International Monetary Fund's Poverty Reduction and Growth Fund.

Germany

Established in 1961, the Federal Ministry for Economic Cooperation and Development (BMZ) plans the government's development policies and disburses about two-thirds of its aid. In 2000, Germany's official development assistance amounted to about \$5 billion, putting it third (behind Japan and the United States) among the members of OECD's Development Assistance Committee. The top five aid recipients were China, Indonesia, India, Turkey and Egypt.[12]

In April 2001, BMZ issued a report titled *Poverty Reduction—A Global Responsibility—Program of Action 2015: The German Government's Contribution towards Halving Extreme Poverty Worldwide.* The Program of Action 2015, as it is known, embodies the government's commitment to helping achieve the first millennium development goal in partnership with other bilateral and multilateral donors, as well as recipient countries themselves.

BMZ implements its development projects and programs through a number of independent organizations. In 1975, the Agency for Technical Cooperation (GTZ), a nonprofit organization, was established as the government's principal executive agency for technical cooperation activities.

Other aid entities include the German Development Bank (KfW) and its subsidiary, German Investment and Development Company (DEG), and InWEnt-Capacity Building International. The latter was created in 2002, as a result of a merger between two long-standing development organizations, the Carl Duisberg Society (CDG), founded in 1949, and the German Foundation for International Development (DSE), founded in 1959. The new organization continues the human resource development and dialogue programs of its two predecessors.

Japan

The Colombo Plan, launched in 1950 to foster economic and technical cooperation in the British Commonwealth of Nations, was significant for Japan. On October 6, 1954, Japan joined the Colombo Plan, thereby beginning its assistance to developing countries.

Subsequently, the Plan extended its reach to countries outside the Commonwealth and Japan began aiding other Asian countries. Beginning with Burma (now Myanmar), Japan worked out agreements with various Asian countries on wartime reparations and economic cooperation.

In 1958, Japan extended official development assistance loans to India. As the Japanese economy grew in the latter half of the 1960s, its foreign aid programs expanded and diversified.

In addition to economic infrastructure, Japan's official development assistance has come to be targeted on basic human needs and human resource development. Geographically its programs take in Asia, Middle East, Africa, Latin America and Pacific regions.

Japan sees itself as interdependent with developing countries since it obtains vital natural resources through trade with them. Its security and prosperity are insured by a peaceful and stable world. It also feels a high degree of international responsibility as an advanced, non-Western power.

In June 1998, the Diet enacted the Basic Law on the Administrative Reform of the Central Government, which included the framework for reform of Japan's administration of official development assistance. It gave the Ministry of Foreign Affairs jurisdiction in the economic cooperation-related affairs of foreign policy; planning with respect to loans; coordination of policy-making on common guidelines for assistance; and policy-making and planning related to technical cooperation.

Japan has evolved into the world's preeminent donor nation. In 1993, it provided $11.3 billion in official development assistance, the highest amount of any country. It was the largest contributor to the Asian Development Bank and United Nations Population Agency and the second largest contributor to the World Bank, United Nations Development Programme, World Health Organization and Office of the United Nations High Commissioner for Refugees.

Sweden

Sweden is a neutral country with no history as a colonial power. Various church and trade union groups provided assistance to developing countries since the early 1950s. In 1962, the Swedish parliament incorporated the activities of these private sector entities.

The Swedish International Development Authority was established in 1965 and placed under the Ministry of Foreign Affairs in 1970. In order to maximize its aid impact, the agency initially concentrated its resources on some nineteen "program" countries, so designated because their priorities democracy, human rights, economic and political independence) were congruent with Swedish aid goals. At the time the government touted the 'Swedish model" as a third way between capitalism and communism and aid promoted this approach.

The largest of the "program" recipients, Tanzania, had a relationship with Sweden dating to the colonial period when Lutheran missionaries were active in East Africa. In 1976 the Swedish Commission was established to aid developing countries outside the "program" recipients. The aid provided is more limited in scope. The agency has a board of directors that includes members of parliament, civil service employees and representatives of industry, trade unions and religious organizations.

While aid specific projects predominated, a new model emerged that stressed structural adjustment, that is, aid for market-based reforms and macroeconomic balance in the recipient countries. This of course reflected an international trend in multilateral and bilateral aid. By the 1990s, the adverse consequences of this approach, most notably worsening poverty and social unrest in the recipient countries, had become manifest. Eradicating poverty stood out as a principal policy objective, as opposed to a secondary (and as it happened illusory) effect of economic reform.

In 1995 the Swedish International Development Authority became the Swedish International Development Cooperation Agency. The kinds of policy analyses conducted by the United Kingdom's Department for International Development were adopted by the Swedish aid agency. This approach stresses the building of aid strategies based on the collection of current data, analyzing poverty trends, assessing a recipient country's power structures and examining the work of other international donors.

United Kingdom

The British aid program was shaped first by its colonial experience and more recently by its role in the Commonwealth nations. The Colonial Development Act of 1929 was recognition of the British government's responsibility for the ongoing development of its colonies. In 1961, a Department of Technical Cooperation was established to deal with the technical cooperation side of the aid program.

In October 1964 the Overseas Development Ministry was set up to formulate aid policy and manage the country's aid programs. Six years later the ministry's functions were transferred to the Overseas Development Administration within the Foreign and Commonwealth Office. In May 1974 the Government announced that the ODA was once again to be a separate ministry under its own minister. However, in November 1979 the ministry again became the Overseas Development Administration (ODA) as a functional wing of the Foreign and Commonwealth Office. By 1981, two-thirds of the bilateral aid program of the United Kingdom was going to former and (then) current colonies and dependencies.

Other entities with aid responsibilities included four "Special Units" for technical assistance, the British Council and Technical Education and Training Organization for Overseas Countries, the Crown Agents (which helps with the disbursement of official development assistance funds) and the Commonwealth

Development Corporation, which invests in the economies of developing countries.

In 1997 the Overseas Development Administration was replaced by the Department for International Development, headed by a secretary of state with cabinet rank, The secretary of state for international development is formally responsible to Parliament for the Department.

As set out in its 1997 White Paper on International Development, the government is committed to the international goal of cutting global poverty in half by 2015, along with related goals like basic health care and universal access to primary education. A second White Paper on International Development, published in December 2000, reaffirmed this commitment. Most assistance is provided to the poorest countries in Asia and Sub-Saharan Africa.

The Department for International Development also contributes to poverty elimination and sustainable development in middle-income countries in Latin America, the Caribbean and elsewhere. The goal of poverty reduction is embodied in the International Development Act 2002, which became effective June 17, 2002, replacing the 1980 Overseas Development and Cooperation Act.

Appendix 5. Selected Multilateral Development Banks

Multinational development banks are autonomous international financial institutions that finance economic and social development initiatives in developing countries. The funds they use for such financing come mainly from the governments of member countries and from world capital markets. Enjoying favorable credit ratings they borrow money from world capital markets on terms that are better than their borrowers, namely developing countries, could negotiate on their own. In this way the banks give developing countries access to foreign currency resources on more favorable terms than would otherwise be possible. While the principal assistance vehicle is direct lending to developing countries, the multilateral development banks also make equity investments, offer loan and equity guarantees and provide technical assistance.

The World Bank Group

The World Bank Group consists of the International Bank for Reconstruction and Development, International Development Association, International Finance Corporation, and Multilateral Investment Guarantee Agency.

The *International Bank for Reconstruction and Development*, established in 1945, provides loans, loan guarantees and technical assistance to middle-income countries and more creditworthy poorer countries. With guarantees by rich members, the United States in particular, the International Bank for Reconstruction and Development can raise money from finance markets at rates lower than many governments.

The Bank lends the money it raises to individual governments at rates more favorable to these governments than they could obtain directly from private finance markets. "Since it was established, the IBRD has only received $11 billion in capital paid by its members, but has leveraged more than $280 billion in loans."[13]

In fiscal year 2000, of its 181 member countries, 98 were borrowers. In that year, the Bank authorized development loans totaling about $10.9 billion. Its five largest borrowers were Indonesia, Mexico, China, Argentina and Republic of Korea.

Voting power is weighted according to the financial contributions of UN member states. Thus for the International Bank for Reconstruction and Development, the vote of the United States amounts to about 17 percent of the total, while that of the United Kingdom is about five percent.

China and India, which together comprise a third of the world's population, weigh in at about three percent each. The more affluent Northern countries collectively control over 60 percent of the total vote. The Bank president is always a United States citizen.

The World Bank was not established as an economic aid agency but rather as an instrument for promoting the flow of investment capital internationally. That may be changing. The World Bank's influence over the process of development is larger than the size of its loan portfolio would suggest.

The audits it and the International Monetary Fund conduct in debtor countries often determine the willingness of other institutions to provide financing to these countries. The Bank has become a leading think tank on issues affecting the poorer nations of the South.

The *International Development Association,* which was created in 1960, is the concessional lending arm of the World Bank Group. It provides interest-free loans, called credits, to the least developed countries, as well as loan guarantees and technical assistance.

Many of the projects it supports address such areas as primary education, health services, clean water, sanitation, environmental protection, private business expansion, improved infrastructure and governmental reform.

Within the World Bank, the International Bank for Reconstruction and Development and the International Development Association share the same staff and headquarters; both report to the World Bank president. A country must be a member of the International Bank for Reconstruction and Development before it can join the International Development Association.

The International Development Association lends to countries that have per capita incomes of less than $885 in 2000 and lack the financial ability to borrow from the International Bank for Reconstruction and Development. Of the 162 countries that are members, 79 countries are eligible to borrow from the International Development Association.

Together these countries are home to 2.5 billion people, of whom some 40 percent "live" on less than $1 a day.

Some countries, such as India and Indonesia, are eligible for International Development Association credits due to their low per capita incomes, but are also creditworthy for some International Bank for Reconstruction and Development borrowing. These countries are known as 'blend" borrowers.

Over the years, twenty-two countries have seen their economies develop and grow beyond the IDA-eligibility threshold. These countries, that are now too prosperous to qualify for IDA funds include China, Costa Rica, Chile, Egypt, Morocco, Thailand, and Turkey.

IDA credits have maturities of 35 or 40 years with a 10-year grace period on repayment of principal. There is no interest charge, but credits do carry a small service charge of 0.75 percent on disbursed balances. In fiscal year 2001 (which ended June 30, 2001), IDA commitments totaled $6.8 billion and disbursements were $5.5 billion.

Since 1960, IDA has lent $107 billion to 106 countries. It lends, on average, about $6-7 billion a year for different types of development projects. In fiscal year 2001, $6.8 billion was committed to IDA borrowers.

Half of new credits went to Sub-Saharan Africa, 18 percent to South Asia, 15 percent to East Asia and the Pacific, 8 percent to Eastern Europe and Central

Asia (ECA), and the remainder to poor countries in North Africa and in Latin America and the Caribbean.

In fiscal year 2000, the Association's five largest borrowers were India, China, Bangladesh, Pakistan and Ghana. In that year the Association approved approximately $4.4 billion in new credits to fifty-two countries.

The *International Monetary Fund* came into being on December 27, 1945 and commenced operations in 1946. Membership was opened to governments that controlled their foreign policy and subscribed to the Fund's Articles of Agreement.

Each member has a quota, expressed in Special Drawing rights (SDR). Voting power is weighted. A member has an allotted number of votes plus additional votes related to the size of its quota.

The Fund's top level structure includes a board of governors, composed in most instances of the minister of finance or central bank governor of the member states, and an executive board that handles day to day business.

The executive board consists of executive directors, eight appointed by the members with the largest quotas in the Fund and the other sixteen elected by those members who do not have the appointment power.[14] The eight members representing their individual countries are China, France, Germany, Japan, Russia, Saudi Arabia, the United Kingdom, and the United States.

A managing director is selected by the Executive Board and serves an initial term of five years. Traditionally, the managing director is a European and the deputy managing director an American.

The International Monetary and Financial Committee consists of 24 governors, corresponding to the members of the executive board. Its primary role is to advise the Fund on the functioning of the international monetary system.

As of June 30, 2002, the International Monetary Fund had credits and loans outstanding to 88 countries for an amount of Special Drawing Rights 66.3 billion (about $88 billion). The Fund makes its financial resources available to its members through a variety of loan programs called "facilities."

The Fund's regular facilities go by various names: stand-by arrangements, extended fund facility, supplemental reserve facility, contingent credit lines and compensatory financing facility. It also offers concessional assistance under its poverty reduction and growth facility and heavily indebted poor countries (HIPC) initiative.

As of February 2003, the International Monetary Fund had 184 members.

The *International Finance Corporation* was established in 1956 to foster private sector growth in developing countries. It provides loans and equity investments to private enterprises when sufficient private capital at reasonable terms from other sources is not available. Such loans are not guaranteed and hence carry a significant degree of risk.

As of June 30, 2000, the Corporation's portfolio was $10.9 billion, of which loans accounted for three-quarters of this total. The countries of its five largest operations were in Brazil, Argentina, Mexico, Turkey and Thailand.

The newest member of the World Bank Group, the *Multilateral Investment Guarantee Agency*, established in 1988, does not make loans to government or private enterprises. Rather it provides insurance and investment guarantees to foreign investors in order to stimulate investment in developing countries.

Generally guarantees can be made up to 90 percent of these investments and serve as protection against currency transfer restrictions, war and civil disturbance, expropriation, and breach of contract within the host country. At the end of fiscal year 2000, the Agency's investment guarantees totaled $4.4 billion. The five countries where the agency had its largest exposure were Brazil, Argentina, Peru, Russia and Turkey.

African Development Bank Group

The African Development Bank Group consists of the African Development Bank and the African Development Fund. Established in 1964, the *African Development Bank* seeks to reduce poverty and promote sustainable economic growth in Africa. It has seventy-seven member countries of which fifty-three are from the region. The Bank focuses on agriculture, rural development, human resource development and private sector expansion. Its financing mechanisms include market-based loans, loan guarantees, equity investments, cofinancing and technical assistance.

Only thirteen of its member countries were eligible for the Bank's resources. In 1999 the Bank's five largest borrowers were Morocco, Tunisia, Nigeria, Algeria and Côte d'Ivoire. During 1999, the Bank approved about $1.1 billion in new loans and equity investments.

The *African Development Fund*, established in 1973, is the Group's concessional lending facility. Of the Group's fifty-three regional member countries, thirty-nine members were eligible only for concessional aid through the African Development Fund. The African Development Fund offers extremely favorable loan terms with no interest and extended repayment and grace periods. During 1999, the Fund approved about $630 million in new financing. Its five largest borrowers were Ethiopia, Tanzania, Mali, Uganda and Malawi.

Asian Development Bank Group

The Asian Development Bank Group is comprised of Ordinary Capital Resources and the Asian Development Fund. *Ordinary Capital Resources* provides market-based loans, equity investments, loan guarantees and technical assistance to middle income and creditworthy poorer countries.

Established in 1966, it has sixty-one member countries, including forty-two from the region. Since its establishment, the Bank has approved loans totaling about $90.0 billion to its member countries. On average it lends about $5-6 billion a year.

Ordinary Capital Resources seeks to reduce Asian poverty through employment-intensive economic growth projects, social programs, and good governance. During 1999, Ordinary Capital Resources approved about $3.9 billion in loans to private and public borrowers. The five largest borrowers were Indonesia, People's Republic of China, India, Republic of Korea, and the Philippines.

The *Asian Development Fund*, established in 1974, serves as the concessional lending arm of the Asian Development Bank Group. In 1999, the Fund approved $1.1 billion in new loans. The five largest borrowers were Bangladesh, Pakistan, Sri Lanka, Nepal and the Philippines. The Asian Development Bank Group, which is headquartered in Manila, has twenty-four other offices around the world.

Inter-American Development Bank

The oldest and largest of the multilateral development banks is the Inter-American Development Bank, established in 1959. It assists countries in Latin America and the Caribbean. The Bank has forty-six members, including twenty-six from Latin America and the Caribbean, plus the United States and Canada and eighteen nonregional countries. Its lending priorities include poverty reduction, social equity, good governance, economic integration and environmental protection.

Most of the Bank's operations are conducted through *Ordinary Capital*. During 1999, Ordinary Capital approved $9.1 billion in loans and loan guarantees. The five largest borrowers were Brazil, Argentina, Mexico, Colombia and Peru. The Bank has never had any write-off of its loans.

The *Inter-American Bank's Fund for Special Operations* provides loans on concessional terms to the region's less developed countries. Like Ordinary Capital, the Fund for Special Operations has never had a write-off, except for debt relief. During 1999, the Fund approved about $417 million in loans. The five largest borrowers were Honduras, Bolivia, Nicaragua, Ecuador and El Salvador.

The *Multilateral Investment Fund*, a part of the Inter-American Bank Group, supports investment reforms and private sector development.

An autonomous affiliate of the Inter-American Bank Group, the *Inter-American Investment Corporation*, established in 1986, fosters economic development in Latin America and the Caribbean through financing small and medium-sized enterprises. It has thirty-seven member countries, of which twenty-six are from Latin America and the Caribbean. The remaining members include eight European countries, Israel, Japan and the United States.

The Corporation serves as a catalyst for attracting other financing, technology and expertise. It does this through methods like cofinancing, syndication, support of security underwritings, and identification of joint venture partners. During 1999, the Corporation approved $192 million in loan and equity investments. The five areas where loans were concentrated most heavily in 1999 were Argentina, Regional projects, Brazil, Bolivia and Peru.

European Bank for Reconstruction and Development

The *European Bank for Reconstruction and Development* was established in 1990 and consists of sixty members, of which fifty-eight are sovereign countries. The Bank seeks to foster market-oriented economies and private entrepreneurship in central and Eastern Europe and within the Commonwealth of Independent States.

The latter was created in December 1991 and includes Azerbaijan, Armenia, Belarus, Georgia, Kazakhstan, Kyrgyzstan, Moldova, Russia, Tajikistan, Turkmenistan, Uzbekistan and Ukraine. Under a September 1993 agreement, these states formed an economic union that promoted the free movement of goods, services, labor and capital and coordinated monetary, tax, price, customs, and related polices.

During 1999, the Bank approved about $2.2 billion in financing, the bulk of which was for private sector loans and equity investments. The Bank has placed special emphasis on strengthening the recipient countries' financial sector. It also invests in agriculture, natural resources, tourism, telecommunications, utilities, transportation and environment. The five countries where the Bank's operations are the largest are the Russian Federation, Romania, Poland, Hungary and the Ukraine.

Appendix 6. Poverty Focus of United Nations System

This Appendix describes the United Nations system insofar as it bears on the goal of global poverty reduction.[15]

As of the end of 2002, the membership of the United Nations consisted of 192 nation states, a 276 percent increase over the original fifty-one. The United Nations operates through six principal organs: Secretariat, General Assembly, Trusteeship Council, Security Council, International Court of Justice and Economic and Social Council. The Secretariat, General Assembly and Economic and Social Council are the most relevant to our present purpose.

General Assembly

The General Assembly (1945), as the main deliberative body within the United Nations system, has functioned as a voice for the world's developing nations. The General Assembly is composed of representatives of member states, each of which has one vote. The decisions of the Assembly have no legally binding force for governments. However, they carry the weight of world opinion as well as the moral authority of the world community.

The General Assembly has weighed in on the war on global poverty through the work of standing committees, sessional committees, *ad hoc* bodies and other subsidiary organizations. Its Economic and Financial Committee, the second of six main committees, provides staff support in the area of poverty reduction.

United Nations Secretariat

The United Nations Secretariat includes a number of departments and offices. Two that address global poverty most directly are the Office of the Secretary-General and the Department of Economic and Social Affairs. The Department of Economic and Social Affairs was established in 1997, consolidating several existing departments within the Secretariat. It has endeavored to articulate a framework for global development, financing and poverty reduction.

Economic and Social Council

Under the United Nations charter, the Economic and Social Council is responsible for promoting higher standards of living, full employment, and economic and social progress. It seeks solutions to international economic, social and health problems, fosters cultural and educational cooperation and encourages respect for human rights and fundamental freedoms.

The Economic and Social Council's purview extends to over 70 per cent of the human and financial resources of the entire United Nations system. It directly oversees nine functional commissions and five regional commissions. It coordinates ten programs and funds, four other related UN entities and five research and training institutes.

Within the United Nations system there are fourteen specialized agencies that are operationally autonomous but fall under the umbrella of the Economic and Social Council.

The nine functional commissions cover the following areas: social development, human rights, narcotic drugs, crime prevention and criminal justice, science and technology for development, sustainable development, status of women, population and development, and statistics.

There are regional commissions for Africa, Europe, Latin America and the Caribbean, Asia and the Pacific, and Western Asia. Additionally there are sessional and standing committees as well as expert, *ad hoc* and related bodies. There is a separate forum on forests.

The "programs and funds" group of the United Nations covers a wide swath. There are United Nations programs for drug control, environment, human settlements, world food and development.

Additionally there is a "conference" on trade and development, an "office of the high commissioner" for refugees, and a "relief and works agency" for Palestine refugees in the Near East. The latter reports directly to the General Assembly

There are several distinct research and training institutes, a generic one and several specialized institutes that focus on the advancement of women, crime and justice, disarmament and social development.

Other entities that fall under the purview of the Economic and Social Council are two offices of the high commissioner, one for human rights and one for project services, as well as the United Nations University and the United Nations System Staff College.

Specialized United Nations Agencies

Fourteen specialized agencies use the machinery of the Economic and Social Council to coordinate with each other and the United Nations as a whole.

- International Labour Organization
- Food and Agriculture Organization
- United Nations Educational, Scientific and Cultural Organization
- World Health Organization
- World Bank Group[16]
- International Monetary Fund
- International Civil Aviation Organization
- International Maritime Organization
- International Telecommunication Union
- Universal Postal Union
- World Meteorological Organization

- ◆   World Intellectual Property Organization
- ◆   International Fund for Agricultural Development
- ◆   United Nations Industrial Development Organization

Selected United Nations Agencies

(A) United Nations Development Programme

By the end of the 1990s, the annual budget of the United Nations Development Programme hovered around $2.16 billion. The budget comes from voluntary contributions by United Nations member states, principally in the form of official development assistance provided by the Organization for Economic Cooperation and Development.

The United Nations Development Programme devotes most of its resources to the world's poorest countries. Its executive board represents both the more prosperous Northern nations and the developing nations of the South.

Conceived by Mahbub ul-Haq, first published in 1990 and annually thereafter, the *Human Development Report* of the United Nations Development Programme exerts wide influence on issues of poverty and development.[17]

The reports have focused attention on global poverty conditions and provided valuable analytical perspectives on the nature, scope and impact of poverty. They have critiqued among other things the neoliberal or private market driven approaches to international finance, trade and development that predominated in the 1980s and early 1990s.

Under the umbrella of the United Nations Development Programme are lodged the Development Fund for Women and United Nations volunteers. Additional parts of the group consist of the United Nations Population Fund and the United Nations Children's Fund.

The United Nations Capital Development Fund helps eradicate poverty through local community development programs and microfinance operations. Since its establishment, the Fund has undergone far-reaching changes.

Its projects favor rural areas, with emphasis on local governance, small business and microenterprise development, small-scale infrastructure building, natural resource management and decentralized microcredit programs. From the beginning its assistance was not restricted to individual projects, but could include "general development plans, where such plans exist, or to meet general development requirements."[18]

The Fund is a member of the United Nations Development Programme group and reports to the UNDP's executive board. Its investments typically lie in the range of $500,000 to $5 million per project.

The United Nations Development Programme has consistently stressed the human toll of poverty, advocated for gender equity, and pushed for balanced and sustainable development. It regards the concept of human poverty as complementary to income poverty.

Since 1990, the United Nations Development Programme has emphasized that economic growth alone is insufficient to assure individual freedom of choice and human development. Hence national and global poverty reduction strategies are incomplete without concern for equity, social inclusion, women's empowerment, and respect for human rights.

While the United Nations Development Programme operates globally, other members of the UN system such as the Economic Commission for Latin America have a regional perspective.

(B) United Nations Children's Fund

The United Nations Children's Fund (UNICEF, 1946) advocates for the protection of children's rights, which includes meeting their basic needs. It started as the United Nations International Children's Emergency Fund.

UNICEF helps children get the care and stimulation they need and encourages families to educate girls as well as boys. It strives to reduce childhood death and illness and to protect children in the midst of war and natural disaster.

The creation of the United Nations International Children's Emergency Fund was in some respects accidental. In 1943, the Allied nations had established the United Nations Relief and Rehabilitation Administration to provide for post-war assistance.

In 1946-47 Europe experienced a bitter winter. Millions of people, including many children, lacked proper food, clothing or shelter. The United States Government refused to continue operating through the United Nations Relief and Rehabilitation Administration because its aid extended to the communist bloc of Eastern Europe.

At the final meeting of the United Nations Relief and Rehabilitation Administration in Geneva, the Polish delegate, Ludwik Rajchman, and others protested the fate of European children. The upshot was a proposal that the agency's remaining resources be used for children through a United Nations International Children's Emergency Fund.

The executive director designate, Maurice Pate, insisted that aid go to children in defeated as well as victorious countries. On December 11, 1946, a resolution of the UN General Assembly established the UN's International Children's Emergency Fund.[19] In effect this established a precedent if not the principle that the needs of children superseded political considerations.

The new agency supported programs in Poland, Romania, Yugoslavia, Germany, China, Greece and the Middle East. Though established to assist children hurt by war, the Fund's mission began to expand beyond meeting emergency needs.

In 1950, when the International Children's Emergency Fund was slated to go out of business, representatives of developing nations advocated for its continuation. The Pakistani delegate, for example, noted that millions of childrerin Africa , Asia, and Latin America suffered from sickness and hunger, due not to war but to poverty. The international community could not in conscience ignore them.

In 1953, the General Assembly confirmed the children's organization as a permanent fixture in the UN system. The words "international" and "emergency" were removed and it was renamed the United Nations Children's Fund (while retaining the acronym UNICEF), with a mission to help children living in poverty in developing countries.

(C) Economic Commission for Latin America and the Caribbean

The Economic Commission for Latin America (ECLA) was established by Economic and Social Council resolution 106 (VI), February 25, 1948. The Commission later broadened its scope to include the Caribbean nations and by resolution 1984/67, July 27, 1984, changed its name to the Economic Commission for Latin America and the Caribbean (ECLAC).

The Commission is headquartered in Santiago, Chile. It fosters economic and social development in Latin America and the Caribbean through research, advisory services, conferences and coordination with the larger UN system.

The Commission has established two subregional headquarters, one in Mexico City in June 1951 to serve Central America and another in Port-of-Spain, Trinidad and Tobago in December 1966 for the Caribbean nations. The Commission maintains country offices in Buenos Aires, Brasilia, Montevideo and Bogotá, as well as a liaison office in Washington, DC. There are 41 member states, with an additional seven associate members.

Every two years in even years, technical- and ministerial-level representatives of the member states meet on issues relating to the economic and social development of the region. Each biannual session is hosted by one of the member States.

(D) International Labour Organization

The International Labour Organization formulates basic labor standards, promotes policies to expand employment at decent pay levels for men and women everywhere and advocates systems of adequate social protection. It has consistently advocated for full employment measures and programs to meet basic needs of the poor. It

The International Labour Organization predates the United Nations, having come into existence in 1919 just after World War I. Its Declaration of Philadelphia published on May 10, 1944 "anticipated and set a pattern for the UN Charter and the Universal Declaration of Human Rights."[20]

The Declaration set forth the Organization's principles, as embodied in the following statements. (a) Labor is not a commodity. (b) Freedom of expression and of association are essential to sustained progress. (c) Poverty anywhere constitutes a danger to prosperity everywhere. (d) The war against want requires to be carried on with unrelenting vigor within each nation, and by continuous and concerted international effort.

In 1946 the International Labour Organization became the first of the specialized agencies in the United Nations. It is the only United Nations agency with a tripartite structure that includes representation at all levels of governments, employer organizations and worker organizations. There is a permanent secretariat headquartered in Geneva, Switzerland. The secretariat employs some 1,900 officials in its headquarters and 40 field offices worldwide, plus 600 experts in technical cooperation projects.

The ILO promotes democracy, fights against poverty for the protection of working people. It emphasizes international labor standards, human rights, gender equality, employment promotion, structural adjustment, rural and informal sectors, environment and the world of work.

At the International Labor Conference 86th Session, June 1998, the ILO reiterated its commitment to these principles. It contended that "economic growth is essential but not sufficient to ensure equity, social progress and the eradication of poverty, confirming the need for the ILO to promote strong social policies, justice and democratic institutions."

For the International Labour Organization, poverty is "a denial of choices and opportunities."[21] It subscribes to the perspective of the UN's Administrative Committee on Coordination for action to eliminate poverty. The Committee believes that economic growth by itself will not rapidly reduce poverty; it therefore must be augmented by specific policies that promote social justice and redress social inequities.

The International Labour Organization endorses the centrality of employment creation as an economic priority. In February 2000, the International Labour Organization established the World Commission on the Social Dimension of Globalization. The Commission explores innovative, sustainable ways of combining economic, social and environmental objectives to make globalization work for all.

Other UN-Sponsored Pathways to Poverty Reduction[22]

Within the United Nations system, a number of individual entities in addition to the UNDP have taken up the banner of poverty reduction while espousing philosophies of growth and development that fit snugly with their institutional missions. The year in which the entity was established as a part of the United Nations system is in parentheses.

The *Food and Agriculture Organization* (1945) has emphasized food security, better nutrition, improved agricultural methods and sustainable rural development. In 1951 the organization moved its headquarters from New York to Rome. In 1960, it launched the Freedom from Hunger Campaign to mobilize non-governmental support. Its 1974 World Food Conference yielded an international commitment to world food security. This theme was reiterated at the 1996 World Food summit.

The *United Nations Educational, Scientific and Cultural Organization* (1945) seeks international collaboration through education, science and culture. To help create national settings conducive to poverty reduction, it supports community-based projects in education, culture, governance, communications, social development and the environment.

The *World Health Organization* (1948) has advocated and sponsored worldwide vaccination campaigns and related public health measures. Headquartered in Geneva, Switzerland, it works to promote positive health outcomes at the country and the global level, with emphasis on reducing excessive mortality, morbidity, and disability in poor and marginalized countries.

The *United Nations Industrial Development Organization* (1985; founded in 1966) engages in research, advocacy and technical assistance in support of industrial development. Through its role as an honest broker between developing countries and outside institutions, it promotes sustainable industrial development. It stresses the three E's—economy, employment and environment. For poverty reduction it has put increasing emphasis on support for small and medium enterprises.

The *International Fund for Agricultural Development* (1977) grew out of the 1974 World Food Conference. The Conference concluded that food insecurity and famine were caused not so much by failures in food production as by structural problems relating to poverty. Given that a majority of the world's poor were concentrated in rural areas, the Fund was created to mobilize resources on concessional terms for programs that alleviate rural poverty and improve nutrition. It has emerged as a credible and influential advocate for rural poverty reduction.

The *United Nations Fund for Population Affairs* (1969) has linked poverty reduction with family planning and population control. The Fund assists countries at their request with reproductive health care, particularly family planning, safe motherhood, and prevention of sexually transmitted infections including HIV/AIDS. The Fund promotes the rights of women and supports data collection and analysis to help countries achieve sustainable development.

The *United Nations Conference on Trade and Development* (1964) aims at integrating all nations into the global economy and has challenged an inequitable trading system that disadvantages poor countries. It is the focal point within the United Nations system for addressing comprehensively the issues of trade, development, finance, technology, public and private investment and environmental protection.

The *World Food Program* (1963), set up as an experimental body, has emerged as the United Nations frontline agency in the fight against global hunger. In 2001, the organization provided food to 77 million people in eighty-two countries, including most of the world's refugees and internally displaced people.

Finally, the *Office of the High Representative for the Least Developed Countries, Landlocked Developing Countries and the Small Island Developing States* was established by the United Nations General Assembly in 2001 under resolution 56/227. Through its advocacy role, the Office seeks to keep the issues of the least developed countries, landlocked developing countries and small island developing States high on the international agenda. It mobilizes international support for the eradication of poverty, capacity-building, economic growth and sustainable development and global integration of these three groups of countries.

Appendix 7. Country Groupings[23]

Sub-Saharan Africa. Angola; Benin; Botswana; Burkina Faso; Burundi; Cameroon; Cape Verde; Central African Republic; Chad; Comoros; Congo; Congo, Democratic Republic of the; Côte d'Ivoire; Equatorial Guinea; Eritrea; Ethiopia; Gabon; Gambia; Ghana; Guinea; Guinea-Bissau; Kenya; Lesotho; Liberia; Madagascar; Malawi; Mali; Mauritania; Mauritius; Mozambique; Namibia; Niger; Nigeria; Rwanda; Sao Tome and Principe; Senegal; Seychelles; Sierra Leone; Somalia; South Africa; Swaziland; Tanzania, United Republic of; Togo; Uganda; Zambia; Zimbabwe.

Middle East and North Africa. Algeria; Bahrain; Cyprus; Djibouti; Egypt; Iran, Islamic Republic of; Iraq; Jordan; Kuwait; Lebanon; Libyan Arab Jamahiriya; Morocco; Occupied Palestinian Territory; Oman; Qatar; Saudi Arabia; Sudan; Syrian Arab Republic; Tunisia; United Arab Emirates; Yemen.

South Asia. Afghanistan; Bangladesh; Bhutan; India; Maldives; Nepal; Pakistan; Sri Lanka.

East Asia and Pacific. Brunei Darussalam; Cambodia; China; Cook Islands; Timor-Leste; Fiji; Indonesia; Kiribati; Korea, Democratic People's Republic of; Korea, Republic of; Lao People's Democratic Republic; Malaysia; Marshall Islands; Micronesia, Federated States of; Mongolia; Myanmar; Nauru; Niue; Palau; Papua New Guinea; Philippines; Samoa; Singapore; Solomon Islands; Thailand; Tonga; Tuvalu; Vanuatu; Viet Nam .

Latin America and Caribbean. Antigua and Barbuda; Argentina; Bahamas; Barbados; Belize; Bolivia; Brazil; Chile; Colombia; Costa Rica; Cuba; Dominica; Dominican Republic; Ecuador; El Salvador; Grenada; Guatemala; Guyana; Haiti; Honduras; Jamaica; Mexico; Nicaragua; Panama; Paraguay; Peru; Saint Kitts and Nevis; Saint Lucia; Saint Vincent and the Grenadines; Suriname; Trinidad and Tobago; Uruguay; Venezuela.

CEE/CIS and Baltic States. Albania; Armenia; Azerbaijan; Belarus; Bosnia and Herzegovina; Bulgaria; Croatia; Czech Republic; Estonia; Georgia; Hungary; Kazakhstan; Kyrgyzstan; Latvia; Lithuania; Moldova, Republic of; Poland; Romania; Russian Federation; Slovakia; Tajikistan; the former Yugoslav Republic of Macedonia; Turkey; Turkmenistan; Ukraine; Uzbekistan; Yugoslavia.

Industrialized countries. Andorra; Australia; Austria; Belgium; Canada; Denmark; Finland; France; Germany; Greece; Holy See; Iceland; Ireland; Israel; Italy; Japan; Liechtenstein; Luxembourg; Malta; Monaco; Netherlands; New Zealand; Norway; Portugal; San Marino; Slovenia; Spain; Sweden; Switzerland; United Kingdom; United States.

Developing countries. Afghanistan; Algeria; Angola; Antigua and Barbuda; Argentina; Armenia; Azerbaijan; Bahamas; Bahrain; Bangladesh; Barbados; Belize; Benin; Bhutan; Bolivia; Botswana; Brazil; Brunei Darussalam; Burkina Faso; Burundi; Cambodia; Cameroon; Cape Verde; Central African Republic; Chad; Chile; China; Colombia; Comoros; Congo; Congo,

Democratic Republic of the; Cook Islands; Costa Rica; Côte d'Ivoire; Cuba; Cyprus; Djibouti; Dominica; Dominican Republic; Timor-Leste; Ecuador; Egypt; El Salvador; Equatorial Guinea; Eritrea; Ethiopia; Fiji; Gabon; Gambia; Georgia; Ghana; Grenada; Guatemala; Guinea; Guinea-Bissau; Guyana; Haiti; Honduras; India; Indonesia; Iran, Islamic Republic of; Iraq; Israel; Jamaica; Jordan; Kazakhstan; Kenya; Kiribati; Korea, Democratic People's Republic of; Korea, Republic of; Kuwait; Kyrgyzstan; Lao People's Democratic Republic; Lebanon; Lesotho; Liberia; Libyan Arab Jamahiriya; Madagascar; Malawi; Malaysia; Maldives; Mali; Marshall Islands; Mauritania; Mauritius; Mexico; Micronesia, Federated States of; Mongolia; Morocco; Mozambique; Myanmar; Namibia; Nauru; Nepal; Nicaragua; Niger; Nigeria; Niue; Occupied Palestinian Territory; Oman; Pakistan; Palau; Panama; Papua New Guinea; Paraguay; Peru; Philippines; Qatar; Rwanda; Saint Kitts and Nevis; Saint Lucia; Saint Vincent/Grenadines; Samoa; Sao Tome and Principe; Saudi Arabia; Senegal; Seychelles; Sierra Leone; Singapore; Solomon Islands; Somalia; South Africa; Sri Lanka; Sudan; Suriname; Swaziland; Syrian Arab Republic; Tajikistan; Tanzania, United Republic of; Thailand; Togo; Tonga; Trinidad and Tobago; Tunisia; Turkey; Turkmenistan; Tuvalu; Uganda; United Arab Emirates; Uruguay; Uzbekistan; Vanuatu; Venezuela; Viet Nam; Yemen; Zambia; Zimbabwe.

Least developed countries. Afghanistan; Angola; Bangladesh; Benin; Bhutan; Burkina Faso; Burundi; Cambodia; Cape Verde; Central African Republic; Chad; Comoros; Congo, Democratic Republic of; Djibouti; Equatorial Guinea; Eritrea; Ethiopia; Gambia; Guinea; Guinea-Bissau; Haiti; Kiribati; Lao People's Democratic Republic; Lesotho; Liberia; Madagascar; Malawi; Maldives; Mali; Mauritania; Mozambique; Myanmar; Nepal; Niger; Rwanda; Samoa; Sao Tome and Principe; Senegal; Sierra Leone; Solomon Islands; Somalia; Sudan; Timor-Leste; Togo; Tuvalu; Uganda; United Republic of Tanzania; Vanuatu; Yemen; Zambia.

Appendix 8. Least Developed Countries

Table A-2. Least Developed Countries (as of December 2003)

01. Afghanistan	26. Madagascar*
02. Angola*	27. Malawi*
03. Bangladesh*	28. Maldives*
04. Benin*	29. Mali*
05. Bhutan	30. Mauritania*
06. Burkina Faso*	31. Mozambique*
07. Burundi*	32. Myanmar*
08. Cambodia	33. Nepal
09. Cape Verde	34. Niger*
10. Central African Republic*	35. Rwanda*
11. Chad*	36. Samoa
12. Comoros	37. Sao Tome and Principe
13. Dem. Repub. of the Congo*	38. Senegal*
14. Djibouti*	39. Sierra Leone*
15. Equatorial Guinea	40. Solomon Islands*
16. Eritrea	41. Somalia
17. Ethiopia	42. Sudan
18. Gambia*	43. Timor-Leste
19. Guinea*	44. Togo*
20. Guinea-Bissau*	45. Tuvalu
21. Haiti*	46. Uganda*
22. Kiribati	47. United Repub. of Tanzania*
23. Lao People's Dem. Repub.	48. Vanuatu
24. Lesotho*	49. Yemen
25. Liberia	50. Zambia*

*One of 30 LDC members of the World Trade Organization, 2002. Nine other LDCs are in the process of joining the WTO: Bhutan, Cambodia, Cap Verde, Laos, Nepal, Samoa, Sudan, Vanatau, and Yemen. Countries with WTO observer status are Equatorial Guinea, Ethiopia, and San Tome & Principe.

Source: United Nations Conference on Trade and Development, World Trade Organization. Office of the High Representative for the Least Developed Countries, Landlocked Developing Countries and Small Island Developing Countries

ENDNOTES TO APPENDICES

1. The unit in terms of which social benefit-cost accounting occurs is referred to as the numeraire. For example, when the Bretton Woods exchange rates were initially pegged to the price of gold ($35 an ounce in U.S. dollars), gold served as the numeraire. The value of other currencies (inflating, deflating) was given meaning in relation to its unit value. For economic analysis, one typically must select the numeraire from among domestic or foreign currency and domestic or border prices.
2. For more on this topic, let me commend to you Asian Development Bank (1997).

3. See www.usaid.gov/about/usaidhist.html.

4. Earmarking refers to the process by which Congress places restrictions on or mandates specifically how an agency is to spend appropriated funds.

5. U.S. Congress, House of Representatives (1989) 27.

6. U.S. General Accounting Office (1993) 4.

7. Foreign Assistance Act of 1961, as amended (P.L. 87-195). Also see International Anti-Corruption and Good Governance Act of 2000 (Title II of Public Law 106-309).

8. U.S. General Accounting Office (1993) 66-67.

9. Lieberson, Joseph and Jonathan Sleeper (2000) 22, 36.

10. See http://www.whitehouse.gov/news/releases/2002/03/20020314-7.html

11. The following year, Mr. Pearson became the founding chairman of Canada's influential International Development Research Centre.

12. Organization for Economic Cooperation and Development (2002) 52, 79.

13. Thomas, Allen and Tim Allen (2000) 205 in Allen, Tim and Alan Thomas, editors (2000) *Poverty and Development: Into the 21st Century*. New York: Oxford University Press in association with the Open University, United Kingdom.

14. President Harry S. Truman named White as its first U.S. executive director. With declining health exacerbated by never-proven charges that he had acted as a Soviet agent, White resigned in March 1947 and died of heart failure the following year.

15. There are many excellent sources for a description of the United Nations system as a whole. See, for example, United Nations (2000). Here we highlight those parts of the system that focus on alleviating global poverty.

16. For years, the "World Bank" was a shorthand reference to the International Bank for Reconstruction and Development. Over time it added several quasi-independent and more specialized components. The World Bank Group is comprised of the International Bank for Reconstruction and Development; International Development Agency; International Finance Corporation; Multilateral Guarantee Agency; and International Centre for Settlement of Investment Disputes. The "World Bank" now refers to the first two of these.

17. An articulate advocate for the developing world, Dr. ul-Haq served in National Planning Commission of Pakistan as chief economist during the 1960s, director of the Policy Planning Department of the World Bank in the 1970s, and in Pakistani cabinet posts during the 1980s. As special advisor to the United Nations Development Programme, he devised the Human Development Index. He authored six books on poverty and development. He died in 1998 in New York.

18. General Assembly resolution 1706 (XVI), December 19, 1961.

19. UN Resolution 57(I). Rajchman is regarded as the founder of UNICEF.

20. Frierson, Eleanor, G., Joëlle Kargul-Maccabez, and Sue Luzy (1995).

21. Statement of commitment of the United Nations' Administrative Committee on Coordination (ACC) for action to eradicate poverty (June 22, 1998).

22. Information in this section was drawn from the various UN agencies' websites.

23. Source: United Nations Children's Fund (2002) 114.

Bibliography and References

Ackerman, Bruce and Anne Alstott. 1999. *The Stakeholder Society*. New Haven: Yale University Press.

Adams, Richard H., Jr. and John Page. 2003. *The Impact of International Migration and Remittances on Poverty*. (December). World Bank Policy Research Working Paper 3179. Prepared for U.K. Department for International Development (DFID) and World Bank Conference on Migrant Remittances, London, October 9-10, 2003. The full paper can be accessed at econ.worldbank.org/view.php?id=31999.

African Development Bank, Asian Development Bank, European Bank for Reconstruction and Development, International Monetary Fund, World Bank. 2000. *Global Poverty Report*. (May) Prepared for the G8 Okinawa Summit in Nago City, Okinawa, July 21-23, 2000.

Agence Française de Développement. 2001. *Rapport Financer 2000*. (May 28) www.afd.fr/english/activite/resultats_financiers_1.cfm

Aghion, Philippe and Peter Howitt. 1998. *Endogenous Growth Theory*. Cambridge, Massachusetts: MIT Press.

Adelman, Irma and Sherman Robinson. 1978. *Income Distribution Policy in Developing Countries: A Case Study of Korea*. Stanford, California: Stanford University Press.

Ahluwalia, Montek S., Nicholas G. Carter and Hollis Chenery. 1979. "Growth and Poverty in Developing Countries," *Journal of Development Economics* 6(3): 399-441.

Allen, Tim and Alan Thomas, editors. 2000. *Poverty and Development: Into the 21st Century*. New York: Oxford University Press in association with the Open University, United Kingdom.

Anderson, Sarah, editor. 2000. *Views from the South: The Effects of Globalization and the WTO on Third World Countries*. Chicago, Illinois:

Food First Books and co-publisher, The International Forum on Globalization.

Asian Development Bank. 2002. *Asian Development Outlook 2002*. New York: Oxford University Press.

Asian Development Bank. 1997. *Guidelines for the Economic Analysis of Projects*. www.adb.org.

Australian Agency for International Development (AusAID). 1997. *One Clear Objective: Poverty Reduction through Sustainable Development*. Report of the Committee of Review, Commonwealth of Australia. This is often referred to as the Simons Report, after the Committee's chair, H. Paul Simons, AM. Canberra: AusAID. Available on the Internet at www.ausaid.gov.au.

Ayres, Robert. 1983. *Banking on the Poor: The World Bank and World Poverty*. Cambridge, Massachusetts: MIT Press.

Baker, Judy L. 2000. *Evaluating the Impact of Development Projects on Poverty: A Handbook for Practitioners*. Washington, DC: World Bank.

Basic Income European Network. 2004. *NewsFlash*. (January) Electronic newsletter for BIEN subscribers. See www.basicincome.org.

Bayliss, Kate. 2002. *Privatisation and Poverty: The Distributional Impact of Utility Privatisation*. (January) Working Paper No. 16. ISBN:1-904056-15-6. Centre on Regulation and Competition, Manchester University. http://idpm.man.ac.uk/crc.

Bergmann, Barbara R. 2002. *A Swedish-Style Welfare State or Basic Income: Which Should Have Priority?* Paper prepared for Conference on Rethinking Redistribution, sponsored by the Real Utopias Project, University of Wisconsin, May 3-5, 2002. See www.ssc.wisc.edu/havenscenter.

Bhagwati, Jagdish. 2004. *In Defense of Globalization*. New York: Oxford University Press.

Bhalla, Surjit. 2002. *Imagine There's No Country: Poverty, Inequality and Growth in the Era of Globalization*. Washington, DC: Institute for International Economics.

Bhalla, A. S. and Frédéric Lapeyre. 1999. *Poverty and Exclusion in a Global World*. New York: St. Martin's Press.

Binswanger, Hans P.; Klaus Deininger and Gershon Feder. 1995. "Power, Distortions, Revolt and Reform in Agricultural Land Relations", Chapter 42 in Jere Behrman and T.N. Srinivarasan, editors, *Handbook of Development Economics*, III-B:2559-2772. Amsterdam: Elsevier Science B.V.

Bird, Richard M. and Susan Horton, editors. 1989. *Government Policy and the Poor in Developing Countries*. Toronto: University of Toronto Press.

Birdsall, Nancy, Allen C. Kelley, and Steven W. Sinding, editors. 2001. *Population Matters: Demographic Change, Economic Growth and Poverty in the Developing World*. Oxford: Oxford University Press.

Bottelier, Pieter. 2001. "Was World Bank Support for the Qinghai Anti-poverty Project in China Ill-Considered?" *Harvard Asia Quarterly* 5:1 (Winter).

Boughton, James and K. Sarwar Lateef, editors. 1995. *Fifty Years after Bretton Woods: The Future of the IMF and the World Bank.* Washington, DC: IMF and World Bank Group.

Brandt Commission. 1983. *Common Crisis North-South: Co-operation for World Recovery.* Second report of the Independent Commission for International Development. London: Pan World Affairs Books.

Brandt Commission. 1980. *North-South: A Program for Survival.* First report of the Independent Commission for International Development. Cambridge, Massachusetts: The MIT Press.

Brzezinski, Zbigniew. 2004. *The Choice: Global Domination or Global Leadership.* New York: Basic Books.

Bruton, Henry J. 1969. "The Two-Gap Approach to Aid and Development: Comment" in *American Economic Review* 59: 566-577.

Burnside, Craig and David Dollar. 1997. *Aid, Policies and Growth.* Working paper 1777. Washington, DC: World Bank.

Canadian Foundation for the Americas (FOCAL). 2001. *Addressing Poverty and Inequality in Latin America and the Caribbean.* Available at www.focal.ca.

Canadian International Development Agency. 2001. *CIDA's Sustainable Development Strategy 2001-2003: An Agenda for Change.* Catalogue No. E94-306/2001. (February). Hull, Quebec: CIDA.

Cassen, Robert. 1994. *Does Aid Work?* Oxford: Clarendon Press.

Catholic Relief Services. 2003. "Creating Peace Amid the Horrors of War," *The Wooden Bell* 14:1 (March) This is a magazine for CRS donors.

Caufield, Catherine. 1996. *Masters of Illusion: The World Bank and the Poverty of Nations.* New York: Henry Holt.

Centre for Aid and Public Expenditure. 2000. *New Approaches to Development Co-operation: What Can We learn from Experience with Implementing Sector Wide Approaches?* (October) Working Paper 140. London, England: Overseas Development Institute.

Centre for International Economics. 2002. *Globalisation and Poverty:Turning the Corner.* (October) Canberra, Australia: Panther Publishing & Printing.

Chaudry, Kiren A. 1997. *The Price of Wealth: Economies and Institutions in the Middle East.* Ithaca, New York: Cornell University Press.

Chen, Shaohua and Martin Ravillion. 2000. *How Did the World's Poorest Fare in the 1990s?* Washington DC: World Bank.

Chenery, Hollis B. and T.N. Srinivasan, editors. *Handbook of Development Economics*, Volume I. 1988. Volume II. 1989. Volume IIIA. 1995. Volume IIIB. 1995, with Jere Behrman and T.N. Srinivasan as editors. Amsterdam: North Holland.

Chenery, Hollis B., Montek S. Ahluwalia, C.L.G. Bell, John H. Dulloy, and Richard Jolly. 1974. *Redistribution with Growth: Policies to Improve Income Distribution in Developing Countries in the Context of Economic Growth.* New York: Oxford University Press and Sussex, England: Institute of Development Studies, University of Sussex.

Chenery, Hollis and Michael Bruno. 1962. "Development Alternatives in an Open Economy: The Case of Israel" in *Economic Journal* 72 (March):79-103.

Christensen, John. 2000. "AIDS in Africa: Dying by the Numbers", *CNN In-Depth Specials.* www.cnn.com/SPECIALS/2000/aids.

Christian Aid. 2003. *Losing Ground: Israel, Poverty and the Palestinians.* (January) See www.christian-aid.org.uk.

Citro, Constance F. and R.T. Michael. 1995. *Measuring Poverty: A New Approach.* Washington, DC: National Academy Press.

Clapham, Christopher. 1985. *Third World Politics: An Introduction.* Madison, Wisconsin; University of Wisconsin Press.

Clark, Charles M. A. 1997. "A Basic Income for the United States of America: Ensuring that the Benefits of Economic Progress are Equitably Shared." *The Vincentian Chair of Social Justice: Volume 3.* New York: The Vincentian Center for Church and Society at St. John's University.

Clark, Colin. 1940. *The Conditions of Economic Progress.* London: MacMillan.

Clark, Robert F. 2002. *The War on Poverty: History, Selected Programs and Ongoing Impact.* Lanham: Maryland: University Press of America.

Cole, John. 1987. *Development and Underdevelopment.* New York: Methuen.

Collier, Paul and David Dollar. 1999. *Aid Allocation and Poverty Reduction.* Working paper 2041. (January 1) Washington, DC: World Bank. Note: The authors emphasize that the paper does not necessarily reflect the official views of the World Bank.

Committee for Economic Development. 2002. *A Shared Future: Reducing Global Poverty.* New York: CED.

Committee on International Relations, U.S. House of Representatives, and Committee on Foreign Relations, U.S. Senate. 2001. *Legislation on Foreign Relations Through 2000.* (June) Volume I-A: *Current Legislation and Related Executive Orders.* Washington, DC: U.S. Government Printing Office.

Consultative Group to Assist the Poorest. 2000. *Annual Report 2000.* Washington, DC: World Bank.

Cornia, Giovanni A., Richard Jolly, and Frances Stewart, editors. 1987. *Adjustment with a Human Face.* Oxford: Clarendon Press.

Creative Associates International, Inc. 2002. *Local Organizations in Development: Background Study- Literature Review and Works Cited.* (May) Report prepared for the U.S. Agency for International Development under Contract No. AEP-I-00-00-00019-00. Washington, DC: USAID.

Deaton, Angus. 2004. *Measuring Poverty in a Growing World (Or Measuring Growth in a Poor World.* (February) NBER Working Paper 9822. Washington, DC: National Bureau of Economic Research.

Deaton, Angus. 2001. "Counting the World's Poor: Problems and Possible Solutions." *World Bank Research Observer* 16:2 (Fall): 125-147.

Deaton, Angus and Margaret Grosh. "Consumption," Chapter 5 in Grosh, Margaret and Paul Glewwe, editors. 2000. *Designing Household Survey Questionnaires for Developing Countries: Lessons from Ten Years of LSMS Experience.* Washington, DC: World Bank.

Deininger, Klaus. 2003. *Land Policies for Growth: A World Bank Policy Research Report.* (May) Washington, DC: World Bank and New York: Oxford University Press.

Deininger, Klaus and Lyn Squire. 1996. "A New Data Set Measuring Income Inequality," *World Bank Economic Review.* September 10(2): 65-92.

Demery, Lionel and Michael Walton. 1998. *Are Poverty Reduction and Social Goals for the Twenty-First Century Attainable?* Washington, DC: World Bank.

Department for International Development, Government of the United Kingdom. 2001. *Poverty Elimination: The Role of Economic and Social Research.* (July). London: DFID. www.dfid.gov.uk.

Department for International Development, Government of the United Kingdom. 2001(a). *Poverty Elimination: DFID's Aim.* (January). London: DFID. www.dfid.gov.uk.

Development Assistance Committee, Organization for Economic Cooperation and Development. 2001. *DAC Recommendation on Untying Official Development Assistance to the Least Developed Countries.* Paris: OECD.

DeVries, Margaret Garritsen, editor. 1986. *The IMF in a Changing World.* (June 15) Washington, DC: International Monetary Fund.

Dollar, David. 2001. *Globalization, Inequality and Poverty since 1980.* (November) World Bank research paper. Washington, DC: World Bank.

Dollar, David and Aart Kray. 2000. *Growth is Good for the Poor.* Development Research Group Working Paper 2587.Washington, DC: World Bank.

Dollar, David and Lant Pritchett. 1998. *Assessing Aid: What Works, What Doesn't and Why.* Washington, DC: World Bank.

Domar, Evsey. 1946. "Capital Expansion, Rate of Growth and Employment." *Econometrika* 14 (April):137-147.

Domar, Evsey. 1957. *Essays in the Theory of Economic Growth.* New York: Oxford University Press.

Easterly, William. 2001. *The Elusive Quest for Growth: Economists' Adventures and Misadventures in the Tropics.* Cambridge, Massachusetts: MIT Press.

Easterly, William. 2000. *The Effect of IMF and World Bank Loans on Poverty.* (October 31) Working Papers—Poverty. Washington, DC: World Bank.

Easterly, William. 1997. *The Ghost of Financing Gap: How the Harrod-Domar Growth Model Still Haunts Development Economics.* (July) Draft working paper. Washington, DC: World Bank.

Economic Commission for Latin America and the Caribbean. 2002. *Globalization and Development.* (April 15) Brasilia: 29th ECLAC Session, May 6-10, 2002. LC/G 2157(SES.29/3. New York: United Nations.

Eckes, Alfred E. 1975. *A Search for Solvency.* Austin, Texas: University of Texas Press.

Emmerij, Louis, editor. 1997. *Economic and Social Development into the XXI Century*. Washington, DC: Inter-American Development Bank.

Emmerij, Louis; Richard Jolly; and Thomas G. Weiss. 2001. *Ahead of the Curve?: UN Ideas and Global Challenges*. First volume in the United Nations Intellectual History Project. Bloomington and Indianapolis: Indiana University Press.

Estes, Richard, J. 1997. *The World Social Situation, 1970-1995: Professional Challenges for a New Century*. See caster.ssw.upenn.edu/~restes/jak2.html

European Commission. 2002. *Annual Report 2001: On the EC Development Policy and the Implementation of the External Assistance*. Brussels: EuropeAid Cooperation Office.

European Network on Debt and Development. 2001. *Putting Poverty Reduction First: Why a Poverty Approach to Debt Sustainability Must Be Adopted*. (October) See www.eurodad.org.

European Network on Debt and Development. 2001(a). *Many Dollars, Any Change?* (October) See www.eurodad.org.

Feinstein, Osvaldo N. and Robert Picciotto, edtitors. 2001. *Evaluation and Poverty Reduction*. Volume 3 in World Bank Series on Evaluation and Development. Piscataway, New Jersey: Transaction Publishers.

Ferreira, Francisco. 1999. "Economic Transition and the Distributions of Income and Wealth", *Economics of Transition*. 7 (2) 377-410.

Fields, Gary S. 2001. *Distribution and Development: A New Look at the Developing World*. Cambridge, Massachusetts: MIT Press.

Fisher, Alan G.B. 1935. *The Clash of Progress and Security*. London: MacMillan.

Food and Agriculture Organization. 2004. *The State of Food and Agriculture 2004: Agricultural Biotechnology— Meeting the Needs of the Poor?*. Rome: FAO.

Food and Agriculture Organization. 2002. *Independent External Evaluation of the Special Programme for Food Security*. Report by independent nine-member team of experts for the FAO's Programme Committee, 87th Session. (May) Rome: FAO.

Food and Agriculture Organization. 2000. *The State of Food Insecurity in the World*. Rome: FAO.

Food and Agriculture Organization. 2000(a). *The State of Food and Agriculture 2000*. Rome: FAO.

Foster, James; Joel Greer; and Eric Thorbecke. 1984. "A Class of Decomposable Poverty Measures," *Econometrica* 52:761-765.

Frankman, Myron J. 1997. *Planet-Wide Citizen's Income: Antidote to Global Apartheid*. Paper published at the author's website. (October) See www.arts.mcgill.ca/programs/econ/frankman.html.

Frierson, Eleanor, G.; Joëlle Kargul-Maccabez; and Sue Luzy. 1995. *Information Services of the International Labour Organization: A 75-Year History* Paper prepared for the 61st International Federation of Library

Associations and Institutions (IFLA) Conference: Proceedings, August 20-25, 1995.

Führer, Helmut. 1996. *The Story of Official Development Assistance: A History of the Development Assistance Committee and the Development Co-operation Directorate in Dates, Names and Figures.* Paris: OECD.

Fukuyama, Francis. 1989. "The End of History?" *The Public Interest.* (Summer)

Gaiha, Raghav. 1993. *Design of Poverty Alleviation in Rural Areas.* Rome: United Nations, Food and Agriculture Organization.

Garfinkel, Irwin; Chien-Chung Huang; and Wendy Naidich. 2002. *The Effects of a Basic Income Guarantee on Poverty and Income Distribution.* (February 22) Paper prepared for Conference on Rethinking Redistribution, sponsored by the Real Utopias Project, held at the University of Wisconsin, May 3-5, 2002. See www.ssc.wisc.edu/havenscenter.

George, Robley E. 2002. *Socioeconomic Democracy: An Advanced Socioeconomic System.* Westport, Connecticut: Praeger Publishers.

Goldin, Ian; Halsey Rogers; and Nicholas Stern. 2002. *The Role and Effectiveness of Development Assistance: Lessons from World Bank Experience.* A research paper from the Development Economics vice-presidency of the World Bank prepared for the United Nations International Conference on Financing for Development, Monterrey, Mexico, March 18-22, 2002. Washington, DC: World Bank.

Gordon, David and Peter Townsend, editors. 2001. *Breadline Europe: The Measurement of Poverty.* Bristol, United Kingdom: The Policy Press.

Greenhill, Romilly and Ann Pettifor (Jubilee Research); Henry Northover (CAFOD); and Ashok Sinha (Jubilee Debt Campaign). 2003. *Did the G8 Drop the Debt? Five Years after the Birmingham Human Chain, What Has Been Achieved and What More Needs to be Done?* (May) London: Jubilee Research. Report is available at www.jubileeresearch.org. Note: CAFOD is the Catholic Fund for Overseas Development, the official overseas development agency of the Catholic Church in England and Wales.

Halvorson-Quevedo, Raundi and Hartmut Schneider, editors. 2000. *Waging the Global War on Poverty: Strategies and Case Studies.* Paris: Organization for Economic Cooperation and Development.

Hammer, Lucia and Felix Naschold. 2001. *Attaining the International Development Targets: Will Growth Be Enough?* Paper presented at the Development Conference on Growth and Poverty, United Nations University, World Institute for Development Economics Research (May 25), Helsinki. www.wider.unu.edu.

Hansen, Henrik and Finn Tarp. 2000. "Aid Effectiveness Disputed," *Journal of International Development* 12(3):375-398.

Harrison, Paul. 1993. *Inside the Third World: The Classic Account of Poverty in the Developing Countries.* New York: Penguin Press.

Harrod, Roy F. 1939. "An Essay in Dynamic Theory," *Economic Journal* 49 (March):14-33.

Henninger, Norbert and Mathilde Snel. 2002. *Where Are the Poor? Experiences with the Development and Use of Poverty Maps.* Washington, DC: World Resources Institute. See pubs.wri.org.

Heston, Alan, Robert Summers and Bettina Aten. 2002. *Penn World Table Version 6.1.* (October) Center for International Comparisons at the University of Pennsylvania (CICUP). Philadelphia: University of Pennsylvania.

Hirschman, Albert O. 1963. *Journeys toward Progress: Studies of Economic Policymaking in Latin America.* New York: The Twentieth Century Fund.

Hirschman, Albert O. 1958. *The Strategy of Economic Development.* New Haven, Connecticut: Yale University Press.

Hooke, A.W. 1980. *The International Monetary Fund: Its Evolution, Organization and Activities.* Washington, DC: IMF.

Horsefield, J. Keith. 1969. *The International Monetary Fund 1945—1965: Twenty Years of Monetary Cooperation.* Washington, DC: International Monetary Fund.

International Bank for Reconstruction and Development. July 1944. *Articles of Agreement of the International Bank for Reconstruction and Development.* Bretton Woods, New Hampshire. Washington, DC: World Bank.

International Development Association. 2002. *Additions to IDA Resources: Thirteenth Replenishment—Supporting Poverty Reduction Strategies.* Report from the executive directors of IDA to the Board of Governors. (July 25) Washington, DC:IDA.

International Finance Corporation. 2000. *Paths Out of Poverty: The Role of Private Enterprise in Developing Countries.* Washington, DC: IFC.

International Financial Institution Advisory Commission (Meltzer Commission). 2000. *Final Report.* Washington, DC.

International Fund for Agricultural Development. 2001. *The Challenge of Ending Rural Poverty: Rural Poverty Report 2001.* New York and Oxford: Oxford University Press.

International Fund for Agricultural Development. 1993. *The State of World Rural Poverty: An Inquiry into Its Causes and Consequences.* New York: NYU Press.

International Labour Organization. 2004. *Global Employment Trends.* Report prepared by Dorothea Schmidt and Marva Corley. (January) Geneva: International Labour Organization.

International Labour Organization. 2004a. *Towards a Fair Deal for Migrant Workers in the Global Economy.* 92nd Session of the International Labour Conference, Sixth Report. Geneva: International Labour Organization

International Labour Organization. 2003. *Working Out of Poverty.* Report by Juan Somavia, Director-General to the International Labor Conference, Geneva 91st Session 2003. Geneva: International Labour Organization.

International Labour Organization. 2002. *A Global Social Trust Network.* Geneva: International Labour Organization.

International Monetary Fund. 2001. *Fighting Poverty and Strengthening Growth: Recent Progress by the IMF and World Bank in Implementing the PRSP Approach and the HIPC Initiative.* Washington, DC: International Monetary Fund.

International Monetary Fund. 2000. *A Better World for All.* Washington, DC: International Monetary Fund.

International Monetary Fund. 1944. *Articles of Agreement of the International Monetary Fund.* (July) Bretton Woods, New Hampshire. Washington, DC: International Monetary Fund.

ITAD Ltd. in association with Oxford Policy Management. 1999. *Evaluation of the United Nations Capital Development Fund: Synthesis Report.* (August) See www.uncdf.org.

Japan, Ministry of Foreign Affairs. 2000. *Japan's Official Development Assistance Annual Report 1999.* (February) Report is available at www.mofa.go.jp.

Jazairy, Idriss; Mohiuddin Alamgir; and Theresa Panuccio. 1992. *The State of World Rural Poverty: An Inquiry into its Causes and Consequences.* New York: New York University Press.

Jones, Charles. 2002. *Introduction to Economic Growth.* New York, London: W.W. Norton and Company.

Kanbur, Ravi. 2001. "Economic Policy, Distribution and Poverty: The Nature of Disagreements," *World Development* 29(6):1083-1094.

Kapur, Devesh, John P. Lewis and Richard Webb, editors. 1998. *The World Bank: Its First Half Century.* Volume I: *History* Volume II: *Perspectives.* Washington, DC: The Brookings Institution.

Keddeman, Willem. 1998. *Of Nets and Assets: Effects and Impacts of Employment- Intensive Programmes—A Review of ILO Experience.* Geneva: Development Policies Department, International Labour Office.

Korten, David. 1990. *Getting to the 21st Century: Voluntary Action and the Global Agenda.* West Hartford, Connecticut: Kumarian Press.

Krueger, Anne O., Constantine Michaloupoulos, and Vernon Ruttan. 1989. *Aid and Development.* Baltimore, Maryland: Johns Hopkins University Press.

Krugman, Paul. 1994. "The Myth of Asia's Miracle: A Cautionary Fable," *Foreign Affairs* (November/December).

Kuznets, Simon. 1955. "Economic Growth and Income Inequality", *American Economic Review*, 45(1): 1-28.

Lal, Deepak and H. Myint. 1996. *The Political Economy of Poverty, Equity and Growth.* New York: St. Martin's Press.

Landes, David s. 1990. "Why Are We So Rich and They So Poor?" *American Economic Association Papers and Proceedings* 80 (May):1-13.

Lerrick, Adam. 2002. "Are World Bank's Claims of Success Credible? It Is Time for an External Performance Audit." *Quarterly International Economics Report.* (March) Pittsburgh: Carnegie Mellon, Gailliot Center for Public Policy.

Lewis, W. Arthur. 1955. *The Theory of Economic Growth*. London: George Allen & Unwin Ltd.

Lewis, W. Arthur. 1954. "Economic Development with Unlimited Supplies of Labor," *Manchester School* 22 (May):139-92.

Lieberson, Joseph and Jonathan Sleeper. 2000. *Poverty: A CDIE Experience Review. PPC/CDIE/POA* (October 30). Paper prepared by U.S. Agency for International Development's Center for Development Information and Evaluation. Washington, DC: USAID.

Lindenberg, Marc and Coralie Bryant. 2001. *Going Global: Transforming Relief and Development NGOs*. Bloomfield, Connecticut: Kumarian Press.

Lipton, Michael. 1977. *Why Poor People Stay Poor: A Study of Urban Bias in World Development*. London: Temple Smith.

Lipton, Michael with assistance from Shahin Yaqub and Eliane Darbellay. 1998. *Successes in Anti-poverty*. Geneva: International Labour Office.

Lipton, Michael and Martin Ravallion. 1995. "Poverty and Policy", Chapter 41 in Jere Behrman and T.N. Srinivarasan, editors, *Handbook of Development Economics*, III-B:2551-2660. Amsterdam: Elsevier Science B.V.

Love, Joseph L. 2001. *Latin America, UNCTAD and the Post-War Trading System*. (November). Paper presented at "Latin America and Global Trade," a conference of the Social Science History Institute, Stanford University, November 16-17, 2001. See sshi.stanford.edu/globaltrade2001/love.pdf.

Lustig, Nora and Ruthanne Deutsch. 1998. *The Inter-American Bank and Poverty Reduction: An Overview*. Washington, DC: IADB.

Maddison, Angus. 2003. *The World Economy: Historical Statistics*. Paris: Organization for Economic Cooperation and Development.

Maddison, Angus. 2001. *The World Economy: A Millennial Perspective*. Paris: Organization for Economic Cooperation and Development.

Martens, Jeans. 2001. *Rethinking ODA: Towards Renewal of Official Development Assistance*. (April) Discussion paper as background for the International Conference of the United Nations on Financing for Development, Mexico, 2002. One of four papers prepared in conjunction with a roundtable on "The Future of ODA", Berlin, December 4, 2000 by the Global Policy Forum, World Economy, Ecology and Development Association (WEED), and Heinrich-Boell-Foundation. Bonn, Germany: WEED.

Mayfield, James B. 1997. *One Can Make a Difference: The Challenges and Opportunities of Dealing with World Poverty—The Role of Rural Development Facilitators (RDF) in the Process of Rural Development*. Lanham, Maryland: University Press of America.

McNamara, Robert S. 1981. *The McNamara Years at the World Bank*. Baltimore, Maryland: Johns Hopkins University Press.

Milanovic, Branko. 2002. "The World Income Distribution, 1988 and 1993: First Calculation Based on Household Surveys Alone," *The Economic Journal* (January):112:51-92.

Moore, John Allphin, Jr. and Jerry Pubantz. 2002. *Encyclopedia of the United Nations.* New York: Facts on File, Inc.

Morris, James. 1963. *The Road to Huddersfield.* New York: Pantheon.

Mosley, Paul. and Ann Booth, editors. 2001. *New Poverty Strategies: What Have They Achieved, What Have We Learned?* London: MacMillan Press.

Munck, Ronaldo and Denis O'Hearn. 2000. *Deconstructing Development Discourses: Of Impasses, Alternatives and Politics.* London: Zed Books.

Murray, Michael L. 1997 ". . . *And Economic Justice for All": Welfare Reform for the 21st Century.* Armonk, NY: M. E. Sharpe.

Nathan Associates, Inc. 2002. *Poverty in India Since 1974: A Country Case Study* (November 29). Report prepared by James W. Fox and submitted to U.S. Agency for International Development under Contract No. PCE-I-00-00-00013-00. Washington, DC: USAID.

Nathan Associates, Inc. 2002a. *Poverty in Indonesia, 1965 to 1997: A Country Case Study* (November 29) Report prepared by James W. Fox and submitted to U.S. Agency for International Development under Contract No. PCE-I-00-00-00013-00. Washington, DC: USAID.

National Commission on Terrorist Attacks Upon the United States. 2004. *The 9/11 Commission Report.* (July 22) Report is available at www.9-11Commission.gov/report/911Report.pdf.

Nussbaum, Martha and Sen, Amaryta. 1993. *The Quality of Life.* Oxford: Clarendon Press.

Organization for Economic Cooperation and Development. 2002. *Development Co-operation Review: Germany.* Paris: OECD.

Organization for Economic Cooperation and Development. 2001. *The DAC Guidelines: Poverty Reduction.* Paris: OECD.

Organization for Economic Cooperation and Development, Development Assistance Committee. 1996. *Shaping the 21st Century: The Contribution of Development Co-operation.* DAC policy statement. (May) Paris: OECD.

Oxfam America. 2002. *Global Finance Hurts the Poor: An Analysis of North-South Private Capital Flows on Growth, Inequality and Poverty.* (May) Boston, Massachusetts: Oxfam America. www.oxfamamerica.org.

Oxfam International. 2003. *The IMF and the Millennium Goals: Failing to Deliver for Low Income Countries.* (September) Oxfam briefing paper prepared by Bethan Emmett and Max Lawson. Washington, DC: Oxfam International Office. Also see www.oxfam.org.

Oxfam International. 2002. *Last Chance in Monterrey: Meeting the Challenge of Poverty Reduction.* Paper written by Kevin Watkins (March) Washington, DC: Oxfam International Advocacy Office. www.oxfam.org.

Pearson, Lester B. 1969. *Partners in Development: Report of the Commission on International Development.* New York: Praeger.

Pemberton, Malcolm and Nicholas Rau. 2001. *Mathematics for Economists: An Introductory Textbook.* Manchester and New York: Manchester University Press.

Persley, G.J and Lantin, M.M., editors. 2000. *Agricultural Biotechnology and the Poor: An International Conference on Biotechnology.* The conference, held October 21-22, 1999, at the World Bank, Washington DC, was convened by the Consultative Group on International Agricultural Research and the U.S. National Academy of Sciences and had twelve co-sponsoring organizations. Washington, DC: World Bank. See www.cgiar.org

Picciotto, Robert and Rachel Weaving, editors. 2004. *Impact of Rich Countries' Policies on Poor Countries: Towards a Level Playing Field in Development Cooperation.* Piscataway, New Jersey: Transaction Publishers.

Planning Commission, Government of India. 2002. *National Human Development Report 2001.* (March) Note: See the Commission's website http://planningcommission.nic.in/reports.

Planning Commission, Government of India. 2002(a). *10ᵗʰ Five-Year Plan (2002-2007).* See http://planningcommission.nic.in.

Planning Commission, Government of India. 2001. *Approach Paper to the Tenth Five-Year Plan.* (September 1) The report is available at http://planningcommission.nic.in.

Planning Commission, Government of India. 1993. *Report of the Expert Group on Estimation of the Proportion and Number of Poor.* (July) The report is available at http://planningcommission.nic.in.

President's Commission on the Management of AID Programs (Ferris Commission). 1992. *Report to the President: An Action Plan.* (April) Washington, DC.

Pyatt, Graham. 2001. *An Alternative Approach to Poverty Analysis, with Particular Reference to the Poverty Reduction Strategies Being Developed in the Context of the HIPC Initiative.* Background paper prepared for the United Nations Conference on Trade and Development's *Least Developed Countries Report 2002* (See below).

Quibria, M.G. 2002. *Growth and Poverty: Lessons from the East Asian Miracle Revisited.* (February) Asian Development Bank Institute. Research Paper Series No. 33.Tokyo: ADB Institute.

Quilligan, James Bernard. 2002. *The Brandt Equation: 21ˢᵗ Century Blueprint for the New Global Economy.* Philadelphia: Brandt 21 Forum. Note: the Forum was established in 2001 to carry on the work of the original Brandt Commission, 1977-1984.

Ramonet, Ignacio. 1998. "The Politics of Hunger," *Le Monde Diplomatique* (November).

Ravallion, Martin. 2003. *The Debate on Globalization, Poverty and Inequality: Why Measurement Matters.* World Bank Policy Research Paper 3038 (April). Washington, DC: World Bank.

Ravallion, Martin. 1992. *Poverty Comparisons: A Guide to Concepts and Methods.* Working Paper No. 88. Washington, DC: World Bank.

Reddy, Sanjay G. and Thomas W. Pogge. 2002. *How Not to Count the Poor.* Paper available at www.socialanalysis.org.

Reitsma, Henk A. and Jan M.G. Kleinpenning. 1985. *The Third World in Perspective*. Totowa, New Jersey : Rowman & Allanheld.

Reynolds, David. 2000. *One World Divisible: A Global History Since 1945*. New York, London: W.W. Norton & Company.

Robb, Caroline M. 1999. *Can the Poor Influence Policy Directions in Development?* Washington, DC: World Bank.

Romer, Paul M. 1990. "Endogenous Technological Change," *Journal of Political Economy* 98(5, part 2) S71-102.

Romer, Paul M. 1986. "Increasing Returns and Long-Run Growth," *Journal of Political Economy* 94(5)1002-37.

Rostow, Walter W. 1960. *The Stages of Economic Growth: A Non-Communist Manifesto*. Cambridge, England: Cambridge University Press.

Rowntree, B. Seebohm. 1901. *A Study of London Town Life*. London: MacMillan.

Sala-i-Martin, Xavier. 2002. *The Disturbing 'Rise' of Income Inequality*, Working Paper 8904 (April) and *The World Distribution of Income*, Working Paper 8933 (May). Washington, DC: National Bureau of Economic Research.

Sala-i-Martin, Xavier and Sanket Mohapatra. 2002. *Poverty, Inequality and the Distribution of Income in the G20*. Discussion paper 0203-10 (November). New York: Columbia University.

Sala-i-Martin, Xavier and Arvind Subramanian. 2003. *Addressing the Natural Resource Curse: An Illustration from Nigeria*. (July) International Monetary Fund Working Paper WP/03/139. Washington, DC: IMF.

Sen, Amartya. 1999. *Development as Freedom*. New York: Knopf.

Singer, Hans W. 1986. "The Terms of Trade Controversy and the Evolution of Soft Financing: Early Years in the U.N." in G. M. Meier and D. Seers, editors. *Pioneers in Development*. Oxford: Oxford University Press.

Singer, Hans W. and Javed A. Ansari. 1988. *Rich and Poor Countries*. London: Allen and Unwin.

Solow, Robert M. 1956. "A Contribution to the Theory of Economic Growth," *Quarterly Journal of Economics* (February): 70:65-94.

Soubbotina, Tatyana P. with Katherine A. Sheram. 2000. *Beyond Economic Growth: Meeting the Challenges of Global Development*. (October) Excellent textbook published by the World Bank's Development Education Program. Washington, DC: World Bank.

Srinivasan, T.N. 2000. *Growth and Alleviation: Lessons from Development Experience*. (December 8) Paper delivered at the High Level Symposium on Alternative Development Paradigms and Poverty Reduction, Asian Development Bank Institute, Tokyo. Also published in French under the title *Croissance et Allégement de la Pauvreté: Les Leçons Tirées de L'Expérience du Développement*, Revue d'Économic du Développement, 1-2, 2001:115-168.

Stewart, Frances. 1998. *Adjustment and Poverty: Old Solutions and New Problems.* QEH Working Paper Series, Working Paper No. 20. Oxford: Queen Elizabeth House.

Stewart, Frances. 1995. *Adjustment and Poverty: Options and Choices.* London: Routledge.

Stiglitz, Joseph E. 2002. *Globalization and Its Discontents.* New York and London: W.W Norton & Company, Ltd.

Strauss, John and Duncan Thomas. 1995. "Human Resources: Empirical Modeling of Household and Family Decisions." Chapter 34 in Jere Behrman and T.N. Srinivarasan, editors, *Handbook of Development Economics*, III-A:1883-2023. Amsterdam: Elsevier Science B.V.

Structural Adjustment Participatory Review International Network (SAPRIN). 2004. *Structural Adjustment: The SAPRI Report - The Policy Roots of Economic Crisis, Poverty and Inequality: A Multi-Country Participatory Assessment of Structural Adjustment.* (January). London: Zed Books. Also see www.saprin.org.

Subbarao, Kalanidhi. 1997. *Lessons of 30 Years of Fighting Poverty.* (September) Paper presented at the Conference on Economic Approaches Against Poverty, August 26-28, 1997 in Quebec City.

Swaroop, Vinaya. 1998. *The Implications of Foreign Aid Fungibility for Development Assistance.* (October) Preliminary draft paper. Washington, DC: World Bank, Development Research Group.

Tarp, Finn, editor. 2002. *Foreign Aid and Development: Lesson Learnt and Directions for the Future.* London and New York: Routledge.

Theobald, Robert. 1965. *Free Men and Free Markets.* New York: Anchor Books. (Originally published in 1963 by Clarkson N. Potter.)

Tobin, James, Joseph A. Pechman and Peter M. Mieszkowski. 1967. "Is a Negative Income Tax Practical?" *The Yale Law Journal* 77(1):1-27.

Townsend, Peter. 2000. *Prisoners of the Global Market: Social Polarisation and the Growth of Poverty.* The Copenhagen Seminars—Review for the World Assembly in Geneva—Working Paper 25. (June) See www.bris.ac.uk/poverty/pse.

Townsend, Peter and David Gordon, editors. 2002. *World Poverty: New Policies to Defeat an Old Enemy.* Bristol, United Kingdom: The Policy Press.

Triplett, Jack E. 1997. "Measuring Consumption: The Post-1973 Slowdown and the Research Issues," *Federal Bank Review.* Federal Reserve Bank of St. Louis. (May/June): 9-42.

Ul-Haq, Mahbub. 1976. *The Poverty Curtain: Choices for the Third World.* New York: Columbia University Press.

United Kingdom. 1997. *Eliminating World Poverty: A Challenge for the 21st Century.* White Paper on International Development. Command Paper 3789. (November) Presented to Parliament by command of Her Majesty. London.

United Nations. 2002. *Implementation of the First United Nations Decade for the Eradication of Poverty.* Report of the Secretary General for 57th Session of the General Assembly. Advance unedited copy. (July) New York: UN.

United Nations. 2002(a). *Report of the International Conference on Financing for Development.* Monterrey, Mexico. March 18-22, 2002. A/CONF198/11. New York: United Nations.

United Nations. 2001. *Report of the High Level Panel on Financing for Development.* (June 26). A/55/1000. Note: The report is attached to a letter of transmittal from the Secretary-General to the 55th Session of the UN General Assembly. The eleven-member panel was chaired by Ernesto Zedillo, former President of Mexico. New York: United Nations.

United Nations. 2000. *Basic Facts about the United Nations.* No. E.00.I.21 New York: United Nations.

United Nations. 1997. *Report on the World Social Situation.* E/CN.5/1997/8 (Part 1). New York: United Nations. www.un.org/esa/socdev/rwss97c0.htm.

United Nations. 1995. *Report of the World Summit for Social Development.* (April 19) Copenhagen, March 6-12, 1995.

United Nations. 1992. *Report of the United Nations Conference on Environment and Development, Rio de Janeiro: Resolutions Adopted by the Conference, Resolution I, Annex II.* Sales No. E.93.I.8. (June 3-14) New York.

United Nations. 1970. *Towards Accelerated Development—Proposals for the Second United Nations Development Decade.* UN publication E.70.II.A.2. New York.

United Nations. 1962. *The United Nations Development Decade.* New York: UN.

United Nations. 1945. *Charter of the United Nations.* (June 26). New York: UN.

United Nations Children's Fund. 2002. *The State of the World's Children 2003.* New York: UNICEF.

United Nations Conference on Trade and Development. 2002. *The Least Developed Countries Report 2002: Escaping the Poverty Trap.* New York and Geneva: UN.

United Nations Conference on Trade and Development. 2000. *The Least Developed Countries: 2000 Report.* New York and Geneva: UN.

United Nations Department of Economic and Social Affairs, Statistics Division. 2003. *Household Surveys in Developing Countries* (Draft). (April) See unstats.un.org/unsd/hhsurveys

United Nations Department of Economic and Social Affairs, Statistics Division. 2002. *United Nations Millennium Development Goals: Data and Trends, 2002.* New York: United Nations. (May 31) Note: This report is not an official UN document but is based on a report of the Inter-agency Expert Group on MDG Indicators, April 2002.

United Nations Development Programme. 2004. *Overview of UNDP's Support to Poverty Reduction Strategies.* (May) Paper prepared by Terry McKinley, Policy Adviser in the Bureau for Development Policy, based on a longer

background   paper   by   UNDP   consultant   Rasheda   Selim.   See
www.undp.org/poverty.

United Nations Development Programme. 2003. *Human Development Report
2003: Millennium Development: A Compact Among Nations to End Human
Poverty.* New York: United Nations.

United Nations Development Programme. 2002. Human Development Report
2002: *Deepening Democracy in a Fragmented World.* New York: United
Nations.

United Nations Development Programme. 2001. *Human Development Report
2001: Making New Technologies Work for Human Development.* New York:
United Nations.

United Nations Development Programme. 2000. *Human Development Report
2000: Human rights and Human Development.* New York: United Nations.

United Nations Development Programme. 1999. *Human Development Report
1999: Globalization with a Human Face.* New York: United Nations.

United Nations Development Programme. 1999. *The Way Forward: The
Administrator's Business Plans, 2000-2003.* (December 15) Report to the
Executive Board of the United Nations Development Programme and of the
United Nations Population Fund, January 24-28 and January 31, 2000.
DP/2000/8. New York: United Nations.

United Nations Development Programme. 1998. *Human Development Report
1998: Consumption for Human Development.* New York: United Nations.

United Nations Development Programme. 1997. *Human Development Report
1997: Human Development to Eradicate Poverty.* New York: United
Nations.

United Nations Economic and Social Council. 1995. *Poverty Eradication and
Sustainable Development: Report of the Secretary-General.* (March 20)
Commission on Sustainable Development, Third Session, April 11-28, 1995.
E/CN.17/1995/14. New York: United Nations.

United Nations Economic Commission for Africa. 2002. *Economic Report on
Africa 2002: Tracking Performance and Progress.* Addis Adaba, Ethiopia:
UNECA.

United Nations Economic Commission for Europe. 2002. *World Robotics 2002.*
Published in conjunction with the International Federal of Robotics. New
York: United Nations.

United Nations Economic and Social Commission for Asia and the Pacific.
2002. *Economic and Social Survey of Asia and the Pacific, 2002/Economic
Prospects: Preparing for Recovery.* (March) Sales No. E.02.II.F.25. New
York: United Nations.

United Nations Population Fund. 2002. *The State of World Population 200 -
People, Poverty and Possibilities: Making Development Work for the Poor.*
New York: United Nations Publications

United Nations Research Institute for Social Development. 1995. *States of
Disarray: The Social Effects of Globalization.* Geneva: UNRISD.

United Nations Secretariat - Department of Economic and Social Affairs. 2001. *Combating Poverty: Report of the Secretary-General*. (March 14) Report prepared by the Department of Economic and Social Affairs of the United Nations Secretariat for the UN Commission on Sustainable Development.

United Nations, Executive Board of the United Nations Development Programme and of the United Nations Population Fund. 2002. *Annual Report of the Administrator on Evaluation 2001*. Second regular session of the Executive Board, September 23-27. (July 9) DP/2002/27. New York: United Nations.

United States Conference of Catholic Bishops. 2003. *Faithful Citizenship: A Catholic Call to Political Responsibility*. Washington, DC: USCCB. See www.usccb.org/faithfulcitizenship.

U.S. Agency for International Development. 2003. "Statement of the Administrator", *Congressional Budget Justification FY 2004*. (February 28) Washington, DC: USAID. See www.info.usaid.gov.

U.S. Agency for International Development. 2003(a). *Poverty Reduction in Honduras: A Background Paper*. PN-ACR-481. (April) Washington, DC.

U.S. Agency for International Development. 2003(b). *USAID's Approach to Poverty Reduction: The Case of Mali*. PN-ACR-352. (January) Washington, DC.

U.S. Agency for International Development. 2002. *Working for a Sustainable World: U.S. Government Initiatives to Promote Sustainable Development*. (July) Washington, DC.

U.S. Central Intelligence Agency. 2003. The *World Factbook 2003*. Available at www.cia.gov.

U.S. Central Intelligence Agency. 2002. The *World Factbook 2002*. Available at www.cia.gov.

U.S. Central Intelligence Agency. 2001. *Long-Term Global Demographic Trends: Reshaping the Geopolitical Landscape*. (July) Available at www.cia.gov/publications.

U.S. Congress, House of Representatives. 1989. *Report of the Task Force on Foreign Assistance*. (February) 101st Congress, 1st Session. House Report 101-32.

Note: Effective July 7, 2004, the GAO's legal name became the Government Accountability Office. In the following citations, I have retained the earlier name since the reports were issued under that name.

U.S. General Accounting Office. 2002. *Developing Countries: Switching Some Multilateral Loans to Grants Lessens Poor Country Debt Burdens*. (April) GAO-01-593. Washington, DC.

U.S. General Accounting Office. 2002(a). *Foreign Assistance: USAID Relies Heavily on Non-governmental Organizations But Better Data needed to Evaluate Approaches*. (April) GAO-02-471. Washington, DC.

U.S. General Accounting Office. 2001. *Foreign Assistance: Lessons Learned from Donors' Experiences in the Pacific Region*. (August) GAO-01-808. Washington, DC.

U.S. General Accounting Office. 2001(a). *U.S. Agency for International Development: Status of Achieving Key Outcomes and Addressing Major Management Challenges.* (August) GAO-01-721.Washington, DC.

U.S. General Accounting Office. 2001(b). *Developing Countries: Challenges Confronting Debt Relief and IMF Lending to Poor Countries.* (May 15) Testimony before the Subcommittee on International Monetary Policy, Committee on Financial Services, U.S. House of Representatives. GAO/GAO-01-745T. Washington, DC.

U.S. General Accounting Office. 2001(c). *International Monetary Fund: Few Changes Evident in Design of New Lending Program.* (May) GAO-01-581. Washington, DC.

U.S. General Accounting Office. 2001(d). *Multilateral Development Banks: Profiles of Selected Multilateral Development Banks.* (May) GAO-01-665. Washington, DC.

U.S. General Accounting Office. 2000. *Developing Countries: Debt Relief initiative for Poor Countries Faces Challenges.* (June 29) GAO/NSIAD-00-161. Washington, DC.

U.S. General Accounting Office. 1996. *Mexico's Financial Crisis: Origins, Awareness, Assistance, and Initial Efforts to Recover.* (February) GAO/GGD-96-56. Washington, DC.

U.S. General Accounting Office. 1994. *Multilateral Development: Status of World Bank Reforms.* (June) GAO/NSIAD-94-190BR. Washington, DC.

U.S. General Accounting Office. 1993. *Foreign Assistance: AID Strategic Direction and Continued Management Improvements Needed.* (June) GAO/NSIAD-93-106. Washington, DC.

U.S. General Accounting Office. 1991. *Foreign Assistance: Progress in Implementing the Development Fund for Africa.* (April) GAO/NSIAD-91-127. Washington, DC.

U.S. General Accounting Office. 1988. *Foreign Aid: Problems and Issues Affecting Economic Assistance.* (December)   GAO/NSIAD-89-61BR. Washington, DC.

U.S. General Accounting Office. 1986. *Foreign Assistance: U.S. Use of Conditions to Achieve Economic Reforms.* (August) GAO/NSIAD-86-157.

U.S. General Accounting Office. 1984. *Sustaining Improved U.S. Participation in the International Labour Organization Requires New Approaches.* (May 3) GAO/NSIAD-84-55. Washington, DC.

U.S. General Accounting Office. 1983. *Donor Approaches to Development Assistance: Implications for the United States.* (May 14) GAO/ID-83-23. Washington, DC.

U.S. General Accounting Office. 1982. *Private Sector Involvement in the Agency for International Development's Programs.* (August 26) GAO/ID-82-47. Washington, DC.

U.S. Government (2002). *The National Security Strategy of the United States of America.* (September). www.whitehouse.gov/nsc/nss.html.

Van der Veen, Robert and Loek Groot, editors. 2000. *Basic Income on the Agenda. Policy Options and Political Feasibility*. Amsterdam: Amsterdam University Press.

Van Parijs, Philippe with Cohen, Joshua and Joel Rogers, editors. 2001. *What's Wrong with a Free Lunch?* Boston: Beacon Press.

Van Parijs, Philippe. 2000. *Basic Income: A Simple and Powerful idea for the 21ˢᵗ Century*. Paper prepared for Basic Income European Network, VIIIth International Congress, Berlin, October 2000.

Van Parijs, Philippe. 1995. *Real Freedom for All: What (If Anything) Can Justify Capitalism?* Oxford: Clarendon Press.

Van Reisen, Mirjam. 2002. *Directing EU Policy Towards Poverty Eradication: From Commitments to Targets to Results* (ECDPM Discussion Paper 35). Maastricht: European Centre for Development Policy Management.

Voth, Donald E. 2002. *Community and Community Development: Parts I to III*. Book for course on community development at University of Arkansas. See website www.uark.edu/depts/hesweb/hdfsrs/rsoc4263/cdbook6.PDF

Welch, Carol. 2001. "Structural Adjustment Programs & Poverty Reduction Strategy," *Foreign Policy in Focus*. 5:14 (September). See www.fpif.org.

Wells, Robert N. editor. 1991. *Peace by Pieces: United Nations Agencies and Their Role: A Reader and Selective Bibliography*, Metuchen, New Jersey: Scarecrow Press.

Widerquist, Karl. 2002. *A Failure to Communicate: The Labour Market Findings of the Negative Income Tax Experiments and Their Impact on Policy and Public Opinion*. (September) Draft of paper prepared for 9ᵗʰ International Congress, Basic Income European Network, Geneva September 12-14, 2002.

Wilson, Harold. 1953. *The War on World Poverty*. London: Victor Gollancz.

World Bank. *Voices of the Poor* Series—

- Rademacher, Anne; Kai Schafft; Raj Patel; Sara Koch-Schulte; Deepa Narayan. 2000. *Can Anyone Hear Us?* (March) Volume I. London and New York: Oxford University Press.

- Shah, Meera; Patti Petesch; Robert Chambers; Deepa Narayan. 2000(a). *Crying Out for Change*. (September) Volume II. London and New York: Oxford University Press.

- Narayan, Deepa and Patti Petesch, editors. 2002. *From Many Lands*. Volume III. London and New York: Oxford University Press. (January) Note: This three-volume series draws from discussions with 60,000 poor men and women from sixty countries. www.worldbank.org/poverty/voices/index.htm.

World Bank. 2004. *Global Development Finance: Harnessing Cyclical Gains for Development - Volume I: Analysis and Summary Tables* Washington, DC: World Bank.

World Bank. 2004a. *World Development Indicators 2004*. Washington, DC: World Bank.

World Bank. 2003. *Global Economic Prospects 2004: Realizing the Development Promise of the Doha Agenda*. Washington, DC: World Bank.

World Bank. 2003(a). *Global Economic Prospects and the Developing Countries 2003*. Washington, DC: World Bank.

World Bank. 2002. *Global Development Finance 2002: Financing the Poorest Countries*. Washington, DC: World Bank.

World Bank. 2002(a). *Poverty Reduction and the World Bank: Progress in Operationalizing the WDR 2000/2001*. Washington, DC: World Bank.

World Bank. 2001. *Global Economic Prospects and the Developing Countries 2002*. Washington, DC: World Bank.

World Bank. 2001(a). *Global Economic Prospects and the Developing Countries 2001*. Washington, DC: World Bank.

World Bank. 2001(b). *World Development Report 2000/2001: Attacking Poverty*. Washington, DC: World Bank.

World Bank. 2001(c). *Global Development Finance 2001: Building Coalitions for Effective Development Finance*. Washington, DC: World Bank.

World Bank. 2000. *Social Dimensions of Adjustment Programs: A Submission to the World Summit for Social Development Five-Year Review*. (June) The paper was prepared as a contribution to the five-year review of the World Summit for Social Development and the Commitments of the Copenhagen Declaration. Washington, DC: World Bank.

World Bank. 1994. *Implementing the World Bank's Strategy for Reducing Poverty and Hunger*. Washington, DC: World Bank.

World Bank. 1993. *East Asian Miracle: Economic Growth and Public Policy*. Washington, DC: World Bank.

World Bank. 1992. *World Development Report 1992: Poverty*. New York: Oxford University Press

World Bank. 1990. *World Development Report 1990: Poverty*. New York: Oxford University Press.

World Bank. 1981. *Accelerated Growth in Sub-Saharan Africa: An Agenda for Action*. Report 3358. (Also known as the Berg report, since it was prepared by the World Bank African Strategy Review Group under the direction of University of Michigan economics professor Eliot Berg). Washington, DC: World Bank.

World Bank, Operations Evaluation Department. 2002. *IDA's Partnership for Poverty Reduction: An Independent Evaluation of Fiscal Years 1994-2000*. Washington, DC: World Bank.

World Bank, Operations Evaluation Department. 2002(a). *Social Funds: Assessing Effectiveness*. Washington, DC: World Bank.

World Bank, Operations Evaluation Department. 2000. "Development Effectiveness at the World Bank: What Is the Score?" *OED Reach*. (Spring) Number 24.

World Bank, Operations Policy and Country Services. 2001. *Adjustment Lending Retrospective: Final Report*. (June 15) Washington, DC: World Bank.

World Bank, Operations Policy Department, Learning and Leadership Center. 1997. *Handbook on Economic Analysis of Investment Operations.* Washington, DC: World Bank.

World Commission on Environment and Development (Brundtland Commission). 1987. *Our Common Future.* New York and Oxford: Oxford University Press.

World Trade Organization. 1994. *Agreement Establishing the World Trade Organization.* (April 1) See www.wto.org.

Yunus, Muhammed (with Alan Jolis). 1999. *Banker to the Poor: Micro-lending and the Battle Against World Poverty.* New York: Public Affairs.

Index

Note: The term poverty appears throughout the text. Only selected uses of the term are included in the index entries.

Robert F. Clark is a writer and consultant living in Fairfax County, Virginia. A retired federal employee, he has a doctorate in public administration and has written or co-authored scholarly articles on program evaluation, disability, aging, long-term care and poverty. He has previously authored two books on antipoverty programs in the United States, *Maximum Feasible Success: A History of the Community Action Program* (Washington, DC: National Association of Community Action Agencies, 2000) and *The War on Poverty: History, Selected Programs and Ongoing Impact* (Lanham, MD: University Press of America, 2002). He has also published two novels.

305726576+